Island Life

Dion Perry

Island Life
The Story of Clarke Island 1984–1990

Acknowledgements

Heather, for her work in correcting spelling and grammar.
Donna and Paula for reviewing an advanced copy of the book
and providing valuable feedback.
Stephen Matthews and Ginninderra Press
for their outstanding work.

Island Life, The Story of Clarke Island 1984-1990
ISBN 978 1 76041 833 5
Copyright © Dion Perry 2020
Cover: Rebecca Bay, Clarke Island

First published 2020 by
GINNINDERRA PRESS
PO Box 3461 Port Adelaide 5015
www.ginninderrapress.com.au

Contents

Foreword	9
Beginning: March 1984	11
Trial Period	23
Arrival	29
Early Days	37
Settling In	46
The Garden and School	55
Radio Telephone	63
Land Development	66
New Dam	68
Fisherman	77
Suzi Wong	81
Abalone	85
Inner-tube Raft	88
Distress Call	90
Isolation Sickness	93
Launceston Museum	100
Blocked Septic Tank	104
The Day of the Mushrooms	107
Our First Milking Goat	109
Tractor Incident	113
UHF Radio	119
Aerial Sowing	121
Preservation Island	124
1080 Poison	127
More Goats	128

The Scallop Boat	133
New John Deere Tractor	135
Stranded Visitor	141
Rolf Harris	145
Medical Emergency	147
Motorbikes	150
Muttonbirding on Preservation Island	152
Caretakers	156
Libby Belle	163
Rescued Crayfish	166
Arrival of the Bees	169
Stranded Kayakers	173
Teeth and Claws	176
Orphan Calf	180
Night Raid	183
The Drovers	188
The Slaughtering of a Beast	194
The Grader	199
Wallaby Cull	201
The Commercial Pilot	207
Leverington	210
Cape Portland	217
Swan Island	225
Major Decision	231
Kangaroo Bay	237
Sheffield	242
The Last Summer	259
The End of an Era	265
Postscript: April 1996	270
About the Author	284

Dedicated to

My father, a hard-working man who could fix anything.

My mother, who deserves a medal for what she put up with on Clarke Island.

My brother and sister, who were the best siblings I could have asked for.

My wife, for her constant encouragement to get this book completed and published.

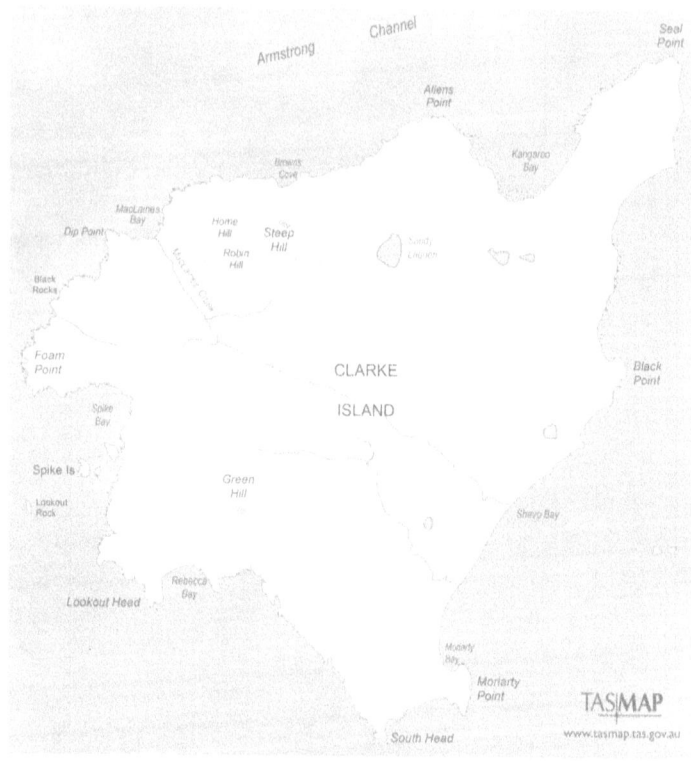

Map of Clarke Island
Base image by TASMAP (www.tasmap.tas.gov.au) © State of Tasmania

Foreword

Between March 1984 and March 1990, my family and I lived on Clarke Island as the sole permanent residents. For years, I had the idea that I wanted to write a book about our experiences. I undertook several planning sessions and wrote a number of introductory chapters, but I could never get the story voice quite right.

In 2011, I was spending a few nights in a shack on Mt Roland in Tasmania with some friends. In front of the open fireplace with a red wine and a pipe, I began to tell them some stories about Clarke Island. They enjoyed them so much that they begged me to write a book about my time there.

At the time, I was particularly interested in capturing the history of Clarke Island and I had access to seven diaries which had recorded the key events of our years. Initially, I wrote a book that was very factual, and although it did refer to the incidents in which the campfire stories were told, they lacked the voice of a storyteller. Those who critiqued the book advised me to try again and to write from the memories of the person I was during the years I lived on Clarke Island.

The redraft was a success. However, it is no longer strictly true, and all names except my own have been changed. The dialogue, although as close to authentic as I can remember, has been made up and some very minor changes have been made to some of the stories. In some cases, the stories also do not strictly follow the timeline of events that was recorded in the diaries.

While these stories come from our time on Clarke Island, they do not belong solely to us. They are a record of events that belong to a larger community. It has been my pleasure to write them and make them available to the world. I hope you enjoy the book and, if you do, please tell your friends and associates about it.

Homecoming

I've been away so long, it seems,
Away chasing elusive dreams,
Things that seem important to me,
But somehow couldn't possibly be.
For here I belong to the Island,
The sun, wind and sea,
At one with myself, allowed to be me.

                                          Marlene Perry

Beginning

March 1984

There's a map on the dining room table. An A4 photocopy of an ink drawing. Judging by the state it's in, the map's seen some mileage before it came to be where it is. Intrigued, I push past my siblings Maree and Stephen in order to get a better look.

'What's that, Dad?' I ask.

He flicks ash from his cigarette into a nearby ashtray and spins the map around so it's the right way up for the three of us. 'Clarke Island.'

Both Maree and Stephen nod. As older children, they've been privy to information I haven't. I hate being seven, the youngest and the last to know things.

'There's a slim possibility of a move there, but nothing's been decided,' reassured Mum from the kitchen where she's busy preparing dinner.

Dad picks up the map and walks off into the bedroom with it. There's a sense of finality about his actions. The mystery will remain for the time being.

I shrug and head through the kitchen and down the back steps of my grandmother's raised house in Woodbridge – a suburb of Brisbane in Queensland. Nana Doris is on holidays in Tasmania and we're housesitting. Our home, a twelve-metre caravan, is parked alongside. It's been parked there since we arrived from Tieri following the death of Granddad in April of 1983.

Elsa is sleeping at the base of the wooden staircase. She's soaking up the afternoon summer sun as only a three-month-old pup can. A white German shepherd, she has a pedigree descended from show dogs. I gently tug her ear. Her modelling career is going nowhere because she's the wrong colour. That's why we have her; unsuitable for showing, she was a giveaway to a good home.

Dad's German shepherd security dog, Oscar, barks playfully and wags his tail. He's secured on a long length of rope to the Hills hoist. Elsa jumps up, grabs his rope in her mouth and begins leading him around. His pink tongue lolls manically. Clearly, he's happy to have someone to play with while he's off duty. I join in the fun and fill out the rest of the afternoon playing with the dogs.

Later that evening, when I'm supposed to be in bed sleeping, I'm actually lying on my stomach in the doorway of the bedroom I share with Stephen. He's pressed up against the wall, also eavesdropping. Dad's on the hall phone; Mum's on the bedroom one. I know they're talking about the Island. Dad's having a phone interview.

'Welding. Of course, I'm a terrific welder.'

I'm perfectly still and in a dark room, but Dad still spots me. He motions angrily for me to go back to bed. Blast, I'm blown. I retreat and consider a different position, but if I get caught a second time, there'll be even more severe consequences. As it is, I'm likely to get a dressing down.

A few days later, Mum and Dad call a family meeting at the dining room table.

Dad lights a cigarette and moves the ashtray closer. He's not stalling so much as trying to come up with the right words. 'I've been offered a job on Clarke Island.'

'Where's that?' I blurt out.

'It's an island off the north-east coast of Tasmania.'

Tasmania? I've never been there because I was born in Townsville, Queensland. My family had a farm on the island state before I was born. They left, I thought, to get away from the place. Why would they go back?

'It's twenty-eight thousand acres.'

I can't imagine that because I have no idea what an acre is.

Dad thumbs out the window. 'The double block is half an acre.'

I try to visualise it in my mind but all I can come up with is big.

Mum grabs Nana Doris's atlas, opens it to the right page and places it on the table.

'It's the third largest island in the Furneaux group,' says Dad.

I zero in on the map and see that he's correct. Flinders, followed by Cape Barren, are the two larger islands and there are literally dozens of others.

'We'd be the only family there, and once we're there, we're there until the plane comes back for us.'

'Isn't there a boat?' I ask, because it doesn't look that far across to Cape Barren which, according to the map, has a settlement called the Corner.

'No boat,' replies Dad. He places a finger on the map. 'We'll fly from Cape Portland. It's about a fifteen-minute flight.'

Seems strange, because Cape Portland doesn't appear to be a town. 'Is there an airport there?'

Dad chuckles. 'No, just a light plane and airstrip.'

'What sort of plane?' asks Stephen.

'A six-seater.'

I visualise a plane in my mind, thinking it's lucky it has six seats, because there are five of us and the pilot will take up the sixth seat. Will there be room for Elsa?

'You'd have to do school by correspondence,' adds Mum.

Away from schoolyard bullies who beat me up regularly. This was sounding better and better. 'What about teachers?'

I'm thinking school of the air through radio like they have in the outback, but my comment causes laughter. My siblings assume I haven't grasped the concept of 'we'd be the only ones there'. I have, which is why I'm so keen for details.

'There'd be mailed lessons and there's a radio telephone, but I'd have to teach you,' says Mum.

I'm genuinely excited, but what's a radio telephone?

'You realise you won't have any friends to play with, don't you?' asks Mum.

I shrug. I've never really had any true friends. Everyone I thought was a friend always turned out not to be.

Mum's worried. I can see it in her eyes.

'We'll be taking Elsa, won't we?' asks Maree.

'Yes, but we can't take Oscar because he's not ours.' There's anger in Dad's tone of voice. He's bonded with that dog whom he's had to rely on during late-night security patrols around Brisbane. The idea of what will become of him in the future is playing heavily on his mind.

'Could we buy him?' asks Maree.

I wince because I know Mum and Dad don't have any spare money.

'Tried, but they wanted a thousand dollars for him,' says Dad, butting out his cigarette more forcefully than required.

My eyes bulge. A thousand dollars is a fortune.

'We'll have to sell the caravan to pay for our move,' says Mum.

I freeze. Aside from this last year, the van, or the ones that came before it, were our home. I'd never lived in a house before this one and this was only temporary. What if the Island didn't work out? What then? I feel a lump form in my throat. The days of living as a nomad are about to end. What lies before us is the adventure of living on an island and there's no plan B.

I don't know what it will be like. I don't even know what the landscape looks like and if Mum and Dad had any photos of the place, they'd be on the table. My mind conjures up images of an isolated utopia. Deserted beaches covered with golden sand. Lush old-growth forests unspoiled by mankind. A haven in the wilderness.

'We'll be driving to Melbourne and catching the *Empress of Australia* across Bass Strait,' says Dad. He again points at a spot on the atlas, this time near the centre of Tasmania. 'There's a six-month trial on the boss's other property, Leverington.'

Six months? That's an eternity.

'Will we have to enrol in a school while we're waiting to go to the Island?' asks Maree.

'Yes, of course,' says Mum. 'The nearest school is Cressy and there's a school bus from the farm gate.'

We all slump. The major appeal of the Island is not having to go to school.

Despondent, we retreat under the house, which is clad only in lattice. A section has been our play area for almost a year. I examine my toy box, which consists mostly of Matchbox cars. We normally move every year or so and sell off or throw away what we don't need beforehand.

When Mum joins us a while later, she looks in alarm at my 'to go' pile. 'Are you sure you want to sell your skateboard and roller skates?'

My body is tall and gangly, which has earned me the nickname Daddy Longlegs. This, combined with an inner ear problem, makes my balance unstable. I've used the skateboard and roller skates only once each and pain and tears were the result. I can't wait to see the back of them. 'Uh huh.'

'What about our bikes?' asks Stephen.

'Your dad thinks there won't be a lot of room on the trip down. We're getting Grace Brothers removalists, but there's limited space.'

Bugger, I was hoping to keep my bike. It's not a cool BMX, just a plain old one-speed, but it's been my wheels since I was four.

Dad appears in the doorway and beckons Mum. Past him I can see a couple of men in suits. Men dressed that way are always bad news. She goes over to Dad and they talk quietly.

'Would it be better not to sell and take the van to Tasmania? We might get a better price down there.'

Dad scowls. 'I'm not lugging the van all the way down there. Besides, the cost of shipping it on the *Empress* would be astronomical.'

They continue whispering.

Mum's close to tears. 'Might as well give it away.' She rushes up the stairs.

Keen to be scarce for a while, I head off for a ride on my bike with my siblings and don't return until dusk.

A few days later, when I return from playing in the park, the van is gone. There's just empty space where it once was and an emptiness within me. We are no longer nomads. Our time as caravanners is over and the time of Clarke Island is about to begin.

*

I awake in a makeshift bed in the back of the short-wheelbase Land Cruiser with my siblings and Elsa. The Old Grey Elephant, as it is affectionately known, is speeding south towards Melbourne. Sitting up, I find a spot where I can stare out the window. The dawn sky is orange and magenta and I love looking at it.

The distance between living places is always marked in days. I know it will take two long days to get to Melbourne and if Dad holds to his normal course we'll be stopping in Dubbo tonight. Dolly Parton is playing on the tape deck. Dad prefers country and western music; the rest of us prefer pop. When Dolly's tape ends, Mum changes it to 'Dumb Ditties'. I was born on the road and this is the only life I've ever known.

In a while, Dad stops for fuel. He uses the stop to examine a map book. Something's not right because I know Dad would know the way to Melbourne blindfolded.

'What's wrong?' asks Maree, who's come to the same conclusion.

'The roads are flooded. We're going to have to find a way around it,' says Dad tossing a packet of potato chips over to us. 'Those are to share.' He closes the map book and heads west.

Maree snatches the packet up. She's the oldest, so she'll have possession until it's empty. As it gets lower, she's able to hold the packet in such a way that her hand blocks access to the contents. When I stick my hand in, I can't reach the chips.

'Stop hogging,' I blurt out.

Dad glances in the rear-view mirror. From where he's sitting, it looks as if Maree's offering them round, but she's really not. Frustrated I straighten my fingers and dive them into the packet. I manage to stab past her closed hand and she drops the packet causing chips to go everywhere.

'If I have to pull up to sort this out, all three of you will get a hiding!' yells Dad.

'He knocked the packet out of my hand,' claims Maree.

It's true I did. 'She was hogging the chips!'

'Was not!'

'Cut it out!' yells Dad.

I know the simplest thing to do is just to drop it, but I feel wronged. 'She was too!'

'I don't want to hear it!'

Never does. I return to staring out the window. Elsa's ended up with the chips, so we've all lost.

Despite the floods, we still end up at Dubbo, it just takes longer to get there. The next day, we're in Melbourne and staying at Alan's house. He's an old work buddy of Dad's.

'We'll be here a couple of days,' says Mum.

I wonder why the delay because, now we're on the road heading to Tasmania, I'm keen to get there.

'Alan is giving your dad a crash course in welding.'

I cock my head. 'I thought Dad was a terrific welder.'

Mum shoots me a look of daggers and I realise I have just confessed to eavesdropping.

Stephen is even more angry. He drags me aside. 'Can't you keep your big mouth shut?'

I stare at the floor. I have a bad habit of blurting things out without thinking. I hadn't done it deliberately. I feel awful and spend the next few days doing my best to be scarce.

Three days later, it's afternoon when we finally say goodbye to Alan and his family and Dad drives us over to Port Melbourne to catch the ferry to Tasmania. The yellow-coloured *Empress* is the largest ship I have ever seen and I can't believe we'll be sailing on it. There is a buzz of excitement as we head through security. We all have to get out of the car, including Elsa, who's on a lead.

'Cars will be loading shortly,' says one of the guards. 'Passengers can head across the gangway now. The dog kennels are on the top deck.'

Mum's face pales, because she realises she is going to have to take us on board herself while Dad drives the car on.

'No food, only water,' says the guard when he sees Stephen holding a can of dog food.

'But she hasn't had her dinner!' exclaims Maree.

'She won't starve to death missing a meal,' says the guard.

Maree's not happy, but she leads Elsa on. The pup is usually a clown on a lead, but right now she has her tail tucked between her legs and is staying close.

We cross the gangway and head straight up to the kennels. The stairs are steeper than normal, but Maree coaxes Elsa up them and she goes into her kennel without a fuss.

Dad's got the car on by the time we head back to the main deck and we head to our cabin. There are only four bunks, but there are five of us.

A steward walking past does a headcount. She stops because she's also noted there's one bed too few.

'I've got a sleeping chair,' says Dad.

'I see,' she replies, 'because there's no sleeping on the floor.'

When the steward moves on, Dad takes us over to check out the sleeping chairs. We each take a turn sitting in it. It lies right back and is surprisingly comfortable.

After we've had dinner, we head back up to see Elsa. She's hunched over and looking dreadfully uncomfortable. It occurs to all of us that she needs to go to the toilet, but won't because she's toilet-trained. There's nothing any of us can do until we reach Tasmania.

In due course, we head back to the cabin and Dad orders us to go shower. He's particular about us showering every night before bed regardless of where we are. Clutching pyjamas, a towel and a wash bag, Stephen and I head off together. Having grown up in caravan parks, I'm used to public amenities with cubicles, but these ones seem ridiculously small and they have handrails.

After I've turned the tap on and stepped under the water, the ship starts rocking violently. I drop the soap and grab the rails. Every time I try to right myself, the ship moves the opposite way. I give up on the shower and do my best to towel myself dry one-handed. I don't do a good job, but I pull on my pyjamas anyway.

Dad comes in. He doesn't seem to be having any trouble with the ship moving. 'You're still wet. Didn't you towel yourself off?'

'The ship started rocking,' I reply.

'It's past Port Phillip Bay Heads and into the open water of Bass Strait,' he replies.

I let go of the railing and almost fall over. He scolds me further about still being wet, but I have bigger concerns than that. Back in the cabin, I discover that an air bed has been pumped up and laid on the floor between the bunks. It seems Dad isn't sleeping in the chair after all and two guesses who'll be on the floor.

The air bed is accompanied by a pillow and sleeping bag. I climb in and try to get comfortable. As the ship rocks, the air bed slides across the floor until in runs into the base of the bunk. It slides the other way crashing into the other bunk when the ship rocks back again. It's going to be a long night.

Despite this, at some point I must have fallen asleep, because Mum wakes me at five a.m. She's keen to pack away the air bed before the steward comes around and sees it. We get dressed. Stephen is insisting on wearing shorts and refusing to put on his shoes.

'You'll have to put your shoes on before we leave the ship,' says Mum.

Stephen shrugs.

'Can we go up and see Elsa?' asks Maree.

'Yes, but stick together,' says Mum.

Elsa's condition has worsened. She's further hunched over and is now whimpering. She's still refusing to go in her kennel. I try to pat her through the mesh, but she's really not interested in being patted. She just wants out so she can relieve herself.

I can see land on the horizon, but it's still a long way off. Unfortunately, she's going to have quite a wait yet.

Dad finishes climbing the stairs and comes over.

'We need to let her out, Dad,' says Maree.

We literally can't because the kennel is secured with a padlock and the guard in charge of dogs has the keys.

'There's nothing we can do. She's going to have to go where she is, or hold it until we disembark.'

Maree's close to tears. While Elsa is the family dog, Maree's been given primary responsibility for Elsa. Sitting down beside the kennel, it's clear Maree's settling in for the rest of the journey.

'Can we go and explore, Dad?' asks Stephen.

'Yeah, but don't go anywhere you shouldn't.'

Stephen and I hurry down the steps and back onto the main deck. The ship is still rocking from a rough sea. On the outside decks it's so windy that it's all we can do to stand up. The wind also has a bite to it and I shiver. Not that I intend to let the cold spoil our explorations.

The ship's passengers are starting to wake up. Red-eyed and zombified, they're gathering on the main deck. Most are holding disposable cups of coffee and or cigarettes.

It's approaching ten a.m. when the ship finally enters the Mersey River and pulls alongside the dock in Devonport. It hasn't warmed up as I'd hoped, and the cold is starting to really seep in. I can't recall it being this cold in midwinter in Queensland and this is only early March. It's not a good omen for how cold it will become when winter arrives.

When the ship docks, Dad helps Maree get Elsa down the stairs to the foot of the gangway.

'I'll go and get the car and meet you in the car park,' says Dad.

We head across the gangway into the terminal. Maree keeps Elsa on a short lead and makes a beeline for the exit. The moment the dog crosses the threshold, she squats.

'Quick, get her over to the grass,' says Mum.

Maree yanks firmly on the lead but Elsa's not budging. She's outside and she's going. A mountain of dog shit is deposited in the doorway and her urine is flowing away from the pile. It's slowly making its way into the terminal. When she's finished, she trots happily over to the grass looking much relieved.

People are staring at us, particularly Stephen, who is still wearing shorts and hasn't put his shoes on. They shake their head in disapproval as they go past.

'Tasmanians are much more conservative than Queenslanders,' says Mum by way of explanation.

I don't know what conservative means and I don't want to ask.

Over at the terminal doorway, passengers are doing their best to step around Mount Crapatoa while waving their hands in front of their noses. A cleaner arrives with a mop and bucket, but he really needs a shovel. He sighs and rubs the bridge of his nose with thumb and index finger.

Red-faced, Mum rushes over to apologise. Maree, who's keen to get the dog away from the scene of the crime, does so on the pretence of taking Elsa for a walk. Now she's relieved herself, she's prancing around being her normal silly self.

Dad arrives with the Land Cruiser. 'What's going on?'

'Elsa's crapped in the doorway,' says Stephen.

Dad appears impressed at the sheer quantity as he heads over to rescue Mum from the cleaner. Until someone finds a shovel, there's really nothing anyone can do. Maree busies herself getting Elsa a drink and feeding her the can of dog food she should have had the night before. She laps up half a bowl before wolfing down her dinner.

Bundling us into the car, Dad drives us west to Burnie. For the next few days, we're going to be jostling around relatives I've never met, which is not a pleasant prospect.

At some point, someone named Aunty Joan looks me up and down. 'So, you're Dion?'

I nod.

'How old are you, then?'

'Be eight in April.'

She rubs her chin. 'So, what do you think about going to Clarke Island and doing school by correspondence?'

I shrug.

'How are you going to cope without any friends? You'll get lonely.'

I shrug again.

Dad's parents, Nan and Pop, come over.

'How are you going to get supplies over there?' asks Pop.

'What are you going to do if one of them is bitten by a snake?' asks Nan before Dad's had a chance to answer the first question.

I see an opportunity to slip away and do so. I'll let my parents answer the 'grown-up' questions. I don't have any answers.

The days in Burnie can't end quick enough.

Trial Period

Gravel crunches under the tyres as Dad turns into Leverington's farm road. On either side of us are grassy paddocks with sheep grazing on them. Further on, I can see some crops, and further still, there's a line of willow trees marking the edge of the Macquarie River.

We pass a weatherboard farmhouse and continue towards a palatial brick one that has been built up on a bank. It's surrounded by formal gardens.

Douglas, our new boss, steps out of the house and Dad gets out of the car and introduces himself. They head away from our car so their conversation will not be overheard by us. It seems like an age before Douglas climbs behind the wheel of an old orange ute. He escorts us past several large sheds to a weatherboard house a couple of kilometres further up the road.

Douglas doesn't come in, he just drops us off. Inside the house, the floors have bare boards and there's no curtains or furniture. In the kitchen there's a wood combustion stove. Upon seeing it, Dad immediately goes outside and begins scrounging kindling and wood from an old woodpile.

It's cool, but not cold, and I wonder what the urgency is.

'There's no hot water if there's no fire,' says Mum, who's getting Maree and Stephen to assist her to unload our luggage from the back of the car.

We don't have any furniture, just sleeping bags and air beds.

Having got a fire going in the combustion stove, Dad is now carrying in some old bricks which he's placing on the floor in the corner of the kitchen. The bricks are accompanied by a plank which he's wrapped in a blue tarp, creating a low bench seat. It's not much, but it's better than nothing.

Mum has decided that we'll all sleep on the lounge room floor for the time being. Used to living in close quarters in a caravan, I don't have an issue with that. That night, Elsa also sleeps with us, as close to Maree as she can get.

Dad goes to work early the next morning. Having commandeered a chainsaw, he returns in time to cut some wood before dark. I've never seen a chainsaw nor had anything to do with wood cutting. Neither has either of my siblings. We stand around with our hands in our pockets.

Dad cuts off a dozen rounds before saying, 'Well, don't just stand there, load it up.'

We look at each other blankly for a moment before cautiously stepping forward to pick up a piece of wood each and place it in the back of the Land Cruiser. Dad hasn't managed to commandeer a trailer or ute but his need to have wood is apparently more important than the mess it will make in the back of the car. Not only do we have to load it, we have to unload it. Dad's cut it; loading and unloading firewood is apparently kids' work.

The next morning, after Dad's gone to work, Mum brings up the issue of us going to school in Cressy.

'I've been thinking about that,' says Maree. 'If we're going to be doing correspondence on the Island, I don't see why we can't get started with that now.'

Mum looks dubious. 'You can't be enrolled in the Tasmanian School of Distance Education until we're living in a remote place where you can't go to school.'

Maree looks thoughtful. 'Yeah, but why can't you just set some lessons. I mean, it would save you having to buy us textbooks and uniforms which we'll only use for a short time.'

I don't need to ask whether money is an issue, because it always is. Perhaps Mum hasn't considered the expense of enrolling us in a new school, or perhaps she has and, like times past, figures she'll manage somehow. However, on this occasion, she seems to be taking Maree's suggestion seriously.

'All right, once you three have washed the dishes, I'll drive you all down to the shearing shed. Then you can all write a composition on it.'

It seems like a strange idea to me, but I'm keen to see the sheep being shorn and so I don't say anything.

Once I get over the smell of the place, the shearing shed is fascinating. There are four shearers, two people picking up fleeces, which they throw onto a large wool table, a classer who sorts the fleeces according to wool quality, one person moving the sheep into the shed, and another counting the shorn sheep and letting them back out again. In addition, there are dogs moving the sheep through the pens towards the shearers.

'So, you're the Clarke Island mob?' says the head stockman, Joe, sizing us up.

'Yes,' replies Mum a little unsure. 'Douglas says he's hoping to send sheep over there within two years.'

Joe raises an eyebrow. 'Really.'

'Do you think it will take longer?'

Joe looks non-committal. 'I guess we'll have to wait and see.'

There's worry in Mum's eyes, but she doesn't voice her concerns. Having thanked Joe for letting us see the shearing, she drives us back to the house. We immediately set about writing a composition, which is no easy task given that we have no desks or even a kitchen table. I write six badly misspelled sentences, Stephen writes ten sentences and Maree manages a page. Now we are playing Uno.

'Right, well, you'll have to do more than play cards for the rest of the day. Write out your times tables.'

'Which ones?' asks Maree.

'Three through to twelve.'

We all groan.

The next day, Dad goes to work as usual, but returns within an hour.

Seeing Dad return home so early, Mum's face pales. 'What's happened?'

'I'm heading to Clarke Island.'

Mum stares blankly. 'When?'

'Now. Douglas's father has a plane on a nearby property. Got to pack and go.'

Mum opens the built-in hall cupboard where we've been storing our clothes and starts stuffing Dad's things into a bag. 'What about food?'

'Yeah, well, I'm going to need some. You're to take the kids and dog to Cape Portland on Friday.'

Mum looks sick. 'But we haven't even sorted food or tools or anything.'

'You'll just have to grab what you think we'll need.'

I know it's more a matter of what she can afford, but I don't voice that aloud.

Having finished packing Dad's clothes, Mum opens the food cupboard, which is only sparsely stocked, and starts tossing food into a box. 'Do you need your guns?'

Dad looks thoughtful. 'Douglas said the plane was only small. There might not be room.'

Within fifteen minutes of coming home, Dad leaves with his clothes and a box of food. We are all speechless. Mum now has to get us ready to go to the Island and she doesn't have long to do it.

Standing in the kitchen, she peers out the widow until Douglas's orange ute disappears out of sight. Then she grabs a pen and paper and starts making a list. 'We'll have to go into Longford,' says Mum.

'When?' asked Maree.

'Now,' replies Mum, grabbing the keys and her handbag.

By the end of the week, Mum has amassed a dozen boxes full of supplies. However, there isn't enough room in the Land Cruiser for all the supplies, plus us three and a German shepherd. Thankfully, Nan and Pop turn up in their panel van.

'One of you three is going to have to travel to Cape Portland with Nan and Pop,' says Mum.

'I'll do it,' I reply, without really giving it any thought.

Both Maree and Stephen let out their breath, leaving me wondering what I again don't know.

'Right, well, make sure you don't swear in front of them, because they're strict Gospel Hall.'

What's a Gospel Hall?

In the back of Pop's panel van are three new foam mattresses and in no time at all he loads as many boxes and bags as will fit.

At dinner, Mum hands out plates, but no one is eating. I go to start, only to receive a not so gentle kick from Maree. I'm confused, but have the sense to desist eating.

'Would you like to say grace, Dad?' asks Mum.

Pop bows his head and speaks a prayer. I've had no exposure to religion whatsoever and the entire ritual seems bizarre. The next morning, we head for Cape Portland.

'I take it you don't normally say grace,' says Nan.

I shake my head.

'And I take it you have not been to Sunday school,' she adds.

My eyes widen. Why would anyone go to school on a Sunday? Crikey, it was bad enough going Monday to Friday. I shake my head again.

Nan spends the next hour talking about Jesus and God.

I stop her at some point. 'If Jesus was such a good man, why did they whip him and nail him alive to a cross?'

'He died for our sins.'

'What's a sin?'

A silence falls over the car. Struth, I'll have to learn to shut up.

There's no more said about God or Jesus for the rest of the trip, but I get the impression Dad's going to cop it next time he speaks to his parents.

We arrive at Cape Portland to discover the weather has deteriorated.

It's too windy to fly over today, so we'll have to see if the weather is better in the morning. The head stockman, Dale, shows us to the shearer's quarters where we'll be spending the night.

Stephen and I spend the next five minutes walking down the side of a fibro building, opening doors. Every room is big enough for two single beds and there are twelve near-identical rooms in total.

'Filthy,' says Nan, wielding a broom she's commandeered from the accompanying laundry. She sweeps and de-cobwebs three rooms.

Stephen and I have to help lift the mattresses outside and beat them with a stick.

In the adjacent cookhouse, Mum is washing down the tables and benches with soapy water. The dining room contains two long tables large enough to seat ten each. The kitchen has a wood combustion stove, in which Pop has lit a fire.

Fearful of being given more chores, Stephen and I go exploring. We discover the hangar right next to the shearers' quarters and we catch our first glimpse of the plane. Yellow and green, it's less than half the size I imagined.

Careful not to touch it, lest I unwittingly cause damage, I peer through the windows. There are only two seats in the plane and less space behind them than there is in the Land Cruiser.

Nan and Pop, along with Mum and Maree, who's leading Elsa, appear. Mum's first impression of the plane causes the colour to drain from her face.

'We're not all going to fit in there,' I say.

'Don't be daft. He'll have to make several trips.'

Oh, right, of course. I walk to the front of the hangar, which has no doors, and peer out. The runway is just a grass paddock. I peer towards the north-east. I can't see it, but Clarke Island is in that direction.

Arrival

The next morning dawns clear and sunny, with little or no wind. A small silver Suzuki ute pulls up beside the hangar and a tall thin man climbs out. He's like a human flagpole. He mumbles a 'Hi' and begins checking his plane.

I've been told his name is Howard, but I've been instructed to call him Mr Miles. He's the boss's brother. When he's finished checking everything from the propeller to the tyres, he fuels the plane from a two-hundred-and-five-litre drum, before meticulously cleaning the windscreen.

Howard opens one entire side of the plane.

'She's a mini cargo plane,' I say.

'A Lockheed Aemacci AL60. The only one of this type around here. She's been re-engineered with a three-hundred-horsepower continental motor.'

'To make her faster?'

'To give her more grunt.'

Howard picks up a pair of bathroom scales and places them on the concrete beside the plane and gestures for me to get on. I do, and removing a pocket notebook and pencil from his top pocket, Howard writes down my weight.

'Excluding my weight, three hundred kilograms a load,' he says before I can ask.

I dash off to assist the others to bring our stuff into the hangar.

Howard sizes it up. 'Four loads,' judges Howard, just from looking at it. 'Don't like to fly more than two at a time, but I'll make an exception today.'

Stephen and I are going in the first load and Howard fits another seat. It slots into grooves in the floor and locks into place.

When loading the cargo, Howard is very particular about where he places things. 'Got to balance the weight,' he says, securing the cargo with another snatchy strap.

He closes the doors and we help push the plane out of the hangar and onto the grass runway. He instructs me to get in the front seat on the right; Stephen is to sit directly behind me. As we're climbing in, Howard heads back to his Suzuki and drives out across the paddock honking his horn. The sheep, who are used to being shooed, head off to one side.

When Howard returns, he climbs in, does up his seat belt and dons a headset. Flicking switches on the dash, which also has dozens of gauges, the engine roars to life. Before he taxis off, however, he leans across and checks both doors are firmly shut.

The plane begins to move forward as Howard lines it up for take-off. Butterflies are fluttering in my stomach and my palms are sweaty. This is it.

The plane speeds down the grass runway and takes off. Howard banks it hard to the left and brings us around in an arc so we're headed north-east. I know this, because there is a compass on the dash. I examine some of the other gauges: altitude, speed, level and a whole heap of others that I'm not sure about.

Below us are grassy paddocks, but very few trees. The absence of trees seems strange to me, but I don't say anything. We leave Cape Portland with its white beaches and head across the water. There's an island approaching, but it's not as big as I imagined. It has no grassy paddocks, just coastal scrub and a lighthouse. I don't recall Dad mentioning anything about a lighthouse.

'Swan Island,' says Howard.

My eyes move to the horizon and I get my first glimpse of our new home. It looks much like the island below us and not at all like I'd imagined. As the distance lessens, I see the mountain range that runs across Cape Barren Island and further north I get a glimpse of Mt Strzelecki on Flinders Island.

When we reach Clarke Island, the plane flies directly over a horseshoe-shaped beach, Rebecca Bay, whose sand has a yellow tinge. The landscape is low undulating hills with distinct types of vegetation in different areas. The south and western parts have large yellow tussocks, the interior is heath, the northern side is tea tree and sheoak and the eastern side has a number of lagoons with a smattering of blue gums and kangaroo tails.

Howard flies low over the house before banking around to line up with the grass airstrip. There are actually two. One runs north–south; the other east–west.

The plane's wheels touch down and bounce several times before contacting properly. I bob in my seat as the plane speeds down the rough strip. Howard brings the plane to a standstill beside a track that disappears into the scrub.

Dad is there standing beside a red-haired man whose name is Wolf. Beside them is an old white David Brown tractor which has a number of dents in its bonnet. Clearly it has seen a lot of action. Attached to it is a flatbed trailer with a wooden tray. Under some trees is an old fishing boat wheelhouse. There's a sign on the side of it that says 'Clarke Island quarantine'. The sign is, of course, a joke.

We pile out and Howard wastes no time unloading the plane and climbing back in so he can head back for the next load. Wolf climbs in with him.

'What do you think?' says Dad.

I'm overwhelmed and somewhat speechless. The place is way wilder than I imagined and reality is setting in. 'It's good.'

Stephen nods. I can tell he also thought the place would be different to what it is.

'How is it good?'

Blast, I was hoping Dad would take the hint and hold the questions. We both shrug.

'Neither of you seems sure.'

We aren't, but there's nothing we can do about that.

Dad places the last our things on the trailer and says, 'Get on.'

I climb onto the trailer. There's no seat and all there is to hang onto is the front panel. The tractor roars to life, sending a cloud of diesel smoke into the air and Dad sets off down a sandy track that winds its way through tea tree and sheoak scrub. We emerge from this at the top of a bank that overlooks a white beach called MacLaine's Bay. Across Armstrong Channel is the mountainous island, Cape Barren. Between the peaks, I can just see the top of Mt Strzelecki.

Dotted across an open grassy area are two weatherboard houses, a large green shed and an old homestead clad in corrugated iron. Dad pulls up in front of the better looking of the two houses and switches off the motor. The house is a perfect square with a steep corrugated-iron roof, a red-brick chimney and a round stovepipe. Attached to the front, affording a view of the beach, is a veranda; across the back is a built-on with a skillion roof. There is also a sleepout with a half dome roof, painted dark green and clad entirely of corrugated iron.

The house has a yard with wooden gates, but there are no gardens and the lawn is mostly cape weed. Entering the yard, Dad walks to the back door and opens it. There is no screen and the porch is unlined. Spiders' webs hang from the exposed rafters and they've been made by evil-looking black house spiders.

There is a step into the main part of the house which is perfectly divided by a hallway that leads to the front door. Its floor is covered in black and white checked vinyl tiles, some of which are damaged. The walls are pine boards painted fluorescent pink.

I suppress a wince and follow Dad into the kitchen. Its floor is covered by red linoleum which has holes in it. My attention is, however, drawn to a wood combustion stove that's going to need a constant supply of firewood. I can already imagine the work that it will require.

Stephen moves his head towards an eight-seater kitchen table which is supporting all manner of condiments and other nonperishable food. He is, however, bringing attention to the ant powder which has been sprinkled around the base of each leg.

Dad leads us to the lounge room, which contains an assortment of old chairs. Across the front are floor-to-ceiling French windows that contain nine panels of glass, each of which is covered in salt spray.

The master bedroom is similar to the lounge, also containing French windows, but with a double bed. The second bedroom contains three single beds which look as if they've been recently repaired with scrounged fence posts and other repurposed timber.

'Did Pop get the mattresses?'

I nod. Something is moving across the floor. Dad sees it, goes into the kitchen and returns with the soft broom. He smacks the broom at the mouse and to my surprise manages to clout it.

'There's a bit of a mouse problem. Wolf is going to bring some traps back with him when he returns in a couple of weeks.' Grabbing the dead mouse by the tail, he carries it into the kitchen and tosses it into the firebox of the stove. Adding another piece of wood, he closes the stove and washes his hands in the sink.

We help Dad carry our stuff into the house before heading back up to the airstrip. Mum and Maree arrive with Elsa on the next load. Maree is looking flabbergasted; Mum looks ill. Neither is saying much. Elsa, who's unclipped from her lead once the plane leaves, is the only one looking happy. Her big pink tongue is hanging out like a grinning idiot.

Dad drives the tractor back to the house, opens the back door and steps in.

Mum follows cautiously. 'Oh, my giddy aunt!'

Maree points at the spiders' webs and black house spiders, who we all know are poisonous. 'And you were worried about snakes, Mum.'

Mum moves through into the kitchen and begins an inspection of the cupboards.

'There's a walk-in pantry,' says Dad, leading the way across the hall. 'It needs some new shelves.'

Mum casts a critical eye at the existing shelves, which are in need of repair, but starts clearing the kitchen table anyway.

'Leave that, I'll show you the rest of the house.' He points to a button on the wall. 'This switch starts and stops the diesel generator, which is located in a shed behind the old homestead.'

'How long can we run it each day?' asks Mum.

Dad scratches his chin. 'About eight hours, depending on how much we fudge the fuel records.'

Mum reluctantly puts down the broom. She walks to the edge of the kitchen where the radio phone and VHF marine radio are. 'Good grief, look at the size of the hole in the wall.'

The hole has been created to pass the cables through from the antennas outside and it's the size of a small coffee mug.

Dad draws her attention to the French windows and spreads his arms wide. 'Look at that view.'

Mum's eyes come to rest on some fresh tree stumps. 'Did you cut down some trees?'

'They were obstructing the view,' replies Dad.

'Did you ask Douglas first?'

Dad ignores her question.

Of course, he didn't. As the Island's new manager, he believes he has the authority to make these sorts of decisions himself. Clearly, Mum isn't so sure about it. She inspects the rest of the house. Judging by her expression, I'd say the Island is not meeting her expectations. I'm of the opinion that things were far worse a week ago, when Dad arrived. I think he's done considerable work since then.

Hearing Howard fly back over, Dad returns to the airstrip and waits up there until the fourth load also arrives. We spend the rest of the morning unpacking our few possessions and settling in as best we can.

Following a lunch of sandwiches, Dad is keen to take us to MacLaines Beach, which is only a five-minute walk away.

'The kids will have to wear boots and long pants as protection against snakes,' says Mum.

I groan. Seriously, is she going to be so concerned about snakes that she's never going to let us do anything?

'I've slashed a track through the bracken ferns all the way to the beach,' replies Dad. 'Besides, the kids know to stand still if they see a snake.'

It was true, we did, and how was this place any more dangerous than where we used to live in Tieri in outback Queensland. In that place, we didn't even wear shoes.

Mum's not happy.

'It'll be fine,' says Dad.

I rush off to find my shorts and thongs, along with a towel.

Dad chuckles when he sees the towel, but fails to let me in on the joke.

We head out the back door and Elsa runs ahead, thrilled to be off lead. She finds a stick, indicating she wants to play fetch. Dad throws it for her and she takes off after it. I stop when we come to a six-strand wire fence.

'This is an electric fence,' says Dad, 'but I've taped some old garden hose to the electric strands so you can step through it.

No one rushes forth, so I step through. When I don't get shocked, everyone follows. We continue to the beach, which is on the other side of a two-metre-high sand dune.

The beach is half a kilometre long with pure white sand. Out in the bay, the water is aqua blue; in close, it is crystal clear. I hurry down the path to the beach and discover the sand is so fine it squeaks underfoot.

Losing my T-shirt and thongs, along with my towel, I charge straight into the water. I'm three running steps in when the cold hits me. I try to gasp, but the water has taken my breath away. Desperate for air, I flee from the water. I can't get out quick enough. My lower half is numb and I'm shivering.

'Thought you were being a bit optimistic,' says Dad. 'You're not in Queensland any more.'

No, we certainly weren't.

The expedition continues down the beach led by Elsa who is discovering that sea gulls are fun to chase. She's also discovered cuttlefish bone which makes a good substitute for sticks. Maree tosses one into the water and Elsa charges in after it, undeterred by the freezing water.

At the far end, we discover a large tidal rock pool about seven by seven metres. Surrounded by high rocks on either side, it's sheltered from the worst of the wind. The water is only waist-deep and not as cold. There's also no chance of being caught in a rip or tugged out by an undertow. Best of all, unless we have visitors, we won't have to share it with anyone.

It's the first bit of Clarke Island's magic that we've discovered and it challenges our first impressions.

Early Days

That evening, Mum and Dad slip out with a dolphin torch and Dad's single shot Lithgow .22 rifle. They return with a couple of wallabies. Chocolate-brown in colour, they're only around fifty centimetres high, with peaked ears and a cute face. I'm horrified when I realise they've been shot and killed, but this is nothing compared to how I feel when I realised they are being skinned for meat.

'There's no supermarkets around here, lad. If we want meat, we have to get it ourselves.'

The realisation hits me like a sledgehammer to the stomach. There is no way I'm eating that. Surely, he's joking.

He isn't and the next day a wallaby stew is cooking in a cast-iron pot on the combustion stove. The pungent smell is travelling through the house and is impossible to avoid. That evening, Mum serves it up with slightly stale bread. I push the meat to one side and eat the vegetables around it. Normally, it's the other way around.

'This meat's still got fur on it!' exclaims Stephen.

He's right, it has.

'A bit of fur won't hurt you,' says Dad. He doesn't normally eat much meat, but he's making a great show of tucking in.

I relent and choose a bit which doesn't appear to have fur on it. It tastes gamey but, having been slow-cooked, it's very tender. I eat most of my dinner and so does everyone else.

Maree, Stephen and I are still washing dishes when there's a commotion in the bathroom.

Dad gets up to investigate. 'Who left the back door open?' he roars.

'I did,' confesses Maree. 'Elsa went out and wouldn't come when I called her. I left the door open so she could get back in.'

'She'll have to bark if she wants inside. We've got to keep the door shut so things can't come in,' says Dad. 'I'll get a screen door next time we go off the Island.' He closes the door and heads into the bathroom to investigate what's in there.

Pulling back the curtain slowly, he discovers Elsa in the bottom of the shower, with its built-in baby bath, and she's not alone. She's caught a wallaby and brought it home unharmed.

Looking unimpressed, Dad grabs the wallaby by the back legs.

'Can we keep him?' my siblings and I ask simultaneously.

'No,' replies Dad firmly. 'You can't keep him. This place will become a farm and the animals won't be pets.' He takes it outside and thankfully lets it go on the other side of the house yard gate, which someone has also left open.

I breathe a sigh of relief because for a moment I thought he was going to kill it and serve it up for tomorrow's dinner. Elsa runs to the gate, which Dad closes, and peers after it. She watches it hop away before coming inside.

The next day, Mum uses the radio phone to call the Tasmanian School of Distance Education in Hobart.

'No, you don't understand, I can't pop down to the nearest school and get a signature from the headmaster. We're on an island… No, we don't have a boat… The plane's not coming back for at least two weeks… Well, what am I supposed to do in the meantime?' Mum rolls her eyes, says goodbye and hangs up. 'Bloody idiot. He won't enrol you all in school until I get a form signed by a headmaster to say you can't attend proper school. It's not as if we can just fly off and do these things. What part of "we're on an island" doesn't he understand?'

'Does it mean there won't be school for a while?' asks Stephen.

'It seems that way,' replies Mum.

'Can we go down the wharf fishing, then?' I ask.

'Might as well,' says Mum. 'See if we can't catch some fish for dinner.'

We don't have any fishing rods, but there are a couple of hand lines on spools about as big as an entrée plate, fitted with cord. Attached are lead sinkers, big swivels and large silver hooks.

The wharf is about the same distance away as the beach, but in a different direction. There's no electric fence to negotiate, but there is a series of stockyards. At the bottom of a steep hill, the yards narrow into a loading race which runs to the end of the wharf.

The timber wharf has been built adjacent to a small cove which forms a natural breakwater. I peer over the end and discover there's about a metre of water, which will increase to twice that as the tide reaches full.

Dad, who's allowed to work flexibly and has thus come with us, jumps off the wharf onto some rocks. He kicks at a couple of limpets, who dislodge. Using his thumb, he removes the shell before threading the tough flesh onto hooks.

We drop the lines over the edge and it's only a few minutes before we're getting bites. Mum's the first to pull in a sizeable parrotfish. A short while later, Maree pulls in a leatherjacket.

'Watch the spine, it's poisonous,' says Dad.

We catch several more parrotfish before we head back. Dad leads us to the outdoor table he used to skin the wallaby on. Of course, it's been cleaned since then. Producing two pocketknives, he gestures to the bag of fish, indicating he wants us to clean them.

Grabbing one by the head, I try to flick the scales off but the fish just shoots across the table.

'You've got to dig your fingers right into its gills so you can hang on to it,' says Dad.

I clasp the fish tighter and this time manage to dislodge the scales, which fly in all directions. It's an icky job and I make a mess. When I'm happy that I've got the scales off, Dad directs me to slit the fish's belly open and rip out the guts. Grabbing hold of it, I tug at it and discover it takes all my strength to rip it out. By the time I finish the first fish, my hands are covered in blood and slime up to the wrist. It's awful.

Stephen and Maree have fared a little better, but not much. Dad removes the heads with a machete and we take them in to the kitchen sink.

'Can we have chips with them?' I ask.

Mum nods slowly. 'Sure, if you're happy to peel and cut the potatoes into chips.'

I sigh as I realise how much effort will be involved to create enough chips for five. There's no slipping to the takeaway shop, because there isn't one.

'Best take the guts and heads away,' says Dad. 'Best take them back down the wharf and empty them into the sea.'

I sigh again and set off with the bucket. Next time, we'll clean them on the rocks. By the time I've walked the bucket to the wharf and back, I've come to the conclusion that Dad wanted me to work that out for myself.

*

A fortnight after we arrive, Howard flies Wolf back over with supplies including some multicoloured hens and a big black rooster. The chickens are let loose in a pre-existing coop with an attached house, which we've cleaned out. Aside from being somewhat stressed, they appear to be in good condition. They're soon scratching up their yard, which is a good sign.

Inside the house, Wolf asks, 'So you have a rifle?'

'Only a .22,' replies Dad.

'That'll do. Come on, we'll go and get some steak.'

'But we haven't got a freezer and won't have one until the *Flinders Trader* brings our furniture from Launceston,' says Mum.

Wolf waves away this inconvenience. 'You can't raise growing kids on wallaby and parrotfish.'

Dad seems unsure, but Wolf is adamant. I watch as they drive off on the David Brown, which has been fitted with a loader bucket and a carry-all. They return an hour later with a headless cow that's been gutted but not skinned. They hang it from the rafters of the workshop.

A few hours later, Mum wanders down to the workshop with a

large enamel bowl. She looks at the horribly thin cow carcass, which has now been skinned, with a sense of hopelessness. Wolf sees her and climbs out from under the D6 bulldozer he's working on. Without washing the grease off his hands, he picks up one of the two pocket-knives and hacks a hunk off a back leg.

I don't know much about cows, but I know this one is not in good condition. Her plight is due to a lack of grazing pasture. The grease aside, the meat doesn't look good. Mum takes it back to the house and spends a good ten minutes washing it off before laying it on a wooden chopping board.

Since there are no knives, other than the two pocketknives, she picks up one and attempts to slice off some steak. The meat rolls unharmed across the chopping board first one way and then the other. She tries the other knife, but the result is the same.

A panicked look appears on her face. No matter what she tries, the knives are simply too blunt to cut off steaks.

'Do you know where the machete is?' asks Mum.

I'm not allowed to use the machete, so no, I don't. I shrug.

'Can you go down to the workshop and see if you can find it?'

Stephen and I head off. The machete is sitting on a wooden bench not far from the cow carcass.

'Mum needs the machete to cut up the meat,' says Stephen.

Dad pauses from unbolting something from a piece of machinery he has on the workshop bench and cocks his head. 'You can't go hacking at the meat with a machete.'

'She can't cut it up with the pocketknives, they're too blunt,' says Stephen.

Dad wipes his hands on a piece of rag and returns to the house with us. Mum has given up on the meat and is sitting at the kitchen table crying. Dad doesn't say anything, he just produces a whetstone from one of the kitchen drawers and begins sharpening one of the knives.

'I can't do this. We need our things. We need decent knives. We need to get the kids' school form signed.'

Dad finishes sharpening the first pocketknife and then phones Douglas. When he hangs up from talking to him, he phones Howard.

'We'll fly off tomorrow for a few days and get these urgent things sorted. Wolf is here, so he can look after Elsa, feed the chooks and keep an eye on the place.'

Mum blows her nose and washes her hands before taking up the now sharp pocketknife. She manages to slice off some strips of meat, but they look nothing like steak. At dinner, she serves up the meat with vegetables. It's so tough that it's all I can do to hack off a piece with a table knife. Of course, we have no steak knives. Chewing it is nigh impossible, but somehow Wolf manages it.

That night, I'm still awake when Dad switches off the generator and the lights go out. It seems like only a few minutes later when I hear footsteps in the hall. There's no torchlight, so I know it isn't Mum who's night blind and thus always carries a torch. I check the other beds beside me, but neither Stephen or Maree have gotten up. It has to be Dad or Wolf. Wolf is sleeping out in the sleepout and I haven't heard the back door open. If he's come into the house, surely it would only be to use the toilet, and that's at the far end of the porch. There'd be no need for him to come into the hall except to pass into the kitchen and if he's left something he needs there, surely he'd have brought a torch with him.

The footsteps go back up the hall before coming back down again. I feel the hair on the back of my neck stand up. A moment later, a spectre appears in the doorway. The form is not fully solid but I can tell it's a woman. She's holding an old-fashioned kerosene lantern.

The woman is also wearing a dress that's a century out of fashion. She glances at each of us in turn before pulling the door shut from fully open to about a quarter. The door, which was open, actually moves. Her footsteps move away from the door and the house falls silent again.

I'm too frightened to move, not even to pull the covers over my head, not that that would help. I must be dreaming. I know I'm not and I know what I saw and heard. I lie there listening intently until I drift off to sleep.

In the morning, Mum instructs us to dress in our good clothes in preparation for going off the Island. This consists of a tracksuit which is butt-ugly and makes me feel silly, but there's no point in arguing.

Dad, having finished his Weetbix, is drinking a cup of tea. 'Did any of you kids get up last night after the power was switched off?'

We all shake our heads.

'Did you come in last night, Wolf?'

He too shakes his head.

I want to speak up but I'm not going to. The last thing I want is to be ridiculed.

Dad notices me looking particularly quiet. 'What did you see, lad?'

I shrug and he repeats the question. 'I saw a ghost. A woman in an old dress with a lantern.' I wait for the laughter, but there is none.

'Didn't want to say anything,' says Stephen, 'but I've seen ghosts too, but down at the other house. A young boy was fleeing something and he opened the door on this end. The one which is nailed shut.'

Dad nods and turns to Maree.

'I haven't seen anything, but I was looking in the old homestead yesterday, reading the newspapers on the wall. I swear I could feel a presence. Then I found the grave of Emily Anne MacLaine up behind the generator shed.'

This is the first I've heard about the grave. 'Do you think it's her?'

Dad looks mystified. His Christian upbringing doesn't accommodate ghosts, yet I can tell he believes us.

'It seems to me like more than one presence, but I wouldn't worry. I don't think they intend any harm,' says Mum, trying to sound reassuring.

I am worried, but I let the subject drop.

Howard arrives soon after and flies us all off in two loads. Mum goes on the first plane, Dad on the second, the idea being that if anything happens, there's always one parent on the Island with whichever child is still there. At the same time, Howard delivers supplies to the Island – in this case, grain for the chooks and forty-kilogram LPG gas bottles, along with other odds and sods.

It occurs to me that Howard doesn't like to fly over empty. This means Mum and Dad will need to coordinate supply drops before the plane comes over to pick someone up. I know that Dad has already set up accounts with the supermarket and hardware in Scottsdale and the hardware has a delivery truck that comes to Cape Portland. As long as there's room on the truck, they're happy to bring a couple of boxes of food along as well, at no extra cost.

Four hours later, we're back in Burnie staying with Mum's sister Aunty Mora. She owns a café and can buy food in bulk at much cheaper prices, which is a godsend. I'm restless. Until now I'd never noticed just how smelly and noisy towns are. I'm not the only one who can't settle. Everyone else is also uneasy.

Thankfully, we only stay two nights, just long enough for Mum and Dad to buy essential things, including decent knives. On the way back, we call into the Gladstone primary school, so Mum can get the school form signed.

Mum's looking stressed when she returns to the car from seeing the headmaster. 'Does no one understand what a sodding island is?'

'Wouldn't he sign it?' asks Dad.

'He did, but not until I got into an argument with him. He seemed to think we ought to be able to bring the kids across Bank Strait in the morning in time to catch the school bus and then bring them back in the afternoon. Bloody moron.' Mum puts the form into an envelope and seals it.

Dad drives to the post office, not just so Mum can post the letter, but so they can drop off a cheque. Thankfully, the postmaster is already up to speed with the need to hold money for future postage costs. The same arrangement is also in place for Cape Portland and a number of other properties in the vicinity. There's also an arrangement with the school bus driver to bring the mail down to Gladstone and drop it off at the post office.

Howard flies us back that afternoon. I can't believe how good it is to be back. Despite the hardship, the place has become our home. When we get back to the house, Mum makes a coffee and takes it out onto the veranda. Her gaze is on the view of the beach and Cape Barren Island. I can tell she's glad to be home and has got over the initial shock of the day of arrival.

Settling In

A few days later, a four-seater low-wing plane lands and we head up to the airstrip on the David Brown. The plane reminds me a little of a Spitfire. A plane version of a sports car.

'She's a Piper Comanche 400,' says Dad. 'She's the plane I first flew over in. She's fitted with a V8 engine and has three propeller blades. Flies like a rocket.'

The door opens over the wing and Joe and two other stockmen get out, along with an old man who is the boss's father. Dad calls him by the initials ED, but I'm instructed to refer to him as Mr Miles, the same as Douglas and Howard.

ED climbs down and opens a compartment which is chock-a-block full of bedding, luggage and boxes of food. I can't believe so much stuff came out of such a small compartment. Dad gets them settled in the bottom house and they drive off across the Island.

They return a couple of hours later with a mob of six stock horses and a Shetland pony. A halter is placed on the pony and he's taken down and shut in the large yard above the wharf. Maree takes us down to have a look at him. The pony comes right up to her and she speaks to it quietly while gently stroking his neck. A good ten minutes later, she grabs hold of his mane and slings her leg over his back. She rides the pony around the yard bareback.

'He's quiet as,' she says. 'Shame he's being taken off, because he's an ideal size to learn on.'

We head back to the house and put the hard word on Mum and Dad.

'He belongs to your Uncle Ernie, who was the manager before us. He's moved to Flinders Island to manage a property up there.'

'Do you think he'd consider selling him?' asks Maree.

Mum sighs. 'I could ask him, but if we do buy him, he'll have to be your Christmas present.'

We all nod eagerly.

That night, following a phone call to Uncle Ernie, Mum and Dad agree to buy the pony, who they discover is called Cheeky. Over the next few days, we take turns riding Cheeky round the little yard. He sure is a placid quiet little fellow. I envision long rides across the Island with a cut lunch in a saddlebag.

That evening, the stockmen, who have been out mustering cattle, bring in a mob of about one hundred and twenty head. They're a mix of Hereford and Angus and they're all in poor condition.

The next morning, the cattle are driven into a set of post and rail stockyards, which are in an adjoining paddock about two kilometres from the houses. Once they're shut in, my siblings and I are allowed to go up and take a look.

'Make sure you stay on that side,' says Joe. 'These are wild cattle and they'll take to you like a loose propeller.'

We find a good spot where we can see but won't be in the way. The stockmen are separating the older calves from the breeding cows. There don't appear to be any bulls.

Even so, the cows shake their heads and dig up the dirt with their front hooves. On several occasions, one of the stockman has to run for the safety of the fence and leap over. The drafting continues for much of the day. In the end, it comes down to one stubborn bull calf. They've got him separated, but he's refusing to come out of his pen and join the others. Dad's doing his best to shoo him.

'Leave him be,' says Joe.

The bull calf snorts and digs the dirt with his front hoof. Given that he appears to be only a few months old, it's quite comical.

Dad shakes his head and turns around to walk off. That's when the calf charges. He butts Dad up the backside, lifting him up in the air. Dad goes sprawling but luckily stays on his feet. The calf turns on a dime and charges a second time, but Dad manages to get out of the way.

'You little beast. I'll have you for steak.'

The calf takes umbrage at Dad's threats and charges a third time. By this time, Dad is climbing out.

The sound of laughter fills the air and I look up to see that all three stockmen are so hysterical, they're crying. To add insult to injury, the calf now happily trots out of the pen and joins the others.

Joe closes the gate behind him. 'We won't be able to bring them down to the wharf until we've unloaded the incoming cargo and we'll have to move the pony out of the way.'

We head back to the house and discover the *Flinders Trader* is anchored in the bay.

'What sort of boat is she, Dad?' I ask.

'She's an auxiliary ketch, thirty-one metres long and six metres wide with a one-hundred-and sixty-seven-tonne capacity,' replies ED, matter of factly. He turns to address Dad. 'There's an issue with the stock on Leverington. I have to leave immediately and take Joe and Peter with me.'

Dad glances at the sky. 'You going to have enough time before dark?'

'There's fifty-five minutes of official light left. I only need forty-five.'

I suck air through my teeth. That's cutting it fine. There's a rush to get them up to the airstrip. Once airborne, I watch him fly into the distance, wondering if he'll be forced to land in Launceston, where the airstrip is lit by lights.

Back at the house, we have a cup of tea. Afterwards, Dad grabs a saddle and bridle from the bottom house and heads down to the wharf paddock. Maree soon has Cheeky bridled and saddled. She gets on and Dad opens the gate. Nudged forward, the pony walks on happily. Three lengths clear of the gate, he bolts.

If I didn't see it, I would not have believed the speed the pony could gallop. Maree manages to stay on until the pony turns at a right angle. She sails off, but luckily lands on the sandy ground. We run over to her. She's angry but not hurt.

'He just took off,' she exclaimed.

Dad runs a hand across his bald patch and walks over and grabs the pony by the reins. He happily trots along as Dad leads him up to the house.

'It might be just because he hasn't been ridden in a while,' says Maree.

'Let me have him,' says Scott. 'He just needs a firm hand.'

Scott climbs on and nudges the pony forward. He again bolts and again turns at a right angle. Somehow, Scott manages to stay on, and the pony breaks into a gallop again. Three times the pony tries to throw him. By the time they return to the house, Cheeky is frothing at the mouth.

Scott gets off and he's shaking. 'That pony's crazy,' he says.

Maree gets a stubborn look in her eyes. 'I'm getting back on.'

'Be careful,' says Mum.

Maree climbs on and nudges Cheeky. He walks forward and I wait for him to break into a gallop. She kicks him in the flank with the heels of her boots, but Cheeky's exhausted and refuses to go faster than a walk.

When she returns, I climb on and take him for a walk around the paddock. Stephen does likewise after me.

'The only way you're going to be able to ride him is if you gallop him first,' says Scott.

'Yeah, but what's the point of that? If he's exhausted, we're not going to be able to take him far.'

'True,' he says, pointing to the other horses who are in the generator paddock about five hundred metres away. 'See that chestnut with the white stripe down his face. He's called Horse. You can ride him, but I'd be careful with the others.'

I sigh. 'No point keeping Cheeky if we can't ride him.'

'Too late now,' says Dad. 'I've already agreed to take him. Can't go back on my word.'

Blast. Cheeky's our Christmas present and he's a lemon. Dad and Maree lead him over to the generator paddock, unsaddle him and turn him loose with the others.

That night, we all sit around the table discussing the plan of action for unloading the boat, which will be docking with the incoming tide at dawn. The boat will need a half tide to dock and we'll have to unload her before the tide goes back past half again.

'Six hours isn't long. We're going to have to push it along,' says Dad.

'The furthest tie-off point can't be got to once the tide's over quarter,' says Scott. 'Someone will have to row out and tie off the stern rope.'

'You mentioned it,' says Dad with a sly grin.

'Don't mind, but I can't do it on my own.'

Dad rubs his chin. Two of the men who were supposed to be here to help with the boat just left, which leaves just Scott and him, plus Mum and us kids.

'I'll do it,' I blurt out.

'Yeah, I'm thinking you and Maree. Stephen can take the bowline up to the hook on the rocks besides the wharf. I'll take the other stern line to a tie-off eye on the opposite side of the wharf, which leaves Joy on the wharf.

'I don't know the first thing about docking a boat,' exclaims Mum.

'You just have to drop the lines over the bollard,' says Dad. 'It'll be fine.'

Mum's not so sure. She's also worried about Maree and me being in the dinghy. If something goes wrong, the *Trader* could easily crash into us and there are no life jackets on the Island, so obviously we won't be wearing one.

That night, I'm so excited I can't sleep. I'm only eight, but I already feel the beginnings of becoming a man. Tomorrow I won't be just an onlooker, I'll actually have a role to play.

At dawn, Scott, Maree and I launch the Island's dinghy, *Marianne*, off the wharf beach and Scott rows the boat the ten metres to the wharf and lets us drift.

Maree dips the long measuring staff into the water to test the depth. 'Six foot one,' she says.

'Just a few more inches should do it,' replies Scott.

Dad is using the larger tractor, a 1066 International, to reverse a single-axle truck-trailer down the ramp onto the wharf. Because there's no room to turn round, there's about half a kilometre of reversing to do and there's little room for error. Dad manages it easily.

'Super piece of reversing that,' says Scott, genuinely impressed.

'He used to drive semi-trucks,' I reply.

Dad climbs out and Maree hands him up the staff. Once she has, Scott rows out towards the *Trader*, which is lined up and ready to pull in. There's a marine radio back at the house, but there's no one up there and, even if there was, there's no way to talk to them from here. So communication the easy way is impossible. When we're closer, Scott waves his arms in a beckoning motion.

Black diesel smoke puffs out of the *Trader*'s exhaust as the skipper revs the motor. She comes towards the wharf a lot faster than I expect and it's all Scott can do to row us out of the way. As the *Trader* slips past, we bob around like a cork in her backwash.

The line, which is attached to a buoy and leader, is thrown out and Maree manages to lean out and grab it.

'When we reach the rocks, jump out and hold the dinghy, while I secure the line to the tie point,' says Maree.

I grab the dinghy's lead rope and prepare to jump out. The surge is still considerable and I realise it's not going to be easy. If I mistime this, I could easily slip and hurt myself or end up in the water.

'Hurry up with the stern line!' shouts one of the crew.

I can see that the stern is drifting towards the natural breakwater and realise the urgency. Scott heaves on the oars and the dinghy reaches the rocks. I jump out. My foot slips, but I'm able to steady myself to avoid falling over. Maree, who's defter on her feet than me, jumps out and begins hauling on the ship rope, but it's too heavy for her.

'Hold on to her, boy,' says Scott. 'If she gets away, you'll have to swim after her.'

I don't mention that I can't swim more than dog-paddle. He jumps out and helps Maree haul the line in. The crew are still yelling at us, but there's nothing more we can do.

Once the line is secure, Scott rows us back to the wharf beach and we drag the dinghy up above the high tide mark. Although the wharf is only ten metres away, there's no quick way back to it. We either have to clamber across the rocks or walk around the track, which will take a good fifteen minutes. We elect to clamber across the rocks and it's not easy going.

By the time we get onto the wharf, the place is in chaos. The *Trader*'s jib crane is lifting larger items onto the trailer, but smaller boxes are simply being dumped on the wharf anywhere there's room.

'Careful with our things,' says Mum.

She's ignored. All we can do is start moving stuff further up the wharf and into the stockyards, where it's at least out of the way.

Once the trailer is full, Dad runs it up to the workshop, where he has made space. There's no time to sort out what's what. All we can do is put it in a pile. Worst of all, there's no crane or forklift to lift the stuff off the trailer. Everything has to be done by hand.

Maree and I are helping as best we can, but we're not strong enough to lift fifty-kilogram bags of superphosphate. All we can do is drag them to the edge of the trailer for Dad and Scott. Stephen's a lot stronger, but even he can't manage the heavy bags.

Five and a half hours later, the captain is yelling at everyone to hurry up. He's watching the height of the water as it slowly drops.

'How much more is there?' asks Dad, trying to peer into the hull.

'This load should do it,' comes the reply.

'Stephen, you stay with me. Scott, take the other two and go and grab the dinghy.'

I fall into step with Stephen and Maree. We've decided it will be quicker to foot it around to the wharf beach. By the time we row out to the rocks, the captain is ready to cast off. We unhook the lines and the *Trader* steams out faster than she came in. A moment later, she's at full speed crossing Armstrong Channel. I expected them to re-anchor in the bay.

'Where are they going? I thought we had to load the calves on.'

'We do, but the captain's worried about rough weather. If it does cut up rough, God only knows when she'll be able to dock again.'

When we get back to the house, Mum is flat out trying to cook a hot meal, while also unpacking. I sigh and look helplessly around at the mess. I want to help, but don't know where to start.

Dad drains his mug of tea. 'Maree, Scott wants to know if you think you could handle one of the stock horses and help him bring the calves down to the wharf.'

Maree nods. 'Yeah, I'll give it a go.'

They catch and saddle three horses. I knew Maree could ride, but I didn't realise Dad could. Then it occurs to me that he can't. Short of riders, all he can do is learn on the job. At least he has the sense to choose Horse. Maree's on a black mare called Candy; Scott's on a grey called Pistol.

From the saddle, Scott points. 'We'll try and bring them straight down the track. They're not going to want to go, so spread out and do what you can to stop them peeling off.'

I realise that he means we're to help on foot. Not good. I've already seen one of the bull calves charge Dad. I make a plan to run if need be, but the reality is I'm already exhausted. I'm not going to be able to out-run even a calf.

The three riders manage to get them almost to the wharf paddock, when the bull calf who got angry with Dad decides to cause trouble. He breaks from the mob and makes a run for it. Scott cracks his stock whip and causes the bull calf to think again. Still the mob doesn't want to go into the wharf paddock, and they mill around the gate.

'Steady,' says Scott. He doesn't want to push them too hard, lest they break.

All we can do is keep pressure on them from behind and hope a leader will take the initiative and pass through. The stand-off lasts a good ten minutes. Then one moves forward, followed by a second, and the rest follow. Stephen swings the gate closed behind them.

I smile, pleased with the effort.

'They're not off the Island until they're on the *Trader*,' says Scott. He points towards Preservation Island, where the *Trader* was last seen. She's not there, which means she's likely returned to Flinders Island.

Since Dad hasn't put up the television aerial, which has only just arrived, there's no television reception. All he can do is phone the Bureau of Meteorology to get a forecast.

Dad puts the receiver down and shakes his head. 'Not looking good.'

The next morning, there's a westerly and the sea is too rough for the *Trader* to sail down from Flinders Island, let alone dock. There's no water trough on the wharf and by noon we're forced to let the calves go. The forecast indicates the westerly has set in and isn't likely to change for a week. Unfortunately, the opportunity to get the calves off the Island is lost. They're turned loose and the muster has been for naught.

It's just the way things are.

The Garden and School

The next day, Dad emerges from the workshop with a length of galvanised pipe. Climbing the ladder onto the house roof, he secures it to the main chimney with fencing wire.

'Pass me up that antenna,' says Dad, who seems to have no concern about being on the steep roof.

Stephen passes it up to him and Dad fastens it to the end of the pipe before returning to the house and climbing into the manhole. Once he's fed the ribbon through the roof, he secures it to the television before getting back onto the roof. Mum stands in front of the television, Stephen stands in the hall, I stand at the back door and we relay messages about the reception.

'Nothing,' I yell.

Dad's got the antenna pointed in the direction of Launceston. He moves it a smidge.

'Still nothing,' I yell.

Red-faced, Dad climbs down the ladder to see for himself. Frustrated, he climbs back up and slowly turns the antenna a half turn.

'There, but only ABC,' I relay.

Dad lights a cigarette and casts his gaze at Home Hill. 'Flipping signal is bouncing off the boulders up there.'

That night, Dad lights a fire in the open fireplace and we all cram into the lounge room to watch the ABC. The show is reaching the point of high drama, when the phone suddenly rings. The reception completely cuts out.

'Stupid radio phone,' says Dad getting up to answer it.

Seeing there will be no reception while the phone is in action, we groan and head into the kitchen, where Stephen finds a pack of cards. We start playing the same as we have every night since arriving.

The next day, Dad heads over to the fenced-off garden, which is full of weeds. It's tucked in behind a tea tree and sheoak shelter belt which spares it the worst of the westerly wind created by the Roaring Forties that the Island is located in. Having hoed down the weeds, Dad begins to turn the soil. It's mostly sand mixed with subsoil, making it an unhealthy orange colour. If there was ever any topsoil, it's long gone now.

'We're going to have to build it up with manure and mulch,' says Mum.

Dad leans on his shovel and nods. He disappears and returns on the David Brown. 'Well, don't stand about, grab a shovel.'

I sigh and do as asked. For the next few hours, we walk around the paddock shovelling horse and cow manure into the bucket of the tractor, which Dad tips over the garden fence. When we've got a sizeable pile, Dad announces that we now need seaweed. He drives the David Brown, which is towing a trailer, down to the wharf beach.

There are great rifts of seaweed half a metre deep. I'm hoping Dad is going to magic a pitchfork from somewhere, but he doesn't.

'Well, pick it up,' he says.

There's no point picking up a handful at a time. I get down on one knee and gather up an armful. My front is instantly covered in seawater and sand and much of it gets beneath my shirt.

'Ooo, it's got lice in it,' says Maree, brushing frantically at her arms.

'They won't hurt you,' replies Dad.

He's probably right, but they still feel horrible when they crawl across your skin.

Mum stops picking up weed and starts digging in the sand. 'Pipis.'

I lean across to take a look and see that she's referring to shellfish that look like mini-clams. They're about the size of a one-cent piece. Retrieving the bailing tin from *Marianne*, she fills it up.

After we've unloaded the seaweed, we clean up and have lunch.

'There's got to be more of those triangle huts around here,' says Dad.

He's referring to the one that Uncle Ernie dragged over to use as a chook house. They have a wooden base and plywood sides held together in the shape of a triangle by sawn-in-half treated pine logs. It occurs to me that Dad has been so busy working that he hasn't had time to explore.

'There's at least a dozen of them,' I reply. 'They're tucked into the bush behind the bottom house across from the old toilet block.'

'What were they used for, Dad?' asks Stephen.

Dad grins. 'Used to be a nudist colony here. They set up a bit of a commune.'

Since I'm still acclimatising from Queensland, I think it's awfully cold here to be getting around nude.

Dad gets up. 'Best show me. I want to bring some more over. We're going to need more than one chicken coop, plus we need a grain shed. Too far to be trudging down to the workshop every day to get grain for the chooks.'

'Can we get some ducks, Dad?' asks Stephen.

He shrugs. 'Can't see why not, but you'll be looking after them.'

Of course.

Dad uses the David Brown to tow some sheds over and gently nudges them into position with the bucket of the tractor.

That night, for dinner, we have pipi chowder that contains seaweed and limpet along with chunks of parrotfish. The soup's surprisingly good, once I got used to having a bowl full of shells which I have to suck the meat out of. It occurs to me that I'm growing accustomed to eating Island foods, which is a good thing, because there aren't any shops.

The next day, Howard arrives with a load of supplies, including a number of boxes that have a Tasmanian School of Distance Education stamp. Maree and Stephen have learned to drive the David Brown and Dad's left us to handle the airstrip run.

'Looks like your lessons have arrived,' says Howard.

I groan. I've gotten so used to not having to do school that I'd almost forgotten that it would be a temporary respite. Back at the house, we carry the boxes in and sit them on the school desk that Dad has set up in the corner of the lounge room.

Mum immediately grabs a pair of scissors and cuts the boxes open. There's an accompanying letter which she takes a moment to read. 'You have a box each and each booklet is a week's work.'

The sound of hammering echoes through the house. I glance out the window to see that Dad is fixing corrugated iron on the end of the veranda.

'Come and give us a hand,' he yells.

Dad has grown used to having us at his beck and call and doesn't realise that's about to end now that our lessons have arrived. Mum gets a stern look in her eyes and goes out to tell him. We sneak along to eavesdrop.

'Didn't know the school stuff was going to arrive today. I need a hand to get the iron on.'

'I don't think you understand. You can't be calling out for us any time you need a hand. The kids have their schoolwork to do, and they'll be busy from nine to three every weekday. If they're called away, they won't do their work, then they'll get behind.'

Dad lifts his hat on and off. 'Yes, but I still need a hand to get the iron on.'

'Can't you leave it till later?'

'Not now I've started.'

'Fine, but this is the last time.' She fixes us with a stern stare. 'School starts tomorrow at nine. If you're not at your desks on time, I'll send you all out to live with your grandmother and you can go to a proper school.' She storms off in a huff.

We help Dad get the iron on and spend the rest of the day, our last day of freedom, down at the beach.

The next day, we're all at our desks by five to nine. I open my grade three booklet and discover there's a contents page, which is also a checklist of work that I have to complete that week. The work is broken into four topics: English, maths, science and social studies. I sigh, lay out some fresh sheets of paper and begin working on some writing exercises.

Mum wanders through about an hour later, looking pleased that we all have our heads down. 'How is it?' she asks.

Both Stephen and Maree screw up their noses.

'There's nothing practical,' I reply. 'It's all theory. How are we supposed to learn anything real?'

Mum's taken aback. 'What do you mean by real?'

'I mean practical stuff like music or art or cooking.'

Mum stares out the window for a moment taking in what I've said. 'Well, I can teach you to cook. You can start by getting up early tomorrow and helping me bake bread.'

'Whoa,' says Maree. 'I never said I wanted to learn how to cook.'

Mum looks disappointedly at Maree, but leaves us to it.

The next morning, Mum gets out her large enamel bowl and adds the dry ingredients for bread. She adds water and mixes it into a dough. Having lightly dusted a patch on the kitchen table, she starts kneading it. 'Right, knead that for twenty minutes.'

I blink. 'How long?'

'Twenty minutes.'

I gulp and set about kneading. Five minutes later, my arms are burning. After ten minutes, I stop. Thankfully, Stephen takes over. When he's done his ten minutes, Mum puts the dough on a tray and places it in the warming oven of the combustion stove. To my horror, she then starts making another batch.

'How many are you going to do?' I ask.

'We eat nearly a loaf a day, so I might as well do six loaves, which is a week's worth. That's three batches.'

I check to see if she's joking, but she definitely isn't.

'Maree, come and do your share of kneading.'

Maree drags her feet into the kitchen and gives me a foul look.

'Don't look at your brother like that. You want bread, we have to make it.'

Maree kneads for about five minutes, then we take it turn about. When we're done, Mum pulls the now risen dough out of the oven and to my horror begins kneading it again.

'You don't mean to say it has to be done twice,' I say.

'Uh huh, and we'll have to bake every week, unless the plane brings some over.'

I close my eyes. I had no idea how much work went into making bread. I'd never feel the same way about it again.

At nine, we stop because it's time to start school. I have to write a page on an activity I've done this week. I write about baking bread.

When the first loaves come out of the oven, Mum turns them out. The smell is wafting through the house and making my mouth water.

'Stop for morning tea and one of you go down to the workshop and tell your father.'

Stephen gets up and goes over to the marine radio. He pushes a button on it and speaks into the mike. His voice sounds through a loud-speaker.

'Didn't realise we had a PA,' says Mum.

Dad appears a short while later and Mum serves up hot tea and warm bread with margarine and jam. I've never tasted anything like it. When I get back to my desk, I add some extra sentences to my composition. My teachers need to know how good homemade bread is.

The following week, I'm sitting at my desk when the phone rings. I look around for Mum but she's not there and neither are my siblings. As the youngest, I only answer the phone as a last resort. I pick up the receiver.

'Hello.'

'This is Mrs Blacker from the correspondence school in Hobart. How are you this morning?'

'Good.'

'And who am I speaking with?'

'Dion.'

There's a rustling of papers. 'You must be the youngest.'

'Uh huh.'

'You mean yes.'

'Yes.'

'Well, I'm just calling to see if your schoolwork has arrived and how you're getting on.'

'It has and we're good.'

'What's been your favourite thing so far?'

Going to the beach afterwards. 'It's all been good, but I'm a bit confused about something.'

'Well, that's why we're here to help.'

'It says I have to find all the ice shelves in Antarctica.'

'Yes.'

'Well, there's nowhere in the booklet about Antarctica.'

'You'll have to look that up in an atlas.'

'We don't have an atlas. It also says I have to write a page on octopus and we haven't caught any octopus yet, so I can't write about that.'

'No, you're not to go catching them. You'll need to look them up in a reference book.'

'Don't have any of those.'

'You'll need to go to a library.'

'No libraries here – we're on an island.'

'When you go off the island.'

'Right, we only go off every few months and when we do there's no time for libraries. We're too busy shopping.'

The phone went deathly quiet.

'If we catch an octopus, I can write about it. We caught some fish and I can write about how you scale and gut them. Would that do?'

I turn and realise Mum has walked in. Her face is ashen.

'Who're you talking to?' she whispers.

'Mrs…' Crap, what was her name? 'Teacher.'

She holds out her hand for the phone.

'Mum's here now. I'll put her on.'

I strain my ears, but I can't hear what the teacher is saying.

'Yes, we plan to get an encyclopedia set as soon as we can afford it, along with some other reference books… Yes, they've done the first week's work, but it's still on the bench waiting for the plane to come in… Every two to three weeks… Well, I can't do anything about that. In the meantime, I'll get him to write about something else and, no, it won't be about gutting fish or skinning wallaby… Talk soon, bye now.' She put the receiver back in its cradle.

'Mum, I've already written about skinning and gutting wallaby.'

Mum takes off her glasses and rubs her face in her hands.

Radio Telephone

That night, Dad goes to use the phone and discovers that there's no dial tone. Going outside to the phone's antenna pole, he tries to open a metal box about twice the size of a fuse box but discovers it's locked. Frustrated, he heads back inside.

'Can't fix it?' asks Mum hopefully.

'No, it's all locked up.' He picks up the microphone for the marine radio. 'Flinders Island Police Station, come in.'

There's no reply.

'Anyone on Flinders or Cape Barren Islands, come in.'

Again, there's no reply.

'This thing working?' he asks, scratching his head.

'Ernie said he couldn't contact Cape Barren or Flinders due to the mountain range on Cape Barren,' says Mum.

Dad rubs his chin before pressing the microphone button. 'Can anyone hear me?'

'Receiving you,' comes back a reply.

'Whereabouts are you?'

'Fishing boat in the Gulf of Carpentaria.'

Dad's eyes widen. How was it that he could speak to someone in Australia's far north, but not raise anyone locally? 'We're on Clarke Island. That's off the north-east coast of Tasmania.'

The man's voice is broken by laughter as he replies, 'What's up, mate?'

'Radio telephone is on the blink and I need to get a message to Telecom.'

'No worries, mate. I'll contact the Port Authority in Darwin. They'll relay a message for you.'

'Thanks, mate.'

A week later, we receive a message relayed through a fishing boat's marine radio that Telecom technicians will be arriving on the next fine day. Luckily, we get sunny weather a few days later and a seven-metre runabout pulls into the wharf with six men aboard. My siblings and I meet them on the wharf with the David Brown.

It seems to me that there's an awful lot of them. Certainly too many to fit on the carry-all, so instead they place a toolbox on it and proceed to walk. At the house, two of them unbolt and lower the radio telephone pole. Having moved the single solar panel further up the pole so that it sits above the aerial, which looks like a mini television aerial, they stand it back up.

'The cause was lack of power,' says the head technician. 'When the battery runs down to a certain level, it trips a switch which has to be manually switched back on.'

'So the solar panel was being shaded by the aerial,' replies Dad.

'A bit, but too many cloudy days is the real issue. I'm also fitting an electric charger which will give it a boost when the generator is running.'

Dad nods and helps to feed the power cord, which has been lengthened, through the giant hole in the wall. The technician and his assistant pack up their toolbox and place it back on the carry-all.

'You blokes got other jobs on?' asks Dad.

'No, this job will take us all day.'

I climb onto the David Brown, which I have now learned to drive, and head down to the wharf. Everyone else, including Dad, begins walking.

At the wharf, the head technician slaps his forehead. 'Damn, I forgot to lock the phone box. How silly of me. If the fuse switch should trip, you wouldn't be allowed to switch it back on, but I wouldn't know if you did.'

Dad nods slowly.

The technician picks up his toolbox and steps onto the boat.

I peer in and now realise there's a lot of diving gear on board. 'Are there underwater phone cables around here.'

'No, lad, it's all radio phones.' The technician's face reddens as he realises what I was angling at. 'We're going diving on the wreck of the *Sydney Cove,* which came to grief near Preservation Island on 28 February 1797.'

My eyes open wide. 'So you're going diving for the day?'

Panic flashes in the technician's eyes. 'You wouldn't dob us in, would you?'

'Goodness no. I wag school every chance I get.'

The technician's face splits into a grin. He shakes hands with Dad and the boat sets off across Armstrong Channel.

Land Development

The next school day, I see Dad drive past on the 1066, to the rear of which he's fitted dual wheels. He's towing a twenty-six-furrow plough. I glance at Stephen and Maree and we head out to see what's going on. By the time we get outside, the sound of splintering wood can be heard. Dad is driving straight into two-metre-high tea tree scrub and attempting to plough it straight under.

'What the...?' I say.

'His job is to clear land and sow pasture for sheep,' replies Stephen.

The tractor rears up onto its back wheels, but keeps moving forward. There's a crunching sound before the front wheels drop back onto the ground.

'I know that, but wouldn't you push the scrub up into heaps with the dozer first?'

'The dozer uses too much diesel. Douglas thinks you can plough the scrub straight in.'

I shake my head in disbelief. Maree runs inside and returns with Dad's thirty-five-millimetre camera and takes some photos.

'How's he steering?' I ask, since the front wheels don't appear to be on the ground much.

'With the brakes,' replies Stephen. 'They unlock to become two separate pedals.'

Now that he's mentioned it, I can see periodically one set of wheels are locking while the other set keep turning, causing the tractor to pivot.

Mum comes out. 'Right, you lot, back to...oh, my giddy aunt!' She stares in disbelief. 'That's no way to treat a tractor.'

We head back inside. Before day's end, something has broken on the tractor. I can hear Dad hammering steel along with the periodic noise of the welder, which runs off the PTO shaft of the David Brown. Between breakdowns, it takes over a week for him to plough up the paddock.

Once he has, I see him drive past on the David Brown towing a seed drill. As usual, we rush outside to take a look. Dad hasn't gone far and he's already pulled up and cursing. He jumps back on again and drives back towards the workshop. Resting on the bonnet is a broken piece of drill blade.

'The machinery isn't up to it,' says Stephen.

No, it's not. He should have dozed the shrub up into a heap first. 'The place needs a wood chipper.'

'The place ain't got one and besides, you want to stand there all day feeding scrub into a chipper?' says Stephen.

I wrinkle my nose. 'Be better than smashing machinery all day long.'

At three o'clock, when we knock off, we find Dad mixing up a large pile of grass seed and superphosphate. Nearby is a one-tonne spreader. When he's finished mixing it, he proceeds to load the mix into the hopper of the spreader using the bucket on the David Brown. Once he's filled the spreader, he attaches it to the back and proceeds to empty it on the newly ploughed paddock.

Once he has, he has to unhook the spreader so he can use the bucket on the David Brown to fill it again. It's a slow painful process. What Dad needs is more machinery, but he can only work with what he has.

New Dam

I shiver and pull my coat around me a little tighter as I walk over to the garden. According to Mum and Dad, the climate is mild here compared to other regions of Tasmania. The warm temperate climate of the Island is buffeted by the surrounding seawater, reducing the incidence of frost to only a few mornings a year. The issue for me is: I'm a Queenslander and I haven't adapted yet.

Despite the lack of topsoil, Mum and Dad have planted a garden of potatoes, brassicas, lettuces and silver beet. They are growing in a fashion, but require watering every day. I turn on the tap, but no water comes out. My gaze immediately shifts to the two concrete head tanks, located up on the hill. No water means they're empty.

I tell Mum, who switches on the generator, and I set off with Stephen and Maree to MacLaines Creek. The dam, which is two kilometres from the house and about three metres square, is held back by a two-metre-high concrete weir. Maree turns on the electric piston pump. I know that even pumping for eight to ten hours, which is all the generator runs for, the pump will barely fill the tanks by a quarter. This wasn't such an issue previously, but now we have a garden, our water needs have more than trebled.

'Douglas sent over rolls of poly pipe on the *Trader*,' says Dad that evening. 'We're waiting on the new pump, a Honda firefighter, but the pipe will also need to be laid. I won't lay it from the existing dam, I'll build a new one in the creek closer to the house.'

'Do you think that's a good idea? I mean, the MacLaines lived here from 1862 to 1943. Surely during that time they'd have found the best water supply.'

'It's the same water further down. Besides, we won't have enough pipe to run from the existing dam to the tanks.'

'Can't we get Douglas to send more pipe over? The *Trader is* due to come again in a few months.'

Dad shakes his head. 'We can't wait. The *Trader* mightn't come again for six months.' He moves into the lounge room to watch television.

The next Saturday, my siblings and I set out with Dad to find a new dam site. We start at the beach where the creek ends and head upstream. Unless it has recently rained heavily, the creek doesn't flow into the sea and I note that the water this low down is stagnant. The smell is quite overbearing and I wave my hand in front of my nose.

Dad doesn't seem to notice and continues his exploration for about seven hundred metres. There he finds a bit of a hole about a metre deep and bends down to scoop some up. 'Just as good here,' he says.

I taste the water and quickly spit it out. The water's stained with tannin from the tea tree and sheoak, and it's brackish. It's also winter when rain is more plentiful. What will the water be like in summer?

Dad beats his way up the bank and walks back to the workshop. He returns with a bag full of empty superphosphate bags and a shovel. Taking off his boots, socks and trousers, he stands in the middle of the creek. Using the shovel, he digs a dam, placing the fill in the bags to make a new weir.

A week later, Howard flies Scott over. He's brought the new petrol pump with him along with a box of fittings. Dad fits a trench digger to the three-point linkage of the 1066 and he cuts a trench from the dam to the hill tanks. Over the course of the next few days, the pipe is laid and the trench backfilled. Using scrap packing timber, which can be found washed up all along the northern shoreline, Dad's even built a cover for the new petrol pump.

'I reckon a tank of fuel should fill the tanks,' says Dad. He sets it going.

A few hours later, when the pump has stopped, I climb a wooden ladder and discover the tanks are full. Heading back down to the new dam, which has been pumped dry, I discover it's refilling.

Our water problem now is that the rainwater tank is leaking.

'I'll have to drain it and paint sealant in it,' says Dad, examining the leaks. He runs his eye over the wooden tank stand, which is looking rotten and unstable. 'I'll pour a concrete slab for a new stand while I'm at it.'

'What will we do for drinking water in the meantime?' asks Mum.

'We'll have to bring it up in twenty-litre drums from the small tank on the workshop,' replies Dad. 'If that runs dry, there's also the concrete tank on the bottom house.'

When the sealer arrives on the plane a few weeks later, Dad drains the tank. With all of our help, we manage to get it on its side. Dad crawls in through the top hole and proceeds to paint sealer on. Once he's finished the inside, he does the outside.

Dry sand is brought up from the beach and we spend the next Saturday mixing concrete and pouring a slab for the new tank stand. By Sunday night, the tank is sitting on its new slab and plumbed into the roof guttering.

We all breathe a sigh of relief. Having to haul drinking water in drums has been a big job. The water in the workshop tank is also full of insects, which have to be strained out before use. We're all over it and just want our rainwater tank back.

Nan and Pop arrive the next weekend for a two-week stay. They bring with them three Muscovy ducks and a drake, along with some rhubarb tubers, raspberry canes and strawberry runners. The ducks are settled into one of the triangular sheds about five metres along from the chook house. The chooks are doing well, laying regularly and free ranging within and along the edge of the shelter belt.

'I'd have thought there'd be a well here,' says Pop after dinner that evening.

'Looked all around the old homestead, but I couldn't find one,' replies Dad.

'I know where there was one,' I say. 'It's down near the wharf beach.'

Dad screws up his face. 'They wouldn't build one down there that close to the sea. Might be a hole, but I doubt it's a well.'

I feel hurt, because I'm sure it is one.

The next day, Pop asks me to show him the well and I lead him to it. Rather than being planked, the sides have been secured with fist-sized stones.

'You're right,' he says, 'it is a well. Well, at least it was. Been a long time since it's had water, though.'

The well is only about a metre deep now.

'It's possible the sides caved in,' says Pop, scratching his head, 'but why would they build it here?'

'There's a spring not far away,' I reply.

'Where?' he asks.

I walk to a little cove halfway between the home beach and the wharf beach and step onto the sand. Here I point to the bank, which is damp. 'It's fresh and way better than the creek water.'

Pop gets down on one knee and scoops up the fresh spring water which is pooling in little holes in the muddy bank. 'Well, I'll be darned.'

We head back to the workshop, because Pop needs a shovel.

En route I ask, 'Do you know much about wells?'

He puffs out his chest. 'Dug and planked forty wells by hand.' He smiles. 'With the aid of a bit of gelly of course.'

By gelly, I assume he means gelignite.

We retrieve the shovel and back at the spring, Pop proceeds to dig a sizeable hole just above the bank. Half a metre down, he hits water and his hole begins to fill up. The water is pure spring water.

Dad shakes his head when we tell him about the spring. 'We can't build a water supply that close to the sea. First storm and it'll be full of saltwater.'

My heart sinks. Dad's probably right.

'Wouldn't matter,' replies Pop. 'The spring water is seeping out under pressure. If it does get salt spray, as long as it has a level sill spillway, it will run off.'

Dad shakes his head. 'Got nothing to build a dam with, except a flipping shovel and, besides, I've already built a new dam and laid pipe to it. I'm not digging it up and moving it.'

I want to point out that the water in the spring is far better quality, but there's no point. The subject is closed.

Since it's the weekend, we don't have to do school. Pop has decided that he'll show us kids how to build and set a wallaby snare. Along the creek bank is a stand of tea tree that's about two metres in height and straight. With the use of an axe, Pop cuts down two trees and proceeds to trim the branches. When he's done, we're left with bendy poles about fifteen millimetres in diameter.

Back at the workshop, Pop makes some wooden stakes out of fifty-by-fifty-millimetre packing timber and secures it to the long poles with fencing wire. At the other end of the poles, he knots two pieces of cord. One piece is quite long and has been tied in a loop; the other is shorter and attached to the end is a tiny piece of whittled stick. Having cut some additional wooden stakes, along with some pieces of wire, Pop gathers up the snares and we head to the shelter belt behind the house to find a wallaby run.

Wallaby are plentiful and finding a run is not difficult. Using the back of the axe, Pop drives the stake attached to the snare into the ground. On the other side of the run, he hammers in the other stake. The snare is bent over and Pop hooks the whittled stick into a notch he's cut into the stake. Carefully, he lays the loop across the run before gently placing the wire between the two stakes.

I can see how it works now. The wallaby will hop along, hit the tripwire and be caught by the loop. Pop sets up the second snare and all we have to do is wait.

After dinner, Pop grabs Dad's dolphin torch and he takes us to the snares. The first one has been tripped, but the wallaby managed to escape. The second one has a wallaby whose back leg has been caught in the noose.

Pop scruffs him, pins him down with one knee and cuts his throat with a razor-sharp pocketknife. Back at the house, Pop hooks the wallaby's leg through a one-hundred-millimetre nail which he's hammered into a fence post. I notice the difference in skinning technique. Dad has been skinning them like a rabbit – that is, standing on the feet and peeling the skin up the body. That works, but it makes it difficult to keep the meat clean.

Pop peels downwards and the carcass is always suspended in the air. He also removes the liver and kidneys with care and places them on a clean plate.

'We normally throw the offal away,' I say, because I'm sure he doesn't intend to.

He shakes his head as he carefully trims off the gall bladder. 'I'll have us some liver fry for breakfast and a wallaby and kidney pie for dinner.'

The next morning, Nan dices up the liver along with some bacon and fries it up in dripping. I'm given a tiny bit to try. It feels mushy in my mouth and the flavour is all wrong. I swallow it, but I don't want any more. Neither do Maree and Stephen.

'The problem with you young ones is you're too well fed,' says Pop. 'During the war, if you could get hold of a rabbit or wallaby liver, along with half a rasher of bacon, you had a feast to behold.'

'Why wouldn't you just eat the meat? Why bother with the offal?'

'Rabbits were worth sixpence a pair. Couldn't afford to keep the meat unless it was a special occasion.'

Whoa, that sounded harsh. In that case, we had it pretty good here really. Well, we would if only it would rain and we could get some water in the tank.

'What you need is a meat safe,' says Pop when he's finished eating and is helping himself to a top up from the teapot.

Dad rubs his chin. 'I've been meaning to drag that old wheelhouse down from up at the airstrip. It's been built with strong beams to withstand a storm. It should be strong enough to hang carcasses in.'

Pop drains his mug. 'Let's have a look at it, then.'

Since Dad's already sold on the idea, he takes the sled up behind the 1066. We follow on the David Brown and Dad uses her bucket to manoeuvre the wheelhouse onto the sled without damaging it. Back at the house, they unload it with the bucket and Dad gently shunts the wheelhouse into the shrub. It's now within walking distance but not so close that the smell of curing meat will waft to the house.

Pop smiles happily when he examines the salvaged timber store. He begins to toss lengths aside which he'll need to make a few repairs to the wheelhouse.

Unfortunately, it's a school day and it's after nine, so we head back to the house.

'Pop will need a hand,' I protest to Mum. I really don't want to do my work when there is a major project happening.

'You need to do your lessons. You're all already behind,' says Mum firmly.

'Well, it would be school in a fashion,' I retort.

Mum folds her arms. 'Explain that.'

I gesture to my lesson book. When she leans over, I tap the butt of my pencil on a heading that says 'Making and Doing'. The lesson involves making kites out of dowel and pieces of material. They haven't supplied the dowel and we can't obtain any, so the lesson is not happening.

'What's your point?'

I sigh as if it's not obvious. 'The lesson's not about making a kite, it's about doing something practical. In this situation we're in, we have to be prepared to improvise.'

Stephen grins slyly. He's impressed by my argument.

'I think you should just get on with your work,' says Mum.

She turns to walk away but I'm not done. It's time to go for broke. 'The thing is, Pop's not getting any younger, which means he's only got a limited time to pass on his skills. That's why he taught us how to make the snares.'

Mum pauses. She's no longer sure of herself.

'Pop's generation knows old skills, but once he's gone…'

'All right, fine, but I expect you to be at your desk on Saturday and if you utter one word of complaint, it'll be Sunday as well.'

I'm across the room quicker than a startled rabbit fleeing down a burrow. Nan is pottering in the kitchen. She says nothing but tears of pride are brimming in her eyes. I'd only been making excuses, but now I'm determined to make my grandparents proud. At the wheelhouse, I expect to find Dad helping but he's gone ploughing. I expect Stephen and Maree to follow me, but they haven't. It's just Pop and me.

Pop is using a high-lift jack to raise the wheelhouse at one end. 'Don't you have lessons?'

'I can catch up another day. Besides, I think I'll learn more here with you.'

'On that, we can agree,' he replies. 'Keep your eye on the bubble in that level and let me know when it's centred.'

For the rest of the day, I help Pop level the wheelhouse, repair holes and remove the windows. Once we've done that, we build a door and fit it with salvaged hinges. Dad then welds some tabs onto a length of steel pipe and we bolt it to the centre beam. Now all that's left to do is to fill in the window holes with fly wire on the inside and small-gauge mesh on the outside. Since we don't have either, it will have to wait until we get some.

When we come back into the house, we find Mum, Maree and Stephen gathered round the sink. The water coming out of the tap is brown and it's stagnant.

Mum waves her hand in front of her nose. 'We can't use that water. It's foul.'

We head down to inspect the dam and discover the creek water is not only stagnant, but has an algal bloom. Dad runs a hand across his bald patch. No amount of enlarging the dam is going to improve the water quality. The reality is that a new dam will have to be dug further up the creek.

Pop again mentions the spring, but Dad is adamant that there isn't enough pipe. He brings down the last of what he has and rolls it out along the high bank about seven hundred metres on. The water here is somewhat better, but still not good. Dad digs a new dam and, while he's doing that, we drain the tanks. No one wants to say it, but the truth is the pipe should have been laid to the original dam. Or better still, the freshwater spring.

Fisherman

Elsa wakes with a start, gets up and heads to the French windows, where she starts growling. While we're doing school, she tends to sleep under the school desk. Elsa doesn't tend to growl and she's somewhat of a coward. Thunder sees her hiding in a dark room under someone's bed.

'What's wrong, girl?' asks Maree.

The hair is standing up on the back of her neck and her tail isn't wagging.

Two men come walking along from the wharf.

'Those men are no good,' says Maree, patting Elsa, who is baring her teeth.

Rather than come to the house, they go to the workshop, where Dad is working on a piece of machinery. He's begun to clear land in the interior, and breakdowns are so frequent that he spends more than half his time in the workshop doing repairs.

A couple of hours later, Dad comes up to the house with the two men. 'This is Frank and his deckhand Shaun.'

Mum proceeds to make coffee and place some home-baked biscuits on a plate. Elsa, who'll normally climb back under the school desk and snore once the greetings are over, stays close. She doesn't growl, but she doesn't go to sleep either and her eyes remain on Frank.

'You're fishermen obviously,' says Mum.

'Cray fishermen. We dock in Bridport.'

Frank looks to be in his late sixties; Shaun looks to be only about seventeen or so.

'Are there many crayfish around here?' asks Mum.

'Not what it was twenty years ago, but still enough to make a decent living. Be happy to take you all out in the morning while we haul in the pots if you like.'

'That'd be good,' says Dad.

'And I'll get you some fish for fixing the grab haul.'

The next morning, Dad has us down on the wharf before dawn. He's rubbing his hands together. 'We'll be eating cray for lunch.'

Mum doesn't look so sure about that.

Frank pulls his boat into the wharf, which surprises me because there's less that a metre of water.

'Cray boats have a shallow draft,' says Dad, 'It's so they can get in close to the rocks.'

We climb aboard and Elsa tries to get on as well. Maree has to tell her to stay. She obeys, but keeps her eyes fixed on us as the boat pulls out. Frank steers it straight towards a buoy and hauls in a fish trap which contains half a dozen parrotfish and a leatherjacket. Once they are removed, Shaun tosses it back overboard and Frank heads for the next buoy.

For the next hour or more, they haul in craypots and toss the catch into the boat's well, which has about forty centimetres of seawater in it. We've never seen the Island from the Channel and Maree takes photos with Dad's camera as we head across the bay.

When we get back to the wharf, we discover that Elsa hasn't moved. We climb off and Frank goes to cast off.

'You mentioned some fish,' says Dad.

'Sorry, almost forgot,' says Frank.

Retrieving a filleting knife from the wheelhouse, he grabs the parrotfish and proceeds to scale and fillet them. He's quick about it, but I notice he's not cutting close to the bone. When he's finished, he hands over the fillets in a plastic bag. Anger flashes in Dad's eyes, but Shaun is already casting off. The boat pulls out at a rate of knots and motors out into the bay.

'Miserable old coot,' says Dad. 'If I wanted parrotfish, I could have tossed a line in myself.'

'Why was he cutting so high on the fillets?' I ask.

'He wanted the fish for his cray pots,' replies Dad.

Seriously, parrotfish are plentiful. All you have to do is toss a line in and you'll catch them.

That evening, Frank has the audacity not only to call back in, but to ask how the fish were.

'Not bad,' replies Mum, not caring to elaborate further.

His look implies he's expecting a hot meal. It's too bad, because we've already eaten, not that he was invited.

'Mind if I take a look at your garden?' asks Shaun.

'No worries at all,' replies Dad getting up.

I'm suspicious, because Dad would normally have sent one of us kids on such a trivial errand. I quickly figure out that Dad has spoken to Shaun and there's mischief afoot.

Frank's come to the same conclusion, because he keeps looking expectantly at the door for Shaun and Dad's return. He might have gone looking for them, but Elsa's between him and the door. She isn't the slightest bit interested in Shaun; her attention is solely on Frank. Dad and Shaun are gone a good thirty minutes.

The moment they get back, Frank gets up. 'Thanks for the coffee, Joy.'

Mum nods curtly, but fails to say, 'Most welcome.' I'm quite sure she hasn't forgotten her manners.

Ten minutes after they leave, Dad goes out and comes back in whistling 'Dixie'. He removes two crayfish from a sack and places them in the kitchen sink, where he proceeds to drown them in fresh water.

'Be the last time he'll tie up at the wharf,' says Dad. 'According to Shaun, the old coot is a multimillionaire who just doesn't know when to retire. He lies through his teeth and tries to take everyone down.'

'Why'd he take us out on the boat, then?' I ask.

'Because I asked him to,' replies Dad. 'He couldn't really refuse given I helped him fix the grab haul. He'll be back and we'd best keep an eye on him whenever he's ashore.'

Dad cooks the crayfish in a big boiler the next day. The expert way he cleans them and gets the meat out suggests he's familiar with crayfish.

'Used to work on a cray boat called the *Jean Nichols*,' says Dad. 'That was when I was about sixteen. We used to fish all around Three Hummock and Hunter Islands, which are off the north-west coast of Tasmania.'

Mum serves the cray up with fresh lettuce and some thousand island dressing. The meat is exotic-tasting, but nothing to rave about. Certainly not worth getting Shaun in trouble for. I'm pretty sure a miser like Frank would know exactly how many cray he has on board. When they get into port and he discovers there's two missing, he's probably going to dock Shaun's pay. Still, if Frank had promised Dad a crayfish for fixing the grab haul, then he should have delivered on that.

Suzi Wong

In early December, Nan and Pop agree to caretake so we can go off the Island and do our Christmas shopping. Howard flies us to Cape Portland and Dad drives us down to Ulverstone, where Nana Doris has moved to after selling her house in Woodridge.

'You kids want to take the empty cordial bottles down to the shop and cash them in? They're worth twenty cents each.'

We get up from where we're slumped on the couch. Just being back in civilisation where it's noisy and smelly is depressing. The chance to make a few dollars will give us something to do.

Nana Doris has a trolley which we use to haul the bottles down to a milk bar and we cash them in for nine dollars. Maree hands Stephen and me three dollars each and we immediately spend the money on ice cream and fizzy drink. Taking it over to the nearby park, we sit on a bench and pig out.

Ten minutes later, I'm feeling queasy. By the time we get back to Nana Doris's house, I think I might vomit. Several months without junk food and then all that in one go and my stomach is revolting. Maree and Stephen don't look any healthier and we lie around for the rest of the day groaning.

Mum and Dad arrive back from shopping in a light blue Volkswagen Kombi van. They've sold the Land Cruiser for something they can use to haul supplies back to Cape Portland in. We rush out to have a look and we all agree she's a beast. We'll all miss the Old Grey Elephant, but the Kombi is more suitable for our current needs.

'Did you still want to get a dog?' Dad asks me.

'Yes,' I reply.

'Right, let's go up to the Burnie pound and have a look.'

Dad drives us all up to the pound. Since I'm not allowed to get a big dog, there are only two to choose from. Both are mongrels: a shagpile carpet and one who has a fair bit of fox terrier in her. Since I don't want to spend all my spare time combing the living carpet, I point to the other one.

'But you haven't even looked at this one,' says Mum, who's patting him through the mesh.

The kennel hand gets out the one that I point to and hands her to me on a leash. I take her for a short walk and she trots along beside me.

'Seems to be a good dog,' I say when I get back.

'You don't want to take this one for a walk?' says Mum.

'No.'

Mum is clearly upset and she walks away to talk to Dad, who's shaking his head. I can't hear what's being said, but from body language and tone of voice, I can figure out that Mum wants to take both of them. Dad's insisting we're only taking one home and it's my choice which one.

The discussion ends and we leave with the dog I chose. Back at Nana Doris's house, I bath the dog in the laundry sink and towel her off.

'What you going to call her?' asks Stephen.

'Dunno yet,' I reply as I set her up in the woodshed for the night.

Two days later, we're on our way back to the Island. I still haven't made a decision as to what to call my new dog. I've bounced a few names around but none of them seem like a good fit.

'For goodness sake, just call her Sexy Sue,' says Dad.

'Suzi, yeah that works,' I reply.

'But I thought you agreed on Wong,' says Maree.

'Suzi Wong,' I reply testing the way it sounds. 'That's her name.'

There are nods of agreement.

When we arrive back on the Island, Elsa is pleased to see us and delighted at the fact that she now has a new playmate. I keep Suzi on a lead, because I don't want her to run off and get lost.

Down at the house, Dad instructs me to let her off. An hour later, I see Suzi heading out across the paddock while looking over her shoulder. Whatever she's up to, she clearly knows she shouldn't be doing it. She heads straight for the horses and begins to yap at them. I call her, but she refuses to listen. I have to go and physically get her and drag her back to the house.

Mum purses her lips. 'If she's a stock worrier, she'll have to be put down.'

I sigh. Suzi is middle-aged and is not likely to be easy to train. I close the yard gate so she can't get out.

The next day, we head down to some rocks along from the wharf to do some fishing. Within minutes of arrival, I realise Suzi has run off. I sigh. I'm about to call her, when I hear a high-pitched yap, which sounds like 'help help'.

Elsa cocks her head from side to side before running off to investigate. She returns with a wallaby in her mouth and a big grin on her face. It seems that Suzi is a hunting dog, but she's not big enough to kill the wallaby, only run them down. With Elsa, they're a tag team duo.

I'm worried, however, about the chooks and ducks, who are free range and free to leave. My worry is for naught, however, because Suzi trots past both off lead on her way back to the house and pays them no notice.

The next day, by the smell of her, Suzi has clearly rolled in horse manure.

'Just take her down the wharf and throw her into the sea,' says Dad.

I clip her onto a lead and walk down to the wharf. Suzi keeps giving me a look as if to say, how could you. Somehow, she knows what's coming. When we arrive, I throw her off the end. She swims round to the rocks and climbs out. She still stinks, so I throw her back in again.

This time she swims to the wharf beach, where she proceeds to roll in seaweed and sand before running around like a maniac. I laugh. She'll still stink, but at least she's having a good time.

The next weekend, Dad drives us out to the tussock country on the western side. He's keen to see if the dogs will hunt wallaby together. The moment we arrive, Suzi jumps off, runs into the tussocks and begins her high-pitched yap. Elsa runs after her, but discovers she's too big to run along the wallaby runs between the tussocks. She has to leap over them. Each time she leaps in the air, she moves her head from side to side, trying to see which way to go. Ironically, she's bounding like the wallaby she's chasing. It's quite comical.

They catch six wallaby and we skin them out for dog food before heading back. En route, Elsa finds a large puddle which she wallows in, turning her white fur black. Suzi, however, high steps around it. She's not getting wet for anyone.

A few weeks later, Suzi is outside and barking incessantly at something. I assume one of the horses has come up to the fence, but when I step outside, they're nowhere to be seen. I take a closer look and realise she's barking at a tiger snake which has come onto the lawn. I call Suzi to me and I take her inside and tell Dad.

He gets up, goes into the back porch and removes his four-ten shotgun from a shelf and inserts a shell into the breach. When he steps outside, there's a loud bang as Dad shoots it. The snake is nigh on two metres long and easily ten centimetres in diameter.

'Be dead in under an hour if that thing bit you,' says Dad. 'Be no hope of the flying doctor getting here in time.'

That day, he takes us all out in the paddock, including Mum, and shows us how to handle both the shotgun and the .22 rifle. He explains the difference between the two firearms. The rifle fires a single projectile which will travel up to a kilometre; the shot gun fires a spray of pellets and has a range of about fifty metres. In other words, the rifle is for shooting wallaby and the shotgun is for snakes.

Abalone

School finishes up a week before Christmas. Mum, however, has us all in the kitchen, teaching us to cook biscuits and cakes, in lieu of cooking classes we're missing by not being at a proper school. Stephen and I don't mind cooking, but Maree loathes it. She's so cranky about having to learn that when it's time to turn out the sponge cake, she thumps the bottom of the tin. The top half breaks away, leaving the bottom stuck to the tin.

'You've got to be gentler with it,' says Mum, who's managed to get the bottom out without further damaging it. 'I'll have to stick it together with jam and whipped cream now.'

Maree couldn't care less if the cake ends up going to the chooks. She just wants to get out of the kitchen. She slips out a few minutes later on the pretence of running an errand and doesn't return until the cooking is finished.

On Christmas Day, my presents consist of a number of reference books and novels. I've been given Harry Butler's two wildlife books and Colin Thiele's *The Valley Between* and *Blue Fin*. Stephen has received a number of Murry Ball's *Footrot Flats* comics and Maree has received a pair of riding boots and other clothes. All three of us also receive a snorkelling set.

For lunch, Mum cooks up the biggest feast I've ever seen. Roast beef, along with roasted and boiled vegetables and a whole raft of deserts including plum pudding and Christmas cake. I can't remember Christmas ever being this grand.

After lunch, we head down to the beach. It's a lovely fine day and Stephen and Maree are keen to try out their snorkelling gear. I haven't forgotten how cold the water is and I haven't been in since that first experience. Not wanting to think I'm not grateful for the present, I test out the water in the large rock pool at the far end of the beach. It's bearable and I swim around in waist-deep water.

I didn't intend to spend more than a few minutes snorkelling, but I discover that the underwater world is fascinating. Aside from parrotfish, there are schools of little garfish, all manner of different seaweeds, shellfish, starfish, anemones and even crabs. I stay in until the cold finally gets to me and I climb onto a hot rock to warm up. When school starts back, I'll have something else to write about.

Stephen and Maree have left the rock pool and have headed further out.

'We've found a bed of abalones,' says Maree when they come back.

Dad, who's not going anywhere near the water, looks excited. He magics a big old flat-tipped screwdriver from the bottom of the fishing bag he brought with him. 'You've got to hit them on the curved edge. You'll only get one chance to dislodge them from the rocks before they suck on too tight to move.'

Maree takes the screwdriver and heads back out with Stephen. Dad heads along the rocks which extend into the water and I go with him. When I arrive at the spot, I peer into the water, which is about two metres deep. The abalone are a grey shellfish about as big as a teacup saucer and, like Dad said, they have a curved edge and a flat side.

Maree takes a deep breath and manages to swim down to them. She stabs frantically at one but it won't dislodge. In desperation, she manages to get the one off beside it, but she's out of breath. Stephen swims down to it, but he also has difficulty. Maree surfaces and manages to get the one she's dislodged. On a subsequent dive, she manages to get a second one, but then she's exhausted.

I decide I want to have a go and take the screwdriver. Taking a deep breath, I dive in and swim downwards as hard as I can. It's way deeper than I thought and with every centimetre I descend, the water gets colder. By the time I reach the bottom, the current has taken me off course. My lungs are burning desperate for air, but I stab at the abalone on the fringe of the bed. I miss the curved bit and the screwdriver just slips past. I try again with a different one and manage to dislodge it, but I can't reach it and I know I have to resurface or I'm going to pass out.

It seems to take forever to come back up and I feel myself panicking. When I reach the surface, I breathe in too soon and take in a mouthful of water. Choking, I begin to cough uncontrollably. There is no hope of re-diving; I have to get out.

Maree dives down to get the one I dislodged, but it has disappeared beneath the kelp and she can't find it. 'It's just too deep. We need to wait until a really low tide and then try.'

I curse because I know the abalone I dislodged is about to become parrotfish food, which is a real waste.

Back at the house, Dad shows us how to remove them from the shell with a thin paint scraper, which Mum uses as a spatula. The shells themselves are quite beautiful and Mum takes them outside, where the ants will finish cleaning them out, so she can keep them as ornaments.

Stephen, who has a penchant for cleaning and cooking meat and fish, cuts off the guts and slices the meat into thin strips. He fries it in hot oil for thirty seconds a side. Unlike the crayfish, I think the abalone are a prize worth pursuing.

Inner-tube Raft

With summer comes some unusually nice weather. The wind drops, so that the water in the channel is calm and the days are sunny. Mum is no longer as nervous about snakes as she was, but she doesn't like us going off on our own. The novelty of going to the beach and fishing has worn off and we're bored, yet keen to avoid Dad, who will find us work to do.

Maree is flicking through a *Grass Roots* magazine, which Mum has subscribed to. She pauses on an article which is about how to make a raft out of inner tubes and a plank. 'Can we build one of these?'

Mum returns a non-committal look. 'You'll have to ask your father about using tractor tyre tubes.'

When Dad comes up from the workshop for lunch, Maree waves the article in front of him.

He runs a hand over his bald patch. 'Got some old tubes that are heavily repaired, which I discarded. They might work.'

There's a long plank which has been brought up from the rocks. It's been stored in a timber pile in the original homestead, which is being used as a shed. The three of us go over and get it and carry it across to the workshop. We find Dad blowing up three inner tubes with the compressor.

Using salvaged rope, also collected from the rocks along the shore, we lash the tubes to the plank. Using salvaged timber, we also build three paddles. This is the first time that I have ever worked with timber and I realise it's an activity that I enjoy.

When the raft is built, we lift it onto the trailer behind the David Brown and we drive it down to the wharf beach. The water is really calm, which is unusual. We launch the raft and sit on the plank with our legs in the water inside the tubes and paddle it to the wharf.

Mum has walked down with the camera and she takes some photos. 'I'll send these off to your teachers. Be good to show them that you're doing some practical things and recreation.'

I shrug because I couldn't care less what my teachers think.

Maree dips her paddle again and we follow suit, taking the raft out into deeper water.

'Don't take that out too much further,' says Mum.

'I thought we could paddle round to the main beach,' says Maree, glancing over her shoulder back at the wharf.

'No,' says Mum. 'Just paddle around near the wharf.'

Maree cocks her head, 'Where's the fun in that?'

'I thought we could slip across to Cape Barren. It doesn't look that far.' I shade my eyes against the glare. It really doesn't look that far, but it is probably deceptive.

Mum's face turns ashen. 'Definitely not. I think you should turn that raft around now. That's quite deep enough.'

'What's the issue with paddling round to the beach? Perfect day for rafting.'

Mum folds her arms. 'The channel is a shark breeding ground and there are also barracuda in these waters.'

Maree screws up her nose, 'Geez, if it's not snakes, it's flipping sharks or barracuda.'

We turn the raft round and paddle it back to the wharf beach. If we can't take it out on an adventure, that's boring, and there's really no point.

Distress Call

I press my face up to the glass of the French windows. The weather is awful and has been for several days. There's a westerly blowing and the beach is so rough that the surge is washing up onto the high sand which is normally dry even when the tide is fully in. Too dangerous to go down there even if I did brave the weather.

'Mayday. Mayday. Mayday.'

I spin round to look at the marine radio, which has just received the emergency distress call. Dad gets up from the table so fast that he almost knocks his chair over.

Grabbing the microphone of the radio, he presses the button. 'Clarke Island base receiving.'

'My motor has cut out and I'm taking on water.'

Dad has the phone book and is frantically flipping pages. 'Roger that. What's your location?' He continues to fight with the phone book.

Mum grabs it off him before he damaged it.

'Spike Bay, Clarke Island.'

'Police number,' says Dad, because Mum's not sure whose number he is looking for.

She nods, realising that it should have been obvious. While we can talk to the man in distress, we can't facilitate a rescue.

Mum finds the number.

Dad picks up the phone receiver. Dialling the phone on the circular dial mechanism seems to take forever. With each number, he has to wait for it to return to neutral before he can enter the next one.

'Copy, boat in distress,' says Dad. There's no answer. Dad talks into the phone. 'Received a mayday call. Boat in distress near Spike Bay… No, I haven't got his name yet.'

I swallow. This is serious. I wonder what size boat it is and why he's out in this weather.

Dad is looking concerned. 'Copy, boat in distress.'

'Yeah, copy.' There's a strange noise.

I realise suddenly that the man in distress in violently seasick and isn't able to respond because he's vomiting.

A voice comes over the marine radio. 'This is the *Biminy*. We are on the south side of Preservation Island coming to your aid.'

Dad exhales and talks into the phone. 'Yes, that's confirmed. A boat in the vicinity has responded and is en route.'

'This is the *Biminy*. Please confirm location.'

In the background, the sound of a fog siren can be heard. There's no reply.

'Boat in distress. This is the *Biminy*. Please respond.'

'Roger, *Biminy*.' There's the sound of further vomiting. 'Visibility low. Exact location unknown.'

Dad lights a cigarette. 'Yes, I'm still here… No, he hasn't provided his name or boat name… Yes, I'll stay on the line.'

Every minute seems like an hour as Dad stands by the phone and radio.

'This is the *Biminy*. We have visual. Moving in closer to attempt a rescue.'

Dad butts out his cigarette and lights another.

'This is the *Biminy*. We have distressed seaman on board. Towing boat en route to Lady Barren, Flinders Island. I repeat, distressed seaman is on board.'

Dad again talks into the phone. 'Yes, that's correct. They're making a run for Lady Barren… How big?' Dad provides his phone number before hanging up. 'It's thirty-foot waves out there.'

Running a hand across his bald patch, he sits down and Mum sets a fresh cup of tea in front of him.

He takes a sip of his tea. 'We need to put emergency numbers in the front of the daybook. An emergency call could come in at any time. One of the kids might be the only ones available to answer it.'

Mum nods and Maree begins to transfer phone numbers into the daybook.

An hour later, the phone rings and Dad answers it. He speaks in a low voice as he again confirms that he responded to the mayday call. When he hangs up, he shakes his head before sitting back down. 'According to the police, that's the second time that bloke's gone out in foul weather on his own and has had to be rescued.'

I can't believe it. The water around these islands is some of the roughest in the world. He's lucky we were there to take the call and even luckier that the *Biminy* was willing and able to respond.

Isolation Sickness

In February 1985, Dad's friend Alan, whom we'd stayed with in Melbourne, decides to come over for a holiday with his family. Dad flies off the island and drives to Launceston airport, where he picks them up and drives them to Cape Portland. Howard flies them all over in three loads the next day.

Stephen and Maree meet them at the airstrip with the David Brown and drive them down to the bottom house. A short while later, Dad returns looking serious. He takes Mum off to one side. I can't hear what's being said, but I can get the gist of it. The bottom house was too rustic for Alan and his family and they're wanting to stay in our house.

In some ways it's fair enough, because we imposed on them. On the other hand, it seems a little cheeky, because our house is also spartan and having nine people in it for two weeks is going to be cramped.

Mum relents. Stephen moves out to the sleepout with Maree and I'm placed in the end of the hallway in front of the door we never use. Alan and his family are accommodated in Stephen's and my room and extra beds and mattresses are brought up from the other house.

It's after lunch when Alan's daughter Tara, who's five, comes into the kitchen crying. 'The television doesn't work,' she sobs.

'The generator isn't on,' replies Mum matter-of-factly.

Alan's wife Beverly looks at Mum bewildered. 'You mean there's no power?'

'There's power. Three to four hours in the morning, four to five hours in the evening.'

'When will it come back on?' asks Beverly.

'I'll switch it on about five,' says Mum.

Beverly looks at Alan, who appears pale. Tara has moved from crying to the early stages of a temper tantrum. Clearly used to getting her own way, the idea that she won't on this occasion is an anathema to her.

'Could you possibly make an exception just for today?' asks Alan.

Mum's shaking her head, but Dad sighs, gets up and presses the green button on the wall. Heading into the lounge room with Alan and his family, he switches on the television.

'We can only get the ABC,' says Dad, 'and it cuts out if the phone rings.' He picks up the receiver to demonstrate.

'You're saying there's no Channel Nine or Seven.'

I thought it an odd question, because northern Tasmania only has two stations. ABC and Launceston's commercial channel, whatever that's called. Except for times off the island, I barely watch television. The only shows I'm really interest in are David Attenborough and Harry Butler.

Dad shakes his head.

Tara, who'd initially stopped crying, now completely loses it and has to be taken into the bedroom.

Dad switches the television off and Mum switches the power back off.

The next morning is one of those rare fine days where the wind isn't blowing hard. Mum, who's made tea and toast, invites Alan and Beverly out onto the veranda to sit in the sunshine. On days like this, the bay, with Cape Barren Island in the background, is a postcard-worthy view.

I sit in one of the antique rocking chairs. These are the moments that make the island worthwhile. Alan and Beverly sit quietly as if they've just come from a funeral and barely notice the view. A few minutes later, they head back inside.

Considering their actions strange, I look at Mum, but she returns a 'don't ask me' look. I roll my eyes. She goes to investigate, but I remain where I am.

Dad comes out a little while later. 'We're going over to Rebecca Bay for a picnic. Can you help your mother with the food while Stephen and I sort out some gas for the portable barbecue.'

I drain my mug, nod and go inside to help Mum butter bread and pack drink bottles full of cordial. I can only assume Maree is holed up in her sleepout. Outside, Dad has turned one of the large gas bottles upside down and is filling the small green gas bottle that goes with his portable barbecue.

Having packed the esky with meat from the freezer, I begin to lug stuff out to the trailer of the David Brown. In preparation for Alan and his family coming over, Dad has removed the seats from some old dead cars lying around in the bush. He's bolted them to the trailer to make it more comfortable for passengers. However, I don't need to be a mathematician to work out that there aren't enough seats to go around.

Despite this, fifteen minutes later we're all on the trailer and the David Brown is headed to the western side of the island, where Rebecca Bay is. In terms of distance, it isn't that far, less than seven kilometres as the crow flies. But there are no roads, only rough tractor tracks and the trailer has no suspension.

Driving the tractor at a fast walk, it takes an hour to get there and you feel every bump. Not that it matters to us – we're used to the slow pace and rugged terrain. The city slicker visitors, however, are not.

Dad, who is driving, is blissfully unaware of the frayed tempers and general unimpressed state of the visitors. In due course, he pulls up at the top of the bank which affords a view of Rebecca Bay. Switching off the tractor, he stretches his arms out to indicate the magnificence of the place. With its horseshoe shape and yellow-coloured sand, it's arguably the best beach on the island. In my opinion, it would give any beach in Australia a run for its money.

The visitors get off, look at the beach and then back at Dad as if to say, tell me again why we endured an hour of pain to come here. It's at this point that Elsa comes thundering out of the tussocks carrying a wallaby in her mouth. Dropping it on the ground, she looks around for approval. Tara bursts into tears and her brother Adam just stares with his mouth open.

Stephen has the sense to drag the dead carcass away. Maree and I, deciding it's too early to eat, lead the party onto the sand. The tide is low and in the bay is a small rocky island.

'I reckon we could get out there today,' I say.

Maree raises a hand above her eyes and squints. 'Might be the only chance we get.'

Turning round, we head back towards the tractor to find our bathers.

'You going swimming?' asks Mum.

We point to the island.

'Be careful of rips.'

Maree rolls her eyes.

'At least she didn't say snakes or sharks.'

Maree smiles and we wait for Stephen before setting off. It's trickier than it looks. Although there's a deep V of exposed sand which leads to the island, the waves cover it as they come in and the undertow is significant. The last section is also a deep trench. Although it's only five metres across, I'm not a good swimmer.

Rather than turn back, I keep going. I now discover the rocky island is guarded by large boulders with no easy purchase. Maree, however, finds a way between two boulders and we continue our assault.

There's nothing here, just a few yellow tussocks on a patch of sandy ground surrounded by orange-coloured rocks. But that's not the point. The point is we made it here and now we feel like conquering explorers.

I don't stay long, because I know the tide is coming in and I have to recross the trench. Back on the beach, I frolic in the shallows waiting for my siblings. They arrive back about half an hour later.

When we get back to the others, we find the visitors sitting on a sand dune gazing across Bank Strait towards Cape Portland. Midway, there's an ocean liner, but I'm pretty sure that's not what's holding their focus. Their longing gaze is reminiscent of an old war film where there's a soldier in France gazing across the English Channel towards his homeland. Just one little bit of water between them and civilisation, but it's uncrossable. They're trapped here. Imprisoned with savages who don't have the trappings of modernity.

I wonder why they've come. What did they expect it would be like? Dad surely would have briefed them. Had they not listened, or was it that they had no frame of reference for what he was saying? City slickers always have strange notions about how romantic islands are. Their fantasies bear no resemblance to reality. Islands are wild untameable places that dictate the conditions. You have to accept that or you don't make it.

Tara begins mumbling something about going swimming. It occurs to me that Alan and Beverly probably think us kids rude for not offering to take their children swimming with us. I strangely don't care.

The thing with beaches is that the water is the temperature it is. You can't turn up the temperature like you can in a heated swimming pool. The sand always sticks to your wet body regardless of how much you brush it off. And if you don't respect the sea it borders, it will sweep you out and drown you. On an island, if you get in trouble, there's no one to come help you. It's not a place for spoilt brats.

Dad, wrestling with his portable barbecue, brings me out of my thoughts. It's a good barbecue in that it's robust and dependable. It has been with Dad since before I was born. The issue with it is that bits tend to fall off when you try to unfold its stand to set it up. Dad, however, gets it sorted and soon after has the burners hissing under the hotplate.

He tosses on meat. Not the normal fare of island beef in the form of steak or patties. Today there's the rare treat of sausages and bacon. Food's difficult to get here because of its perishable nature and the uncertainty of weather and pilot determining plane departure times.

As a growing lad, I'm always hungry. I quickly obtain a plastic plate and bread and butter so I'm ready the moment the meat is. Mum's fussing with weeds she calls salad, but my focus is on the barbecue. Dad's not a good cook and he's likely to burn the bacon and undercook the sausages. Thankfully, Stephen edges him out of the way and takes over the cooking.

I'm chowing down on a bacon and sausage sandwich when I have cause to do a double-take. Tara has taken one bite out of her sandwich before feeding it to the dogs. It isn't just the waste of bacon and sausage, it's that she now has the audacity to ask for more.

'Oi!' yells Dad, his face red with anger.

'They looked hungry,' retorts Tara in a tone I would never have tried on with my father.

Dad's a strict disciplinarian. Mostly hard and fair, but he has a tendency to yell first and ask questions later and he doesn't tolerate back-answering. As for the dogs, they're like people and will snack at every opportunity. Hunger has nothing to do with it.

'Don't you speak to my child like that,' says Alan.

Dad's face gets even redder. As far as he's concerned, Alan should be supporting him and disciplining his daughter. Back-answering from a parent is worse than from a child, because the parent should know better.

'You don't give good food to the dogs and then ask for more. We're on an island. We can't get more!'

There's a trace of real fear in Alan's eyes and he backs down. The reality that we only have what food we have, and no way of getting more is sobering. There's a chance they might starve. It's unlikely. We can always go hunting and fishing and we have a garden, such as it is. But this is wild food, not the processed provisions of supermarkets. If their children have a hissy fit, there's no appeasing them with pizza, chips or ice cream.

Not surprisingly, the picnic, which should have continued into the afternoon, is cut short. The journey back is quiet and awkward. The return home is made worse by the fact that the visitors can't pull back to their own house. Instead, they shut themselves in their assigned bedroom feigning headaches. Mum offers them books from our growing library, but the idea of reading to pass the time is an alien concept.

That evening, my sleeping spot in the hall ensures I overhear a conversation between my parents.

'I don't know what's got into them,' says Dad.

'They can't handle the isolation,' replies Mum.

Dad tsks.

'It's quite serious,' says Mum. 'It's not just the lack of mod cons. They're afraid of this place.'

Dad mumbles something incoherent.

'They could snap at any time,' replies Mum. 'I really think we should discuss with them cutting their visit short.'

There's no discernible reply.

They don't, however, leave, and two weeks later Howard arrives with Nan and Pop, who are again flown over to caretake.

As I help carry the supplies to the tractor, I ask Pop, 'So you don't mind it here, then?'

He returns a smile. 'It's got its challenges, with our health and so forth, but it's like being back in my time away from all the craziness.'

I nod. I'm coming from a different perspective, but I know what he's talking about. As long as you accept it on its own terms, the island is a sanctuary away from the problems of society.

At Cape Portland, we all manage to fit into the Kombi and Dad drives us all to Launceston airport. The goodbyes are plastic. I know that whatever friendship Dad once had with this family is gone. From the way Dad speaks and acts, I can tell he's cut up about it. It's as if he feels responsible for the experience they had. Or maybe it's watching the sun go down on a friendship he no longer has.

It's not something I can relate to. Born on the road, I'm so used to moving on that I have no lifelong friends. Friendships are left behind in the place that grows smaller from the view out of the back window of the leaving car. Friends, to me, are like ships that pass in the night. You wave and let it go as the direction we head takes a different path.

Launceston Museum

For the first time ever, we don't drive straight to the north-west coast. Instead, we stay with a different relative in Launceston. I feel awkward as I take a seat on my cousin's couch. He's doing his best to make us feel welcome, but I still feel like we're imposing. Launceston is a larger town than Ulverstone and Burnie and thus feels even more alien.

'I'm planning to take you all to the Queen Victoria Museum tomorrow,' says Mum.

I cock my head and blurt out, 'Why?'

'Because I think you'll get a lot from it,' replies Mum, looking unsure of herself.

I've never been to a museum before, so I can't suggest that it will be boring, but there's no sense of excitement. The truth is, I'm growing to hate civilisation. Opposite to the visitors we've dropped at the airport, I'm suffering from overstimulated senses: flight or fight on high alert, which neither my brain nor body is accustomed to. A quick glance at my siblings and I discern they're fighting their own battles.

The museum is walking distance from my cousin's place and Mum walks us there in time for the ten o'clock opening. Entering the old building, I find myself face to face with a tiger snake. Taxidermied of course, but so lifelike that I find myself checking the glass box to ensure it's sealed.

I've seen plenty, of course. Far more than I'll ever tell Mum, but I've never had the opportunity to take in the details. Even dead, snakes are dangerous if the head's still attached. I examine the mouth, particularly the fangs, with acute fascination.

It's ten minutes before I move on to the copperhead, and a similar time to get to the whipsnake. With the snake exhibits is a pamphlet that details their taxonomy. According to it, these are the only three types in Tasmania. Each type, although somewhat identifiable from size and colour, can be definitively identified by the size of the central scale on their head. The scale doubles in size between tigers and copperheads, and triples between tigers and whips. From a medical perspective, identification isn't necessary, as the same antivenin is used for all three snakes. I didn't know that. The knowledge is gold.

'Your son is very interested in the snakes,' says the curator.

'Alarmingly so,' replies Mum.

I glance around. Maree has finished looking at the taxidermied exhibits and is looking bored. Stephen is about halfway done. I haven't finished with the snakes, but I force myself to move on to the thylacine. A carnivorous marsupial, the last known one, died in the Hobart Zoo on 7 September 1936. Within the glass box is a jar which contains a tiny specimen floating in formaldehyde.

'The future of the species is in that jar,' says the curator, who seems delighted that someone is actually genuinely interested in the exhibits.

I'm not following her. 'How can something dead resurrect the living?'

'Through cloning,' she replies. 'If the science is achieved, the issue will then be genetic diversity.'

My brain is strained because I have a poor vocabulary and I haven't grasped her meaning.

'Inbreeding,' she clarifies.

Now I'm with her. 'Got it. We have a rooster who'll have to go soon, for the same reason.'

I'm surprised to see the woman blush. I pocket a second pamphlet and move on to the Tasmanian Devil.

'Are we done here?' asks Maree, shooting me a look of daggers.

Done? I've barely started and I'll be returning to the snakes. I fold my arms as I prepare for a Mexican stand-off.

'Okay, we'll just be in the other room,' says Mum.

Three hours later, I'm still in the same room. I'm forced to leave because the show in the planetarium is about to begin and I don't want to miss it. Aside from wildlife, my other interest is astronomy. We arrive with a few minutes to spare.

The man in charge of the planetarium looks bored but in an effort to engage asks, 'Who can name the planets in our solar system?'

The names roll off my tongue, beginning with Mercury and ending with Pluto. Not only can I name them, but I can tell him where they fit in the solar system.

The man is taken aback and shifts awkwardly from one foot to the next. 'You planning to be an astronomer when you grow up?'

'No,' I reply. 'I'll be a farmer, but I'll live to see Earth achieve interstellar travel. It's my dream to be a part of that.'

The man blinks and gestures for us to enter. I take a seat and lay it right back so that I'm looking at the roof. My eyes are glued to the screen as we fly past planets. I'm particularly interested in Jupiter and Saturn – or, more correctly, their moons.

'How was that?' asks the man as we're leaving.

'Awesome, but tell me, is it true that Saturn's moon Titan has an atmosphere and cosmic DNA?'

Maree groans audibly. She can't wait to leave and I'm holding us up.

The man adjusts his glasses. 'Yes.'

'There's speculation that it might be habitable with technology. What's the solution to the lack of sunlight?'

'You sure you want to be a farmer?'

'Yep, else I'd have to take school seriously and school's a joke that has its own gravity.'

Concern appears in his eyes and I assume he's missed the joke. By gravity I mean it sucks. But it's not the joke, it's my attitude towards school that has disturbed the man.

'You kids want to head back downstairs,' says a red-faced Mum.

I head off, but linger just out of sight on the stairs.

'We live on Clarke Island and the kids do school by correspondence. The lessons are very basic.'

'They're not working for your boy.'

'It's maddening. He only does the bare minimum to pass his lessons, but then he'll spend the entire evening reading an encyclopedia.'

'That's because the information within produces meaning. Don't hinder him, get him more reference books.'

Mum sighs. 'I think he needs to go to a real school.'

'I think he'll work that out in his own time.'

I fight back tears as I flee down the stairs. I don't want to go back to school, which is full of bullies. I just want knowledge. I make a conscious decision: I will have to learn to keep my mouth shut.

Blocked Septic Tank

Walking back from the garden, I wave my hand in front of my nose. There's a stench like an outdoor toilet might have exploded, but far worse. Upon examining the toilet, I discover it's backfilling rather than flushing as it should be. I tell Dad and, after shaking his head, he goes to investigate.

Judging by the rising damp near the septic tank, there can be little doubt that the outflow is blocked. Digging down beside the tank, it soon becomes obvious that the original cesspit is no longer functioning. This is causing the flow to back up, rise to the surface and cause the stench.

'It will need an entirely new French drain,' says Dad.

Mum closes her eyes. 'How are you going to dig that?'

'Well, given the island has no backhoe, how do you think? I'll have to dig it with a pick and shovel.' He lights a cigarette. 'But that's not the worst of it. The tank will have to be emptied. Otherwise, the tank will overflow pure sewage, rather than the filtered brown-water, which will just back up again.'

Mum looks pale. 'How are you going to do that?'

'It will have to be bailed out.'

This is sounding worse and worse.

'Can't you ask Douglas if he can send over a backhoe?'

Dad snorts. 'I need it now, not in a few years' time.'

The toilet door is closed and a sign put on it to remind everyone it's out of use. When we need to go, we'll have to track down to the bottom house.

The next day, Dad begins the horrendous task of digging the new

French drain with a pick and shovel. According to him, it needs to be a metre deep, a metre wide and about ten metres long. Periodically, Stephen and I jump into the trench and shovel out some of the picked ground. For the first time ever, there's something worse than school.

It's several days before Dad declares the drain is big enough. Now it has to be filled with stone which, thankfully, is plentiful in the interior where Dad has been working up ground. Having loaded the tractor trailer, we have to unload it into the trench. Having done so, Dad uses the loader bucket to cover it over and remove the excess dirt.

When he returns from dumping the last load, he's accompanied by a length of chain from the workshop. This he uses, along with the strength of the loader bucket, to remove the cover from the septic tank. The smell is bad, but there's just something skin-crawlingly evil about looking into an overfull septic tank.

As he so often does when there's a major problem to solve, Dad rolls a cigarette and smokes it before doing or saying anything.

'Right,' he says driving off on the David Brown.

He returns with a 205-litre drum with the top cut out and an empty twenty-litre stainless steel grease bucket also with the top off. When he said the septic would have to be bailed out, he hadn't been using an analogy. He meant it literally.

Bailing is bad enough, period, but it gets worse as the level drops. Tying a piece of rope to the handle doesn't help, as the sewage is so viscose that the bucket won't sink in order to fill it. I'm thinking pushing it under with a pole will do it. Before I can suggest it, Dad jumps in.

He figures it's a 'just do it' moment. I'm not convinced it is. When he passes up the first full grease bucket, there's no time to draw straws on who's going to pour it into the drum. The task isn't just smelly and beyond disgusting, it's hard work. Dad isn't the only one who's thankful when the concrete bottom appears.

'Right,' says Dad climbing out. 'I want to tip this last drum on the garden.'

Seriously.

Dad's too mucky to get on the tractor, so Stephen drives the tractor carrying the drum over. As it pours out, Dad spreads it around.

'That's going to have to be covered over,' says Mum.

Damn, that means a load of seaweed.

Once the tank cover's put back on, there's the issue of what to do about Dad. Mum emerges from the house carrying an old soft broom and a cheap bottle of shampoo. Dad's hosed off, soaped up and hosed off about five times before Mum will let him in the house to shower.

We're all glad to have the toilet working again but crap. Literally crap.

The Day of the Mushrooms

In autumn, there's a rare still day without a breath of wind. A heavy mist rolls in off the sea and creeps inland. I head up the hill with Elsa and Suzi, determined to gain height in order to look down upon the blanket of white. I walk halfway up the hill towards the airstrip, when I pause. The entire bank on which Dad has ploughed the tea tree scrub is covered in white domes. Rushing back to the house, I tell Mum, who comes out to investigate.

She gently turns one over. 'Mushrooms.'

An entire hillside of them growing on the rotting timber which has been ploughed under.

Returning to the house, all five of us grab sharp knives and a bucket and go forth to harvest them. I'm not sure why we need so many. Caught up in the spirit of harvesting, I don't ask, nor does anyone one say. Slicing furiously, I'm determine to fill my bucket first.

When I've done so, my bucket is replaced with an empty one and I continue to harvest mushrooms alongside my family. At lunchtime, I return to the house to the smell of fried mushrooms, and Mum serves them up on toast. I cannot recall ever eating mushrooms before. I decide I like them and go back for a second helping, which is even larger than the first.

We peel and chop mushrooms for the rest of the day, while Mum fries them up in batches. Each batch is bagged and labelled before being placed in the deep freezer. By mid-afternoon, the entire house reeks of fried mushrooms. There's nowhere in the house to escape it and, since the fog has turned to rain, going outside is not an option.

By four o'clock, I feel nauseous. I take refuge on the veranda, but even there I can still smell them. The nausea turns to stomach sickness and an hour later I vomit.

'They're toadstools!' I exclaim, fearing that we'll all be dead before dawn.

'You just ate too many of them,' says Mum, continuing to process them. 'Why don't you lie down for a bit.'

I want to, but I can't. I have to get away from the stench of them which is causing my stomach to again churn. Donning my coat, I head for the bottom house seeking refuge. Out in the fresh air, I immediately feel better and after a few hours in the other house away from the smell, I concede that I have not eaten a toadstool. It's the quantity I've eaten, and the mushrooms are simply too rich for me.

Three days later, our house still stinks of mushroom and I decide I'm not going to eat a mushroom ever again.

Our First Milking Goat

As our first year comes to a close, our hatred of cheap powdered milk reaches its climax. Stephen and I are avoiding it; Maree is refusing outright to drink it altogether.

'We need a milking cow,' says Mum. 'The children must have milk for calcium.'

Dad pours more of the skim milk onto his Weetbix. 'It'll cost a fortune to buy a milking cow and Douglas won't pay to have it shipped here!' exclaims Dad.

Mum nodded. 'What about goats?'

Dad's face sours. 'They'll still have to be shipped here.'

'It might be worth asking Howard if he'll fly one over,' says Mum.

Dad stands up from the breakfast table. 'He's flying over later this morning. You can ask him.'

To my surprise, when Howard's plane flies over, Mum heads for the airstrip on foot. She arrives just as Howard is about to climb back into his plane to depart.

Mum signals for him to wait a moment and hands him a dozen eggs in a carton. For some strange reason, Howard does not have chooks of his own. Howard nods approval and again goes to get into his plane. He's never been much for small talk and he's a busy man.

Sensing the opportunity's about to be lost, Mum says, 'I'm wondering if you'd fly over a milking goat?'

Howard pauses and glances at each of us kids in turn as if hoping we might reveal the punchline of a joke. The seconds tick by and it occurs to him that Mum's question is genuine. 'Is she quiet?' he finally replies.

'She's secured in a miking stand twice daily, so I would think so,' says Mum.

Howard shrugs. 'Should be all right, then.' Without further ado, he gets into his plane and makes ready to head off.

Back at the house, Mum makes a phone call. 'I'm phoning about the miking goat... Yes, we'd need her in kid... No, I'll post a cheque and arrange for someone to come and get her... Could be a couple of weeks... That sounds great.'

We stand by with eager anticipation of the news, but Mum just busies herself making a coffee.

'How are you going to get her to the Cape?' asks Stephen.

Mum lights a cigarette. 'It's a big property. I'm hoping one of the stockmen will go and get her if I pay their expenses.' She takes a sip of her coffee. 'If not, I'll go and get her myself.'

The idea of Mum getting down the road with a milking goat in the back of the Kombi makes me laugh. Still, when Mum gets determined, things usually work out in her favour. Someone will go and get the goat. Of that, I'm sure.

That night, Mum phones Leverington's head stockman, Joe. When she puts down the receiver she says, 'Joe says he'll take a look at her. He's never had anything to do with goats before, but he knows stock.'

Dad nods.

The next day, Joe phones back.

When Mum finishes talking to him, she says, 'Well, he says she's got big tits and looks healthy enough. He's going to bring her up to the Cape.'

A few weeks later, the sound of Howard's plane flying overhead causes a buzz of excitement. We all rush up to the airstrip, keen to see the latest addition to our farm. The plane pulls up and Howard steps out as he always does. He opens the side door to reveal the goat.

She's milk-chocolate brown in colour, with white stripes down her face. Rather than peaked or droopy ears, her ears stand out like aeroplane wings. She wears a set of horns like a queen wears a crown.

Her legs are not tied. Instead, she lies on a tarp as if it's a royal rug with her head held high like a proud princess.

Howard takes her by the collar and the goat jumps down and walks casually towards the tractor trailer. She looks at the trailer as royalty might look at a limousine and jumps onto the back of it without the need for any coaxing.

It's too much. We all burst into fits of laughter. The goat looks on as if to say, 'Why am I being kept waiting?'

Down at the house, Dad chains her to a steel picket which he's rammed in under the shade of a big pine tree. Within minutes, she's grazing happily.

An hour or so later, I see Suzi sneaking her way over to the goat. Sighing, I go to call her off, but Dad bids me to wait. When Suzi begins to bark, the goat, whom we've named Mandy, does not run to the end of her chain like a harassed animal. Instead, she turns towards the dog and watches intently.

Suzi now seems unsure of herself. Barking twice more, she turns to leave. The moment the dog turns her back, Mandy butts her. Suzi yelps, as much from surprise as pain. Mandy butts her a second and a third time, chasing Suzi until she runs out of chain. Suzi flees, still yelping.

Mum comes tumbling out the back door to see what's going on. Mandy stands there looking after Suzi as if to say, 'Yeah, you'd better run.'

'And that will be the end of that,' says Dad grinning.

The next day, Dad sits looking at a *Grass Roots* magazine which features an article on milking stands for goats. When he has the gist of it, he closes it and gets up. I don't need to ask whether he intends to build a milking stand, as obviously we'll need one. As it's a Sunday, naturally we kids will be called upon to help.

For the next few hours, we ram in posts, saw repurposed timber and nail it together. The platform of the milking stand is raised about the height of a chair's base and wide and long enough to comfortably stand a goat. At the front is a headstall which closes with a swivelling piece of timber which locks in place with a removable bolt. Along one side is a wall as tall as a goat. Attached to the wall is a seat belt with its clip mechanism which Dad has salvaged from an old car. The idea is that the goat is locked into the stand by the headstall and fastened to the side by the seat belt, so she's secure without feeling restrained.

Dad proceeds to roll a cigarette. 'Best bring her over and see if it meets Her Highness's approval.'

I go and get Mandy and lead her to the stand on a lead rope more easily than if I'd been leading Elsa. She examines the stand with a critical eye before jumping up onto it. She even willingly puts her head into the bail. Happy with the inspection, she looks back as if to say, 'It's a bit rough, but I guess it will do.'

Mum rewards Mandy with a couple of leaves of silver beet which she munches down with relish. The decision to get a goat, at least for the moment, appears to be a good one.

Tractor Incident

Displeased with the speed at which land is being cleared and sown with grass, Douglas decides Dad can use a permanent offsider. Although only seventeen, Phil has been working on Leverington for several months and has proved himself to be a competent tractor driver. Without being asked if he'd like to live on an isolated island, he's being sent over.

The arrangement is that he'll live in the bottom house, but will have dinner with us each evening. As the bottom house's combustion stove is unusable, there's no hot water in it. This means he'll also have to use our shower and laundry.

While Phil will provide a hand to Dad, taking the pressure off us kids, we're not consulted about the arrangement. We've come to enjoy the fact that we're the only ones living here and don't relish the intrusion Phil will bring. However, as there's no choice in the matter, we all agree to make the most of it.

In exchange for his evening meal, rather than being charged board, Phil agrees to work in the garden one day a fortnight. He's settled into the bottom house, which we all helped to sweep out and clean, and welcomed into the fold. In doing so, we take him fishing and shooting wallaby, which he seems to enjoy doing.

On Monday, two days after he's arrived, Dad gets him working the 1066, rolling scrub in the interior. Phil handles the big tractor competently, so Dad returns to the workshop. There, he's using the welder to build a bespoke piece of machinery called a smudge. The smudge will drag a set of harrows behind it and it's used to smooth plough furrows before seeding grass.

On Saturday, which is fine, Phil fronts to help in the garden as agreed. I assume he'll be put to work weeding, but Mum begins marking out a section in which she intends to plant a flower bed. Phil is given the task of digging a long trench half a metre wide and about the same in depth.

Bare-chested, Phil digs with gusto. Although Dad frequently complains about Phil's lack of skills, there's no doubt about the fact that he's a hard worker. With Phil labouring on the trench, we're sent to collect manure and seaweed. A mixture of both is placed in the trench. Rather than backfilling it with the poor soil Phil has removed, Dad secures some better-looking stuff from the high bank where we harvested the mushrooms. The garden bed's edges are bordered with quartz conglomerate stones, which are plentiful on the island. Afterwards, Mum plants the new flower bed with seeds and bulbs before watering them in.

A fortnight later, Phil is still here and, as best as he can, he's cutting it. I have to admit he's exceeding our expectations. Earlier, Dad proclaimed he wouldn't last three days. He's been here a month. Since Elsa and Suzi get along with him fine and there's no question that he knows how to look after the chooks and ducks as well as Mandy, we decide we'll go off the island for a week and Phil can caretake. The following Saturday, Howard comes and gets us and Phil is left with some handwritten instructions and the run of the place.

From Nana Doris's house in Ulverstone, Mum phones Phil to see how he's getting on.

'Well?' says Dad, when she's hung up.

Mum winces. 'He's burnt the vinyl tablecloth and broken the sandwich press.'

Dad balls his fist. 'How'd he manage that?'

'Not sure. I'm worried he's too young to be left there on his own.'

Dad snorts and proceeds to tell us all he achieved at Phil's age.

The next evening, Dad phones him. He comes away from the phone call shaking his head. 'Apparently the blade came off the brush cutter. He's lucky he wasn't injured or killed.'

Mum looks seriously worried. 'I'm concerned we might get a phone call to say he's burned down the house.'

Even though the phone is in the house, it's not funny, but we all laugh anyway. With each evening that passes, the list of mishaps grows bigger and bigger. The latest is a wild cow came into the home paddock. Trying to shoo her out, Phil was charged and almost gored. Dad will not hear of it. The wild cattle do not come anywhere near the home paddock so if he's been charged it has to be somewhere else on the Island. This raises the question, what had he been doing to provoke a cow in order to make her charge?

At the end of the week, we return. Phil has requested a week's leave, which has been granted, so he flies off as we fly on. Before we've unpacked our shopping, Dad does the rounds. The chooks and ducks are fine, Mandy is chewing her cud in contentment and neither of the dogs look mistreated. Despite the mishaps, the place appears well. It's just as Mum said: Phil was too young to be left on an isolated island on his own.

Dad, however, still disagrees. Over the next week, he compiles a list of things he finds not how he left them. This includes a key, now back in the door of his bedroom's French windows, which he'd placed in Mum's underwear drawer. Some of Mum's jewellery is also missing.

Dad complains to Douglas but, regardless of what's said, Phil returns after his leave. Although nothing is said to Phil about the missing jewellery or his transgressions, there's tension now that wasn't there before. Dad is shorter with Phil and he no longer hangs around after dinner to watch television as he once did.

Later that week, Phil returns from the interior on foot. Walking home means he's broken down. Not that unusual: breakdowns are common. It's his frightened demeanour that leads me to realise that something is seriously wrong.

As it's lunchtime, Mum sits a cup of tea and a sandwich in front of him.

'What's happened?' barks Dad.

Phil takes a moment to empty his mouth before replying, 'Front axle's come off the tractor.'

Dad's face turns purple and for a moment I think he's going to explode. 'How the f— did the front axle come off?'

Dad swears more than he cares to admit, but never in the house and never at the kitchen table. Mum blinks in shock.

'I hit a stump,' mumbles Phil.

Dad slides his chair back with considerable force and stands. 'Let's have a look, then.'

Phil abandons his cup of tea but clutching his sandwich follows Dad out of the house. Normally, Dad would take several, or all, of us out to a breakdown, but not on this occasion.

'Wouldn't like to be in his boots,' says Maree. 'Not after last night.'

I cock my head in confusion, because I haven't heard about any transgressions from the previous evening.

'Where's the letter?' asks Mum.

'Dad took it,' replies Maree.

Stephen lays a hand on my shoulder. 'You're too young to understand.'

I'm not. I understand perfectly, I just cannot believe Phil would be stupid enough to hand deliver a love letter to Maree. She's only fourteen and not especially pretty as far as I'm concerned.

When Dad and Phil return to the workshop on the David Brown about two hours later, they're shouting at each other and using every swear word there is. Five minutes later, Phil slinks off towards the bottom house.

Dad charges home like an angry bull. 'You kids, out!' he yells as he begins dialling the phone.

I slip out onto the veranda with my siblings, although we might as well have stayed in the kitchen because we hear every word. There can be no doubt that Dad's talking to Douglas.

'No, I've sacked the no-hoper and I want him off the island today.'

Damn, this is serious.

Dad hangs up with more force than is necessary and redials. The second call is to Howard to come and get Phil. It's a risky move, because Howard doesn't like to be told when to fly to the island and he tends to do things in his own time. Howard, however, must have agreed with Dad that the need for a plane is urgent because he arrives an hour or so later.

Stephen escorts Phil to the airstrip on his own and returns with bits and bobs, which Howard's scraped together by way of a load.

'Right, all of you, come with me,' orders Dad, 'and someone grab the camera.'

Maree, the island's unofficial photographer, grabs the camera, along with a spare role of film. Bundled onto the carry-all with the dogs running alongside, Dad drives us out to the breakdown site. I cannot believe what I'm seeing.

The front of the tractor is pushed into the ground. The entire front axle, which has been ripped off, has flown through the air and is now lodged between the dual wheels and bent out of shape. The tree, which is now only a stump, is the diameter of a coffee cup and not big enough to have done the damage it did.

'Only going slow, he said!' spat Dad. 'Slow! Look at the damage he's done!'

Maree takes photos as we circle the tractor.

'Are you going to be able to fix it?' asks Mum quietly.

'Fix it! It's going to need an entirely new axle. How we're going to get that over here I don't know.' He shakes his head in disgust. 'The back wheels have to come off to get this out.'

I know how serious this is. If the new axle is too heavy for Howard's plane, then it will have to be shipped on the *Trader*. Not only will that mean it will be out of action for months, there's another problem: the 1066 tows the truck trailer, which is needed to haul loads from the wharf. With it out of action, the David Brown will have to service the *Trader* pulling much smaller loads. This means valuable time wasted and frayed tempers from the seamen.

Back home, Dad spends over an hour on the phone that evening. He needs to know the weight of the new axle in order to determine whether it can be flown on or whether it will need to be shipped.

It turns out the axle is light enough for Howard's plane, but there's the complication of how to load it in without damaging the aircraft. There's also the added issue of who is going to help Dad repair the tractor and how they're going to do it.

I'm not sure how it's loaded into the plane but when it arrives, Dad unloads it using a jib he's rigged to the bucket of the David Brown. A tractor mechanic is also flown over and using every jack the Island possesses, they somehow manage to repair the tractor and get it going again.

Everyone breathes a sigh of relief when Dad drives the 1066 back into the home paddock. Despite what's happened, Douglas has overruled Dad's dismissal of Phil. He will remain employed at Leverington, but he will not be allowed back to the Island.

UHF Radio

There's one good thing to come from the tractor incident. Douglas agrees to install UHF radios in the house and 1066. He's also supplying a handheld, which will be portable. Having scrounged some galvanised pipe, Dad welds some brackets to it so that it can be attached to the side of the house and fitted with a large base aerial. Once the radio has been installed in the house, Dad fits the other one in the tractor.

They're tested and found to work well. Even from the depths of the interior, it's possible to talk to someone in the house via the UHF. The next time Dad breaks down, he'll be able to radio home for someone to come and get him or to bring tools out to him.

Excited, Douglas attempts to contact Leverington, which he deems should be possible through the repeater towers installed on mountain tops across Tasmania. There's no response. He tries again, this time trying to contact someone closer. Again, there's no response.

'It's the position of the house down in the dip,' says Dad, explaining the incident that occurred with the VHF radio when the phone went out. He'd been able to contact someone in the Gulf of Carpentaria but not on Flinders Island.

Douglas looks miffed. 'I'd thought we'd be able to talk via radio, saving money on long-distance phone calls.'

Dad shakes his head behind Douglas's back and even I think it strange. Dad phones Douglas twice a week to provide an update and receive instructions. Expensive admittedly, but those conversations are not ones you'd want to have across an open airway.

'What if we raised the aerial?' asks Douglas.

Dad shakes his head. 'You're not going to get it much higher. It's already swaying in the wind.'

Douglas disagrees. So Dad lowers the aerial and sets about raising the pole even higher. Standing it up requires the aid of the bucket on the David Brown, and to stabilise it, guide wires are run down to the corner fence posts.

Once it's back online, Douglas tries again to contact Leverington. There's still no response. Nor is there when they tried to contact Little Musselrow Bay, which is just south of Cape Portland.

Upset at having his plans thwarted, Douglas returns home.

A few days later, the generator breaks down. Thankfully, the welder that runs off the PTO shaft of the tractor is a good backup so we're not without power. However, there's another problem. The phone has also lost its dial tone, so Dad can't phone anyone to order the new part. Dad looks inside the phone's box which the technician deliberately left unlocked, but on this occasion it's not simply a tripped switch.

I jump in the 1066 with Dad and he drives us out to the western side of the island, where we have a clear view of Tasmania. Dad manages to contact Little Musselrow Bay as well as Swan Island.

'Can we contact Cape Portland?' I ask.

'No, I think Howard uses FM radios,' Dad replies.

It doesn't matter. We've managed to get a message out and it's good to know we now have another form of communication with the outside world when we need it.

Aerial Sowing

Despite the continual breakdowns, progress is being made to flatten the heath in the interior and plough it under. The seed drill, however, has proved to be unsuitable for the rocky ground and the spreader is deemed too small for the area that needs to be sown.

Douglas has sent over eighty tons of superphosphate in half-tonne bulk bags on the *Flinders Trader*. It was unloaded out of the bags onto the truck trailer and dumped in a pile up at the airstrip. Also sent over was a drum of aviation fuel. Dad has spent several weeks making a special scoop to fit on the loader arms of the David Brown. The scoop has a tapered bottom and will allow the superphosphate, mixed with grass seed, to be loaded into the plane without it going everywhere or causing damage. He's also put out flags to indicate what areas needs to be dusted.

In due course, a crop duster flies across from Tasmania and lands on the airstrip. Looking like a giant bumblebee, it has only one seat. It makes Howard's plane look like an airliner.

'That thing's hysterical,' I say to Stephen, who nods.

The pilot gets out and opens a tiny locker behind the hopper, from which he removes an overnight bag. I take his bag for safekeeping as he isn't heading to the house, he just wants to remove the weight of it from the tiny plane. Apparently, even the twenty kilograms of his bag matter. Besides, he doesn't want to be outmanoeuvred by a grasshopper.

Dad puts on a set of goggles and proceeds to load the plane. For the next two days, the plane spreads load after load of fertiliser and seed onto the paddocks. Finally, the big heap of superphosphate disappears and the job is done. I watch as the bumblebee plane disappears into the distance. He's braver than me. I'm not sure I'd want to cross Bank Strait in that little thing.

Two days later, the heavens open and it rains for nearly a week straight. When it finally lets up, the entire area which has just been sown is now under centimetres of water.

'Won't that drown the seed?' I ask.

'Won't do it any good,' admits Dad, shaking his head. 'Douglas has got me working up the wrong country. The interior's too wet and stony. He'd be better off burning the tussock country to the west and south and seeding into the ash.'

I haven't considered that, but now it makes sense. Post burning, the tussocks will grow green shoots which the stock can eat, and grass will grow between the clumpers.

'You'd have to burn every few years, but if you did it on a rotation, you'd always have green shoots coming on. That's what the MacLaine family did for nigh on a hundred years.'

Now I'm confused. The tussock country is a good third of the island. If a four-wheel drive fire truck is sent over, even an old one, the burn-offs would be relatively simple. Even without it, we could manage in a fashion, although the old tank bolted onto the truck trailer is grossly inadequate. Each time they do a burn-off, the trailer ends up on its side and people are nearly killed. However, with controlled burns, the tussock country could be made ready for stock almost immediately. 'I don't get it.'

Dad grins slyly. 'The eastern side is already reserve. The interior contains rare heath and Douglas is concerned that certain people may wish to extend the reserve.

'So he's ploughing it under.'

Dad nods.

I'm speechless and not just because I'm a conservationist at heart. Ploughing the interior is costly and beyond stupid and I know deep down that it will be our boss's doom. Even in the short time I've been here, I've learned something. One has to work with the Island, not against it. Douglas is going against it and he will lose. Maybe not in the short term, but long term he's going to lose big time.

Preservation Island

The man who holds the lease on Preservation Island, across Armstrong Channel next to Cape Barren Island, is one of the men who helped rescue the distressed seaman some time ago. He's stayed in touch and now he's offering to fly us all over to his island for the day.

'Why is Bryce paying to fly us over?' asks Stephen. 'Does he need a hand to do something?'

Like me, Stephen spent his early years living in caravan parks. We learned, 'No one does anything for nothing', and 'Be cautious of anyone who is keen to make friends', because they have an ulterior motive.

'I told him you were all doing school by correspondence. He's a historian and he believes you might all benefit from a history lesson,' says Mum.

I'm not buying it.

'It's more likely he'll want a hand next muttonbird season,' replies Dad.

'What's that involve?' asks Stephen.

'Well, if he invites us birding, you'll find out, but we can always refuse.'

Now I know Bryce's modus operandi, I'm no longer concerned.

The next morning, a plane is due to pick us up around nine. Bryce has charted Munro Airline to pick us up and fly us over and drop us back later that afternoon. Munro is based in Launceston. They sell individual seats and island-hop until they have a planeload. Aside from chartering planes commercial or private, Munro is the only airline operating in the area.

I dress as I always do in island clothes. Mum takes one look at me and tells me I have to change into one of the hideous tracksuits I wear off the island. She herself is fussing with what to wear. I'd assumed she'd stay behind in case we couldn't get back, but it appears not.

When it lands, the ten-seater twin-engine plane looks like a jumbo compared to Howard's plane. We all get in and the flight is literally only a few minutes. Preservation Island is small and flat and covered in tussocks. Aside from the odd tea tree and sheoak, there are no trees.

We climb out and the pilot says he'll be back about three. Bryce leads us over to a shed-cum-shack where his wife and daughter are. Parked in it is an old bus long-dead but still used for storage. I wonder how such a vehicle has come to be on this island. Even when it was going, it wouldn't have been suitable for the terrain.

'We might as well start down the wharf,' says Bryce, who seems keen to play the tour guide.

It's only a few minutes' walk down a sandy track. The wharf extends a lot further out into the sea than Clarke Island's does, meaning it can dock boats at any time regardless of the tide. It is, however, completely exposed to the westerly winds and so there are few days when it's calm enough for boats to dock. Like Clarke Island's wharf, it has yards and a race for loading and unloading stock.

Bryce leads us down onto a beach that has jet-black sand speckled with silver. 'The sand is magnetic.'

'Is it natural?' I ask.

'It's a phenomenon that no one can explain,' he replies. 'As is this.'

He leads us to some nearby rocks. Within them are perfectly round holes about as big round as a treated pine fence post and up to half a metre deep. They don't look natural to me, but what's made them, I can't say.

Bryce points out to sea. 'Just out there is the *Sydney Cove*. She came to grief in 1797.' He points to a small neighbouring island that's separated only by a small channel. 'That's Rum Island. After the ship ran aground, the officers ordered the rum barrels to be taken over there so the sailors couldn't drink themselves to death.'

'You could swim across to there,' I say.

'You can't. A powerful rip runs between the two islands and sharks frequent these waters.'

Bryce climbs onto a high bank. 'After the survivors, came James Munro. He arrived on Preservation Island in 1820. He lived with a Tasmanian Aboriginal woman from Cape Portland named Rramanaluna. She was one of George Robinson's guides during the 1830s Black Line operation. That was where they rounded up all the Tasmanian Aborigines and took them initially to Swan Island and then to Flinders Island. Wybalenna was where they finally settled. The entire operation was a disaster – all but a few died.'

'What did Munro do here?' I ask.

'He was a sealer and muttonbirder, but he also established a market garden and farm here and he sold the produce locally. Later, he became a merchant who traded seal skins and muttonbirds. He came to be known as the King of the Sealers, as well as the Governor of the Straits. He died here around 1844, we're not sure of the exact date, and was buried here in an unmarked grave. Mount Munro and Munro Bay on Cape Barren Island are named after him.'

Bryce leads us back the way we came. En route he takes a different track, where he leads us onto a patch of green. 'Beneath us is a mass grave.' Bending down, he points to shamrock. 'This island has another strange phenomenon. On each grave was planted shamrock. For some reason it doesn't spread beyond the grave.'

Now that he's pointed it out I can't help but see it. Rather than being an entire field of shamrock, it's patterned, marking each grave. It's creepy to say the least.

Back at the shack, Bryce climbs onto a grey Massey Ferguson tractor and starts the engine. We all climb onto the trailer and he drives us across the island. There's two muttonbird rookeries and hundreds of Cape Barren geese, along with a hundred head of cattle.

At the far end of the island, we stop to eat the picnic Mum has packed. Circumnavigating the island, Bryce brings us back just in time to catch the plane home. It's been an awesome day.

1080 Poison

Despite the heavy rains and flooding which followed, some of the grass seed takes. It produces a green patch of several hundred acres. Some of the cattle, once bone-rattlers, are now beginning to fatten. However, there's a new problem. The abundance of grass has led to an explosion in the wallaby population. Since the island's top predator is the feral cat, an animal too small to kill wallabies, there's nothing to keep them in check.

When next Howard arrives, he brings with him dozens of bags of carrots. For the next few days, Dad chops up carrots with a spade in the bottom of an old cut-in-half drum. Once they're cut, he drives the tractor around the new pasture towing the trailer, and we toss carrots over the side.

'What's the point of free-feeding carrots?' I say. 'The cattle are eating them before the wallaby get near them.'

'We do as we're told, lad,' replies Dad, who's obviously come to the same conclusion I have.

At week's end, a plane lands and a poison expert gets off. He's come to poison the last batch of carrots with 1080. Both Mum and Dad insist we remain at the house while they go with the poison man. They return later that afternoon and the poison man's plane returns and flies him off again.

For the first time ever, the dogs have to be caged at night and kept close during the day. Three days later, Dad drives the dozer out to the new pasture. He returns in the evening, having spent the day burying dead cattle. As predicted, the poison has had little effect on the wallaby. If anything, it's made it worse, because now there are fewer cattle competing for the grass. A new solution is needed and fast, but what?

More Goats

In August, Mandy has her kid. Pure white in colour and female. We name her Shelley. She's born one evening and by morning she's charging around leaping and bucking like a rodeo bull. She wants desperately to drink from her mother's teats, but every time she tries, she receives a swift kick followed by a headbutt. A mother refusing to feed her young is strange behaviour, but ironically beneficial. It means Shelley can stay with her mother because she won't drink any of the milk.

Mum milks Mandy and we bottle-feed Shelley. It's a pain because she has to be fed six times a day. Despite that, there's still a surplus of milk. Mum pours us all a small glassful.

I take a cautious sip and it's all I can do not to spit it out again. The milk tastes like it's been mixed with turnip juice. It's awful.

'We can't drink that!' I exclaim.

Mum looks crestfallen. She's gone to a lot of trouble to get us a milking goat and the milk is undrinkable. Thankfully, a few days later the taint disappears and we change our minds about the milk.

As Shelley grows and begins to eat grass, we reduce her milk intake and the surplus increases. Mum now begins to make yogurt and custard.

'We're going to need a billy,' says Dad.

Without a billy, once Mandy goes dry, there'll be no more milk. The only other option to get her in kid is artificial insemination. While there's a vet who's also a pilot with his own plane servicing the islands, we can't afford to pay him to artificially inseminate Mandy.

When next Mum speaks to her brother Uncle Ernie, he tells her about two goats for sale on Flinders Island. A white Saanen nanny and an Anglo-Nubian billy. Both are reported to be three years old.

'Sounds like a reasonable deal,' says Mum.

'How are we going to get them here?' replies Dad, again bringing up the main problem with living on an island.

'Ernie says the seller will arrange transport at a reasonable price.'

Dad looks dubious and for good reason. It was Uncle Ernie who'd sold us the Shetland pony Cheeky whom we can't ride. Despite her reservations, Mum agrees to buy the goats. We need a billy and we have few options.

With the sale complete, it's arranged that the goats will arrive tomorrow. I assume they'll be brought down on a runabout like the Telecom men use. Thus, I keep an eye on the Channel all day but no boats appear.

About three o'clock, I hear the noise of a plane and rush outside to see one of Munro's twin-engine ones circling to land. It's odd, because we aren't expecting anyone. Stephen rushes to get the David Brown. Whatever the reason for landing, it's impolite to keep the pilot waiting.

We arrive just as the plane is pulling in. Before the propellers stop turning, every door on the aircraft opens and passengers begin spilling out. Although it's not unusual for passengers bound elsewhere to get off for a hurried cigarette, most just wait patiently in the plane. Something's wrong. Is the plane on fire? Has the pilot made an emergency landing?

It takes about four seconds to reach me. A stench like fermented urine mixed with manure. What can make such a stink? It isn't until I hear a bleating sound that it hit me. The goats. The seller has flown the goats down on Munro.

Wishing I had a bandana to cover my mouth and face, I move in for a closer look. The goats are in the very rear of the plane but they can't be our goats. These ones look ancient. I glance at the pilot for an explanation.

'Well, get them out, boy!' he barks.

I rush forward to comply. Neither of them is wearing a collar and both have their legs tied. Thankfully, Stephen steps forward. Cutting the leg ropes of the nanny with a knife permanently belted to his right hip, he repurposes the rope to form crude collars. Without them escaping, we manage to get them out of the plane and over to the tractor. Now they won't jump up onto the trailer the way Mandy had.

'I might need to lead them down,' I say.

Standing there with a goat in each hand, I turn to see what's happening with the plane. Normally, planes take off again as soon as they can. In this case, the passengers stand around with their arms folded, refusing to get back on.

'Right. Everyone back on,' orders the pilot.

'Bugger that,' says one. 'You'll have to bring us another plane.'

The stench is bad, but hanging onto the foul git, I'm slowly becoming accustomed to it.

'I'm leaving with or without you,' says the pilot firmly. He isn't joking and he begins closing doors in order to take off.

One passenger, fearing being stranded, moves forward and slowly the others follow.

As the plane begins taxiing, I again try to coax the goats up onto the trailer. Finally, the billy jumps up followed by the nanny. I hold them while Stephen slowly drives down to the house. He stops alongside like he normally does.

'What's that stench?' asks Mum as she comes out the back door. 'Oh, my giddy aunt.'

'Ew, are you touching him?' asks Maree.

I roll my eyes. 'We had to get them out of the plane and down here, didn't we.'

Mum casts her eyes over the goats the same way I had and it occurs to her she's just been robbed.

'They look a bit older than three, Mum,' says Maree.

I go to lead the goats off the trailer.

'What are you doing?' asks Mum.

'I can't leave them on the trailer,' I reply irritably, my patience wearing thin.

'Don't unload them here. They're putrid.'

'Well, what am I supposed to do with them?'

Dad comes up from the workshop. He reaches out for the nanny and I hand her over. 'Take the billy over to the generator paddock.'

Stephen restarts the tractor and drives over there, where we let the billy go. The paddock has its own plumbed-in water trough and there's plenty of grass and shelter, so he should be all right on his own.

Rather than get back on the tractor, I walk back over to the house.

'You'll need to get straight into the shower and soak your clothes,' says Mum.

The smell is bad, but I've gotten used to it to some degree. 'No point showering yet. I haven't done my chores.'

'I don't care. You'll need to shower and change your clothes straight away.'

I'm cranky but do as I'm told. I'm just finishing unloading a wheelbarrow of wood for the combustion stove when Dad walks up.

'Did you take the billy over any food or water?'

'No,' I reply. 'He's got plenty of grass and a water trough.'

'Did you show him where the trough was?'

'No,'

'Best take him over some chaff with a few oats and show him where the water trough is so he feels welcome.'

I sigh, but do as I'm bid. I find the billy urinating on his beard, hence the stink. Rather than get in with him, I show him the bowl of chaff and oats over the fence. He's interested and I lead him round to the trough, which is next to the fence. Dropping his bowl over, I'm careful not to let him touch me.

I've barely stepped into the back porch when Mum shrieks. 'Have you been near that billy again?'

'Dad said I had to feed him. I never touched him.'

'You must have. I can smell him on you.'

He hadn't touched me, I was sure of it

'You'd best shower and change your clothes again.'

Rage bubbles inside me at the injustice of it. 'We have to have a billy. No one else is going to feed him or look after him and I can't be showering and changing every time I toss his food over the fence.' I rage for a good two minutes.

'Enough,' says Dad. 'Go and do as your mother asks.'

'I never touched him.'

'I said enough.'

I storm off towards the shower.

The next day, I refuse on principle to tend to the billy, whom we've named Bruno. As I predicted, no one else will go near him either.

Three days later, he breaks out. It isn't such a drama, in that he doesn't run off, but he insists on rubbing up against Mandy, Shelley and the new nanny, Blossom.

Dad and I manage to catch Bruno and take him back but, within the hour, he's back out again. We walk the fence line, but can't find any hole or weak spot in the fence.

Dad rolls a cigarette and leans on a post as he smokes it. 'He'll have to be chained up if we can't stop him getting out.'

I roll my eyes. We chained Mandy for a few weeks when she first got here and she tangled herself around the steel picket and needed to be untangled every few hours.

'I can't be showering every few hours,' I reply.

Dad doesn't reply but we do have to chain Bruno up. He bleats incessantly about how unfair it is. Come milking time, Mum says she can't milk Mandy because of the stench. We've all been trained to milk, so I do it. Afterwards, I wash down the three nannies with soapy water.

It's as predicted: Bruno tangles himself up frequently. Dad and I are the only ones who will tend to him. I learn to do so, carefully avoiding being touched. As time passes, Mum slowly learns to accept the smell, although she never really gets over it.

The Scallop Boat

Mum has got into the habit of raking up around the goat's milking stand every few weeks. She gathers up not only the goat manure, but also the fallen leaves and twigs of the trees nearby. The scrapings are taken to the garden. With the continuous supply of fertiliser, as long as we run sprinklers every day, the garden grows and produces well.

With the beginning of the fishing season, the fishing boats return. When the Channel is calm, it's not unusual for up to a dozen boats to anchor in the bay. One day as I'm doing my chores, half a dozen men come walking towards the house from the direction of the wharf.

Mum invites them in, and makes tea and coffee and puts out home-baked biscuits.

'We've a bit of a problem,' says the captain when the small talk's over. 'We've sailed from Lakes Entrance to fish the scallop beds, but we've left our provisions behind.'

The con smells worse than the billy, but I remain silent. I can tell by Mum's tight-lipped expression that she also knows the captain is lying.

'We've got an abundance of food in the garden,' says Dad clearly not taking Mum's hint. 'You kids find a box and grab some vegetables.'

The three of us go to the garden and return with a large box containing all manner of fresh produce. When we get back to the house, we find Mum removing beef from the freezer. Although it comes from island beef, which we haven't paid for, there's been considerable effort to slaughter and butcher it. Stephen sits the box on the kitchen table with more force than necessary. Like me, he's unhappy with the situation.

'No potatoes?' one of the men comments casually.

'The tops are still green,' I say.

'Joy, haven't we got some dried potato?' asks Dad.

'Yes, but it's terribly expensive.'

The captain produces his wallet, which is thick with fifty-dollar notes. He thumbs at a five, which I think is miserly. Even without the dried potato, what's already on the table is worth at least fifty. I also find it odd that he doesn't go to the Whitemark store on Flinders Island or across to Bridport for provisions.

Dad waves him off. 'I'm happy for you to pay us in scallops.'

Dad's generosity now makes sense. He wants a feed of scallops, which we can't afford to buy. I'm not convinced these fishermen will honour the deal, but I can understand why he's making it. Mum adds a small zip-seal bag of dried potato to the offerings.

'Do we have a deal?' asks Dad, offering his hand to the captain.

'Sounds good,' he replies, shaking Dad's hand.

We escort them to their boat at the wharf but never see them again.

New John Deere Tractor

A few months later on a lovely sunny day, a barge lands on the home beach. Aboard is a large green tractor with bright yellow wheels. According to Dad, it's an 8430 John Deere. Attached to the front is a heavy steel bespoke noose guard upon which hangs a dozer blade.

Although it's a school day, Mum agrees we can take the day off in place of a Saturday or Sunday and go and watch the unloading. We take off down the beach and find a good vantage point upon the dunes where we'll be out of the way but will still have a good view. Maree brings the camera with her and proceeds to take photos.

Although he frequently left us undermanned when the *Flinders Trader* docked, Douglas has come personally and brought several men from Leverington with him. Although the home beach is only a few hundred metres from the workshop, there's no vehicle access to it from that end. To get to the other end, where you can drive a tractor across the dunes, requires crossing MacLaine's Creek. That requires driving two kilometres inland, a further two kilometres east to the base of Home Hill and then scrub bashing across to the beach.

Pointing, I say, 'That barge is smaller than the *Trader*. Why didn't it dock at the wharf beach, where there's a track down to it?'

There may be a reason, but neither Maree or Stephen can say why. The front of the barge lowers to reveal a hundred drums of diesel which have been shipped with the new tractor. These will need to be moved before the tractor can be unloaded.

A deckhand from the barge rolls the first drum off, but it comes to an abrupt halt the moment it hits the sand. One of Douglas's men tries to roll it further up the beach but finds he can't. Each drum weighs about two-hundred kilograms. They're difficult to roll on firm ground; impossible to move even on the firmer wet sand.

Despite the obvious difficulty the drums are going to provide on the beach, the barge deckhands continue to roll them off. With two men pushing, it's possible to move the drums on the wet sand, but not far and not with any speed.

Impatient to unload and reload, the barge captain backs the vessel up and re-lands it five metres down the beach, where the drums aren't in the way. Douglas climbs into the new tractor, starts it and slowly drives forward. Confronted with the downward slope of the barge ramp and the upward slope of the beach, the tractor's blade digs into the sand and all movement forward stops.

When the tractor is put in reverse, the big wheels, front and back, which were clear of the ramp and on the sand, just spin. The new tractor can go neither forward, nor backward. It's an inauspicious start for the new machine which is supposed to replace both the 1066 and the D6 dozer.

'How are they going to get it up the sand dunes?' I ask.

Stephen's eyes widen but he offers no answer.

Dad, who's driving the dozer, spins around in front of the bogged tractor. A chain is hooked up between the two vehicles and the dozer pulls the tractor forward. Once it's unhooked, Douglas gets to the foot of the sand dunes, where the new tractor again bogs due to the heavy blade on the front, which can only be raised a metre.

'You'd think it would just push its way free,' I say.

Stephen shakes his head. 'Tractors are designed to pull not push.'

I don't understand the physics of it, but the evidence before me shows Stephen is correct.

Dad parks the dozer and switches off the motor. Removing his earmuffs, he leaps off. Douglas is waving for Dad to use the dozer to pull the tractor up the dune, but Dad clearly wants a word. Douglas reluctantly gets out of the new tractor. From our position on the dunes we can't hear what's being said but we get the gist of it. Dad doesn't want the dozer shipped off the island, and for good reason. Without the dozer's help, the new tractor will forever remain on the beach.

'I think he's also arguing to keep the 1066,' says Stephen.

'Well, given the effort it takes to get machinery here, why not?'

Dad stabs a finger out to sea. A dozen of the fuel drums have been caught up in the surge of the waves and are now floating in the bay.

'How are they going to get them back?' I ask.

The only boat we have is the dinghy, and she has no motor. It'll be a tough job pushing floating fuel drums around the bay with a rowboat. Added to that, a westerly is also picking up. The drums need to be retrieved and the barge needs to leave.

One of Leverington's men begins stripping down to his underwear. Plunging into the icy sea, he begins swimming after the drums.

'He's going to be frozen by the time he gets them back,' says Stephen.

I agree and if I'd been him I'd have refused and made Douglas swim after them.

Confrontation over, Dad gets back on the dozer. The new tractor is towed up the bank. The second of Leverington's men gets in the 1066 and drives it onto the barge. Having unhooked the tow chains, Dad drives the dozer down the bank and onto the barge as well. The moment he's back on the beach, the barge door closes and the barge pulls out and begins motoring across the Channel.

Standing up, Stephen shades his eyes. Rather than bring the truck trailer to carry the fuel drums back on, Dad has brought the sled. He'd left it at the top of the dunes, where the new tractor is. The obvious question is how they're going to get the fuel drums up the sand dunes and onto the sled. The dozer could have pulled it up the dunes, but it's now headed back to Tasmania at speed as the westerly closes in. The new tractor couldn't even get itself up the bank, so there's no way it's going to pull a laden sled up there. The reason Dad pointed to the drums is now becoming clearer. He wasn't simply pointing out that they were floating away, he was arguing that the dozer was needed to get the drums up the dunes.

Dad stomps past, heading towards home. An hour later, he returns with the David Brown with its loader bucket attached. He scoops up a drum but, loaded down at the front, the little tractor cannot climb the dunes. Shaking his head, Dad rubs his face in his hands.

A good ten minutes later, he begins to lay out the twitch chains that accompanied the sled. Shackled together, there's enough chain to reach the David Brown from the drawbar of the new tractor. The question is, will the chains be strong enough to take the weight?

Thankfully they are and the new tractor tows the David Brown laden with a fuel drum up the dunes. It takes the rest of the day to get the drums up the bank and back to the home paddock.

Despite the debacle on the beach, Douglas is still convinced the new tractor, now referred to as the 8430, will do the work of the dozer. The next day, the tractor is taken out into the interior to where there's a freshwater spring that Douglas wants dug out to make a new dam.

I'm at my school desk making up for yesterday when the radio call is received at the house. Before its departure, Dad removed the UHF from the 1066 and fitted it to the 8430 last evening.

Stephen gets up to answer it. 'Clarke Island base, receiving.'

'The new tractor is bogged,' says Dad. 'Can someone please drive the David Brown and trailer out here and pick us up.'

'Roger that.' Hanging the mike back up, Stephen just stands there a moment. 'How the blazes are they going to get that out?'

'If I was Douglas, I'd have that barge turn around and bring the dozer and 1066 back,' I say.

'Fat chance of that,' replies Stephen. 'I'd best go and get them.'

Loaded with mud-caked men, the David Brown returns with Stephen driving. There's no time for them to shower before they have to be taken to the airstrip to catch a plane home.

Dad says very little that evening at dinner. Thankfully, his mind is too busy reeling for him to be angry as he tries to figure out how to unbog the 8430. I have no idea what he'll come up with, but I know he'll figure it out.

The next day, my siblings and I go with him to the bog site. The 8430 is bogged to its belly, with mud two-thirds of the way up the large wheels. There's no way it can be pulled out by the David Brown and there's no longer a vehicle large enough to pull it free. I know Dad has a plan, but I have no comprehension of what it is.

Having unhooked the trailer, Dad drives the bucket of the David Brown as deep into the ground as it will go directly in front of the 8430. Getting off, he lays out two lines of chain towards the 8430, securing one end to the bucket of the David Brown. The other end he secures to the lugs of the 8430's large tyres with G-clamps.

'Tell me when the chain has done a full lap,' says Dad, climbing into the 8430.

Having started the motor, he engages the drive and very gently allows the huge wheels to spin a full revolution. Using the hand-held UHF, Stephen calls the spin.

Dad climbs out and removes the G-clamps. Replacing them with shackles, he secures the chain to itself. 'You kids stand well back. If the chain breaks, it will recoil and if it hits you, it will kill you.'

I jog a good ten metres away. Dad's plan is now obvious. He intends to use the 8430's front wheels as winch drums to pull itself out. Two things can go wrong. Firstly, the chain might not be strong enough and secondly, the David Brown, which is being used as an anchor, may not hold.

Dad, having climbed back in, gently engages drive. The wheels spin and the chains pull tight. For a moment, the David Brown begins to move and I fear it won't hold. However, the pull of the 8430's front wheels only digs the bucket in deeper. Slowly, the 8430 inches forward as the chain winds around its wheels. Dad keeps it moving until its front wheels are on solid ground.

Climbing out, he unchains the bucket before driving out with the chain still wrapped around the wheels. Dad manages to get the David Brown to reverse, so its bucket is no longer in the ground. The process is then reversed in order to unwrap the chains from the 8430's wheels.

Throughout the entire process, I stand there flabbergasted. I would never have thought to do such a thing. Dad, on the other hand, has his back to the wall most of the time. On an island, he has to think on his feet because there's no one coming to help and he only has the resources he has at hand.

Maree climbs into the 8430 with Dad. Her driving lessons are to begin immediately. Stephen and I bring the David Brown home. By the time we get back, Dad is already unhooking the blade from the front. Douglas's plan hasn't worked, but we all know he'll be too proud to ship the dozer back.

Stranded Visitor

It's a cold wet day of drizzle. A good day to stay inside by the fire with a book. A plane flies overhead and I hear it circling around to land. By the noise it makes, I know it isn't Howard's plane. It also isn't ED's plane, so why would it be landing?

Maree and I take the David Brown to the airstrip to investigate. The plane is a four-seater Cessna which I haven't seen before. Nor have I seen the pilot, who remains in the plane, or his passenger. I glance at Maree, but she just shrugs. The passenger hands the pilot a wad of notes, shoulders a carry bag and climbs onto the carry-all of the David Brown as if he thinks we know who he is and we're expecting him. Before anyone can say anything, the plane takes off.

'Can you take me to the shop?' asks the bloke.

Maree shakes her head. 'No shop here, mate.'

Undaunted, he asks, 'Can you take me to the police station?'

Maree again shakes her head. 'No police station here, mate.'

He looks confused. 'To the town, then?'

'There's no town here,' I say.

Tilting his head, he says, 'This is Cape Barren Island, isn't it?'

'Nope,' I say. Pointing at the mountains across the Channel, I add, 'Cape Barren is over there, mate.'

He scratches the back of his head as if unable to fathom what we're telling him.

'What's your name, mate?' asks Maree.

'Ralph,' he replies.

'Ralph, I'm Maree and this is Dion and you're on Clarke Island, not Cape Barren.'

'What's on Clarke Island?' he asks.

'Not much,' I say, 'but we can take you to what there is.'

Maree starts the tractor and drives us down to the house. We take him inside.

'This is Ralph,' says Maree. 'The plane dropped him on the wrong island.'

The colour drains from Mum's face. Turning to me she says, 'Go and get your father.'

I foot it down to the workshop wondering what the hell Dad is going to make of this. I'm halfway when it occurs to me that we've messed up big time. We should have stopped the plane from leaving.

Dad can tell from the look on my face that it's grave news. 'What?' he barks.

'The plane's dumped a bloke on the wrong island. We should have stopped the plane leaving. I just didn't think.'

Admitting I've done wrong seems to take the sting out of Dad's temper. We're expected to act like adults, but the reality is, we're not. We're just children forced to learn on the go.

Dad puts down his spanner and wipes his hands on a bit of rag. 'Come on, then, let's get this sorted.'

When we get back to the house, Ralph doesn't look concerned. Mainly because he's tucking into a big plate of spaghetti bolognese along with a hunk of homemade bread.

Dad takes a seat and proceeds to roll a cigarette. 'Ralph, I'm Thomas. I hear you're supposed to be on Cape Barren Island.'

He pauses from eating. 'Was flying over to surprise my brother. It's his birthday tomorrow.'

Dad lights his smoke. 'So, how'd you end up here instead of across the Channel?'

Ralph pauses as if the question is hard to fathom. 'When we were flying over, I thought it was Cape Barren, so I told the pilot I wanted to go down there.'

Ralph might be a bit slow, but as far as I can tell he isn't lying.

Whether the pilot thought Ralph was confused and meant he wanted to go to Clarke Island rather than Cape Barren or whether he'd just had enough and wanted to get Ralph out of his plane, I couldn't be sure. What is sure is that Ralph is now stranded on the wrong island.

'Can you take me over in your boat?' he asks.

'We don't have a boat big enough, Ralph,' says Dad. 'Do you know your brother's phone number?'

'Nah, he doesn't have a phone.'

Dad points towards the phone, but he means the phone book, which Mum passes to him. 'Do you know anyone who has a phone over there?'

Ralph makes a face as if thinking hurt. 'The shop would have one.'

Dad finds the number for the Cape Barren Island store, gets up and phones it. 'I'm calling from Clarke Island. We have a Ralph Cooper here who was coming over to visit his brother... I see... Well, is there someone else who could slip over and get him... Right, well, thanks anyway.'

Dad hangs up. 'Your brother has gone to Flinders Island and he's apparently en route to Melbourne. I asked, but there's no one else who's prepared to come across in a boat and get you in this weather.'

Ralph looks genuinely shocked. He tries to speak but seems unable.

Dad again begins thumbing through the phone book. 'Who flew you here?'

Ralph rubs his forehead. 'I can't remember.'

'Did you fly out of Launceston?'

'No, Devonport.'

Dad dials again. 'Yes, I'm calling from Clarke Island. We have a Ralph Cooper here. I'm wondering if he chartered a plane from you... He did. Excellent. You need to fly back and get him. He was dropped on the wrong island... I don't care whose fault it is. You need to come back and get him... That's not my concern. You need to come back and get him... No, we have no plane or boat. You need to come back and get him... Yes, we can get him to the airstrip.' Dad hangs up and shakes his head. He goes to say something but changes his mind. 'The plane's coming back for you. It'll be about an hour.'

That's good news but I wonder what we're supposed to do with Ralph for the next hour. Mum solves the problem by offering him coffee and cake for dessert.

When the plane lands, Dad accompanies Ralph to the airstrip. The pilot never says a word as Ralph climbs in. It's not until the plane's airborne and flying in the direction of Cape Barren that I breathe a sigh of relief.

'Don't let that happen again,' says Dad.

I won't, don't worry.

Rolf Harris

For the first time ever, I'm excited to be going off the island. Dad has heard that Rolf Harris will be performing live at the Scottsdale Show and he's determined to get us there to see him. As Howard's plane is in Wynyard for a major service, Dad books four seats on Munro Airlines to fly us to Cape Portland.

When the plane arrives, Mum drives the David Brown to the airstrip and we all get in. Two hours later, we're bustling through the show gates. Once we're inside, Dad hands us each twenty dollars and tells us to meet him at the grandstand in time for the show. He plans to meet up with the manager of Scottsdale Websters hardware store, whom he speaks to frequently on the phone.

I head straight for Sideshow Alley, then pause. I don't need to have a go on the air rifles, I frequently use a .22 to shoot at live targets, and the dodgem cars seem lame compared with bombing around on the tractor. Instead, I buy a Dagwood dog and head over to watch the sheepdog trials.

As I watch the dogs obeying commands from their masters, I imagine I'll soon be working with sheep and commanding dogs myself. It has already been two years since we arrived on the island. As Leverington's head stockman Joe had predicted, the sheep haven't arrived yet. Would they ever? Somehow, I have my doubts.

When the sheepdog trials finish, I buy a second Dagwood dog and move across to the main arena. I watch a number of shows including the obligatory clown, which doesn't entertain me, although the karate does. How can anyone break bricks without hurting their hand? I don't know, but I vow to one day find out.

Stephen sees me and comes over. 'Boring, huh?'

'Yeah, I'm hoping Rolf will be all right, though.'

We still have an hour to go before he comes on. I consider a third Dagwood dog, but decide on a bucket of chips instead and wander around killing time. In the end, we headed over to the grandstand early.

It's just as well we do, because twenty-minutes before Rolf comes on, the grandstand is already packed. I laugh until I cry and then laugh some more. It's at that point that Rolf produces a one-hundred-millimetre paintbrush. The way he slaps on different shades of paint randomly, I think he's taking the piss. When the painting turns into an incredible landscape, I'm speechless. He certainly has talent.

'Still telling the same jokes and painting the same picture as he was thirty years ago,' says Dad as he leads us back to the Kombi.

Maybe so, but he was worth seeing at least once in a lifetime.

Medical Emergency

I'm bouncing up and down on the trampoline as I do several times a day, when I hear Dad start yelling for help. I'm unsure what to do. Certainly, there's no point calling triple zero nor the flying doctor until I know what's wrong.

Thankfully, Mum comes barrelling out the back door, but Dad is almost to the house by then.

'What's wrong?' she asks.

'Hydraulic hose burst and I've burnt myself.'

Mum leads Dad straight into the laundry, where she fills the trough with water. Once she has him bent over soaking his burnt upper arm in cold water, she phones the Flying Doctor. Mum frantically scribbles down notes before hanging up and heading into the pantry, where there's a cubic-metre chest full of medical supplies.

She returns with a burn cream, gauze and a bandage. Less than twenty minutes after having been burnt, Dad is swallowing some pain medication and wondering what to do with himself for the rest of the day. It seems surreal because as an accident-prone child I've spent my fair share of time sitting around in hospital waiting rooms waiting to be treated. Here we are physically unable to get to a hospital, yet Dad has been treated in under twenty minutes.

Over the next few days, we discover Dad isn't a good patient. If he's in pain, he doesn't show it, because he moves from room to room as if expecting there to be something different in it from last time he was there. He's never been much of a reader and never one to sit around all day doing nothing. He takes to staring at the blank television screen. Eventually, he starts the generator so he can watch television. Since putting up the antenna, he's installed a booster unit which now allows us to watch the commercial station unless the weather is bad.

Late afternoon, I'm wandering around doing my chores as I do every day. With empty ice cream tub in hand, I enter the chook shed to collect the eggs. Having stepped into the dark from the bright sun, I can't see properly. Too impatient to wait for my eyes to adjust, I grope in the nest boxes for eggs.

I sense danger just a moment before I feel the wind of something move past my arm. There's a thwack sound like a hammer hitting wood. A cold chill runs down my spine. Snake. There's a snake in the chook shed and it has just struck at me.

My first instinct is to remain still. A snake's vision is based on movement and it feels vibration through the ground, or in this case the plywood floor. It can also feel subtle moments through the air through its forked tongue.

The snake is, however, trapped and frightened, which is why it's attacked seemingly unprovoked. It will strike again and next time it mightn't miss. Dropping the eggs, I back away with speed and escape through the door. Outside in the light, I check my bare arm for fang marks. There aren't any; the snake missed.

As I stomp back towards the house, the adrenalin surging through me changes from fear to anger. I go straight to the shelf in the back porch and retrieve the four-ten shotgun along with a handful of shells.

'What's happening?' asks Stephen.

'Snake in the chook house,' I reply. 'It struck at me but missed.'

A concerned look appears on Stephen's face. 'Snakes don't miss, mate.'

'This one did,' I reply, breaking open the shotgun and loading a shell into the breach. Having closed it, I place a finger along the trigger guard and a thumb on the hammer the way I've been shown.

We arrive to discover the snake exiting the chook shed. There's no hesitation. I raise the shotgun to my shoulder, engage the hammer and fire. The shot hits the snake, blowing his head off and causing it to writhe.

Mum and Maree, having heard the report, come rushing over.

'What's going on?' asks Mum.

'It struck at me, but it didn't realise who it was messing with,' I reply.

'Were you struck? You must be struck. Snakes don't miss,' shrieks Mum, insisting on examining my hands and arms.

'I'm not struck,' I exclaim.

'Bloody lucky,' says Maree.

Stephen carefully opens up the chook shed door and gingerly drags the nest box, which is an old wooden apple crate, into the light. Upon close inspection, he points out the fang marks in the wood.

'You should buy a Tatts Lotto ticket next time you're off the island,' says Stephen.

I shrug. He's probably right.

Motorbikes

One day out of the blue, Dad receives a phone call from an old friend he hasn't heard from in twenty years. The man has two 80cc motorbikes for sale and is wondering whether Dad is interested in buying them. For Christmas, just gone, Dad bought us a Honda Z50 which has proved to be the best present ever. I can zip around on it at speed. The problem with it is it's a fraction small for my siblings.

When he hangs up, Dad's excited. Despite the cost, he can see the value in them. From observing us kids riding the Z50 around, he knows the additional motorbikes will be able to travel at speed across the Island's tracks. It means fast transport for running errands.

'I really think we should invest,' he says.

Mum's not sold. 'Motorbikes are dangerous.'

'No more so than riding the stock horses.'

Mum takes a sip of her coffee. 'How are you going to get them over here?'

It was the same old problem we encountered with everything.

'If need be, I'll borrow one of Cape Portland's trailers and drive down to Wynyard and get them.' Dad pauses as if struck by an idea. 'Howard's plane is still in Wynyard. If he's flying it back empty, he might have room for the bikes.'

That evening, Dad phones Howard. When he finishes the call, he's grinning. 'Howard has agreed to fly the bikes from Wynyard.'

It's a rare stroke of luck. They arrive a few weeks later and Dad takes them both for a test ride before he'll let us ride them. That afternoon, my siblings and I set off across the island, heading for Rebecca Bay. The ride takes only about twenty minutes, a third of the time it takes on the tractor. When we return, we burst into the kitchen keen to explain how good the bikes are.

Mum doesn't share our excitement. Instead she returns a black look. 'You shouldn't be riding way out there on your own. What if one of you comes off and hurts yourself or is bitten by a snake?'

Eyes fall on me. The memory of me almost being bitten is still fresh. For some reason, my siblings hold me accountable as if the incident was my fault.

That evening, Mum talks to Dad and at breakfast the next morning he tells us that we're not to ride beyond the creek crossing to the south, or the laneway gate next to the airstrip to the west. It's a major blow, as we'd been planning a longer expedition to South Head, the most southern point of the Island.

Despite that, the bikes do prove to be a good investment.

Muttonbirding on Preservation Island

At Easter, Bryce returns on the *Biminy* with the boat's owner Bill, who'd also assisted with the rescue of the distressed seaman some time ago. They're also accompanied by another man called Sam, whom I do not like the look of. As Dad foresaw, Bryce has invited us to come over to Preservation Island muttonbirding. I'm not sure what that entails, but I'm excited at the prospect of an adventure. As are Dad and my siblings. The only one who doesn't want to go is Mum.

The day we're due to sail dawns fine without a breath of wind. On the trip over, the sea is so calm we could waterski on it. Bill sails around Rum Island and into a horseshoe-shaped bay on the western side of Preservation Island where the *Biminy* is anchored. We go ashore in several loads in a dinghy.

Having wrapped insulation tape around the cuff of his long-sleeved shirt to stop dirt going up it, Bryce leads us up a sand dune to where the rookery is. Without further ado, he plunges his hand into a burrow and removes a muttonbird chick. The chick is of similar size to a bantam hen and Bryce kills it by breaking its neck.

'How do you know there isn't a snake down the hole?' asks Stephen.

'Snakes leave distinct tracks in the sand. You check for them beforehand and if there's a snake in the hole, it'll feel cold.'

Maree folds her arms and Stephen appears unsure.

Bryce, sensing his commandeered labour is about to withdraw, adds, 'A snake needs room to raise its head and strike. Ninety-nine-point-nine per cent of the holes are too small for a snake to strike in.'

Stephen nods at the logic. 'Anything else we should know?'

'Yes, if there are white feathers around the hole, it has a penguin in it which will give you a nasty bite.'

That also makes sense. Despite being the youngest, I'm the tallest, even taller than my Dad. This means I have the longest reach. Without fear of being bitten by a snake, I proceed to thrust my arm into the burrows up to my shoulder. I've removed and killed two dozen chicks when Bryce calls for a count.

'Just a few more and that'll do,' he says.

I go to thrust into the next hole, when my hand bumps into invisible resistance. There's nothing physically there, but I can sense danger the same way I could that fateful day in the chook house. I quickly withdraw. There's no marked difference in the temperature of the hole but I know intuitively that there's a snake in it.

Sam comes wandering over. He goes to put his hand down the hole with the snake.

'No, there's a snake in that one!' I blurt out.

'Doesn't feel cold,' he replies, 'and there's no tracks leading into it.'

Examining the mouth of the hole, I don't see any snake tracks, but there's so many footprints around the entrance it's impossible to know whether there is a snake track or not. 'I just know there is a snake in there,' I say.

'How?' he asks sceptically.

'I just know,' I reply.

He smirks at me. 'Must be grand to have skills us mere mortals can only dream of.'

I'm so angry that for a fleeting moment I want him to get bitten, but it passes. 'If you get bitten, you'll likely die within an hour. I doubt the Flying Doctor will make it in time to save you.'

Sam concedes my point and backs away from the hole.

Stephen crests a dune and comes walking over. 'Whoa, look at the size of that snake track.'

I peer over the low vegetation and see a snake track about five centimetres wide. It's leading towards the holes in front of us. 'Got to be a tiger,' I say. 'Copperheads don't grow that big.'

Stephen pales.

I shoulder my dead muttonbird chicks. 'Come on, let's head back to the beach. Lady Luck is starting to frown and we've all rolled the dice enough for one day.'

At the top of the bank overlooking the beach, there's a commotion. A fairy penguin has latched onto Dad's finger and won't let go. When we arrive, Stephen grabs hold of the bird and manages to prise its beak open. Once he has, he lets it go. It waddles away singing a string of profanities while everyone roars with laughter.

On the beach, Bryce lights a small campfire which he places a twenty-litre drum of water on.

'Is that for scalding the birds?' I ask.

'No, we dry pluck them. The hot water is just to clean up with.' Bryce grabs a bird and demonstrates how to dry pluck. 'You need to be gentle so you don't tear the skin. If you do, they can't be sold as plucked birds and they might as well be skinned.'

While Stephen and Dad lift a large plank of driftwood onto some stones to make a bench seat, Bryce sorts the birds into 'skinners' and 'pluckers'. Holding each bird over a bucket, he squeezes them. An oily gurry comes out of their mouths. It stinks like nothing I've ever smelt before. Almost as bad as the billy goat.

For the next few hours, we dry pluck muttonbirds. Stephen, who is skilled at skinning, works on the skinners, while Bryce removes the guts along with the head, feet and wingtips. It's messy work, but having cleaned my fair share of ducks and chooks, I know there's nothing for it but to just do it.

Bryce steers the boat on the return trip and, rather than go around Rum Island, he chances the narrow passage which separates it from Preservation Island. I can feel the boat sledging as it fights against the current. In the Channel, the sea breeze has picked up and so the water is quite choppy. Not enough to bother the *Biminy*, but enough to make her rock.

Rather than pull into the wharf, the *Biminy* is anchored in the bay and we row ashore. Once we're home, Dad is keen to cook some of the birds. I discern Mum has some prior experience of doing so, because she places a cake rack in the bottom of the electric frying pan, along with some water. The birds are steamed in a way that allows the excess grease to run away before being browned off in the oven.

Having spent all day gathering and cleaning them, I can't wait to try them. Biting eagerly into the flesh, I gag. It's salty, fatty meat that just tastes wrong.

'Yuck!' I say.

'You don't have to eat them,' says Dad.

He needn't worry. I won't be.

Caretakers

It is a usual Saturday morning. We've finished the milking and we're sitting down to breakfast when the phone rings.

Mum gets up to answer it. She's frowning when she returns to her seat. 'Some couple just phoned to enquire about a caretaking job on Clarke Island.'

Dad scratches the back of his head before getting up and phoning Douglas. When he returns to his seat, he says, 'Apparently, Douglas placed ads in all three of Tasmania's main newspapers, *The Mercury*, *The Examiner* and *The Advocate*, advertising for caretakers for when we go off the Island.'

'Nice of him to tell us,' replies Mum.

Dad nods.

The phone rings again and Mum again gets up to answer it. 'No, there's no shop. Once you're here, you have to manage with the provisions you have.' She rolls her eyes. 'No, you won't be able to buy milk and bread every day. There's no shop.' Mum hangs up the phone and sighing, sits down in frustration. 'What part of "it's an island" do they not get?'

All morning long, the phone rings and Mum and Dad take turns answering it. By lunchtime, they've taken twenty-five calls, but only have five possible couples on the list. The next day, Dad is on the main phone, Mum is on the bedroom one, while they interview the potential caretakers. By the time they've finished, they've reduced to three couples.

There's strict criteria because the couples have to be able to come when required without neglecting work commitments, meaning they need to be primarily retired. They need animal husbandry skills, which include being able to milk goats and bottle-feed kids. They need to be able to think on their feet and be able to keep it together if the generator breaks down or the phone goes out. They also need to be able to handle the isolation of being the only ones here, with no means of getting off. In addition, the job doesn't pay: it only covers expenses.

Mum is tired and frustrated. She's reduced her notes to three writing pad pages, one for each couple, and she keeps going over them again and again. 'I think it best if we meet with them in person.'

Dad examines the pages. 'These two couples know each other and they've provided verifiable referees. I'll think they'll be fine. This other couple I'm not so sure about.'

'I was thinking the opposite,' says Mum.

Mum's like me in that she has strong intuition, so she's probably right.

A month later, we fly off the island and the two couples Dad approves of fly on. While we're away, there are no apparent mishaps; everything appears to be going well. We return a week later. All the animals are fine, the garden has been cared for and all appears to be well. It seems Dad was right and the two couples were a good choice.

The next day, Dad returns to the house quite angry. 'The idiot turned the dinghy upside down and the decking was scattered all over the beach.'

Mum sits a cup of tea in front of him.

'They've also used up all the PVC pipe making a weathercock, there are several tools broken in the workshop, and the battery in the 8430 is dead flat because they left the ignition on. They weren't supposed to be driving it.'

'There's bugger all open-fireplace wood left either, which is odd because it shouldn't have been cold seeing as it's summer,' I add.

Dad stares into his teacup clearly disappointed. It could have been worse, but if the caretakers can't follow instructions and rules, then they can't be trusted.

A few nights later, Mum calls the third couple and arranges for them to come over for a holiday while we're here. When the date comes around for them to fly over, Dad flies off as he has to take Maree and Stephen to Launceston where they can catch a bus to Hobart for school camp.

Both Mum and I go to the airstrip to meet the couple and their little dachshund.

The woman hurries over to introduce herself to me. 'I'm Jolan and this is my husband Jack and our dog Schnookie.'

She speaks with a distinct accent which I can't recognise. Unused to friendly people, I shy away and bend down to pat their dog.

She looks concerned about something as if she has been harbouring a secret and now needs to confess. 'I'm German,' she says in a voice that is barely a whisper.

Hence the accent. She's looking at me to gauge my reaction, but I'm unclear of her point.

'From Germany,' she rephrases.

I'm confused. Is she wanted by Immigration for overextending her stay? Has she come here to hide from the authorities? What's the deal?

'Remember the war?' she asks.

There were several and all before my time, so no I don't.

Mum realises there's something wrong and comes over. 'Everything okay?'

'Jolan's from Germany,' I say, my eyes pleading for an explanation of why she's bringing that up and making such a point of it.

Mum gently lays a hand on Jolan's shoulder. 'It's totally fine, the past is behind us.'

Jolan heaves a sigh of relief.

'She was very worried,' says Jack.

Mum pauses. 'Are you English?'

'Yes,' he replies, 'is that a problem?'

'Nah, it'll be fine. It's just my husband won't care about Jolan being German, but he isn't too fond of Poms is all.'

Jack looks indignant; Jolan has to turn her head to hide her laughter.

I drive the David Brown down to the house. Maree has agreed that they can use her sleepout while she's away, so I get them settled in there. Following morning tea, Mum and I show them the garden along with the chook and duck yards.

'There's always seasonal vegetables and heaps of eggs, plus there's plenty of beef meat in the freezer,' says Mum.

'And there's goats,' says Jolan.

'Three milking nannies and five kids to feed. So there's two hours work night and morning to milk the goats and feed all the animals, plus the garden needs to be watered.'

Jack and Jolan look nonplussed, so I gather the handlines and take them down the wharf fishing. Jolan catches several parrotfish, but Jack doesn't catch any. He watches me closely as I clean the fish. I've gained considerable skill since the early days.

'You're very good at that,' says Jolan.

Mum looks proud. 'All my children are proficient at cleaning fish and dressing animals. It's become a way of life for them.'

Back at the house, I grab the filleting knife and fillet the fish.

'Now we're just showing off,' says Mum.

It's true I am, but I also hate picking the bones out of my fish, which is why I prefer to fillet them.

That afternoon, we all go out to milk the goats. Mandy is the matriarch and is always first. She also has the biggest teats and is thus the easiest to milk. Rather than expecting them to show us how they can milk, I give a demonstration first. They watch and listen eagerly, which I'm pleased about. Jolan goes first. She's a little rusty, but it's clear she's milked before. Jack goes next. I'm not convinced he's ever milked before, but he soon learns the squeezing action, so it really doesn't matter whether he has or not. We all had to learn and he will too.

The next day, I take them over and show them the generator.

'When it's going, there's really nothing to it, except pushing the button on the wall,' I say.

'But when it's not?' says Jack.

'You have to use the backup system,' I reply.

I walk them over to the workshop and show them the welding unit which works off the PTO shaft of the David Brown.

Jack examines the lead that has two male ends. I can see he doesn't get it.

'You plug one end into the power point on the welding unit and the other into the outside power point of the house.'

'Is that safe?' he asks.

Of course it's not. 'Seems to work.'

Jolan is looking concerned. 'What happens if both generators fail?'

I smile. 'Then you break out the gas barbecue.'

Jolan cocks her head. 'I don't get joke.'

'He's saying that the freezer will melt, so cook what you can before the meat goes bad.'

Now they're both looking concerned.

'We've never lost both generators at once, but if the worst should happen, don't worry. There's a wood stove to cook on and it heats the water and there's candles, a gas light and torches. It'll be basic, but you'll cope.'

Jolan nods. 'What about if the phone goes out?'

'Happens from time to time,' says Mum. 'We'll call everyday so we'll know if the phone stops working. In an emergency, there are VHF and UHF radios and there's a large medical chest.'

Their apprehension is now slipping away.

'This island will give you everything you need, but on its terms. You can't fight it, you just have to go with the flow and if things go wrong, you move to back up systems.'

They seem to understand.

'We've been thinking,' says Jack that evening after dinner. 'Jolan and I don't have any family in Australia so we'd be happy to caretake over Christmas.'

'What's the catch?' I blurt out.

'Dion!' Mum scolds.

Jolan looks at Jack and I note that I'm correct. They'll want payment.

'We assume you slaughter the Muscovy ducks. We'd like a duck for Christmas Day,' says Jolan.

We slaughter a dozen or more every year. I didn't mind roast duck, but I'm a bit over it. In all honesty, as far as roast meats go, I prefer sheep, one of the meats we don't have access to.

'In Europe, we roast a goose for Christmas,' says Jolan.

'Ah, if you want goose, there's plenty of them here, but getting them is quite challenging.'

'A duck would be fine,' says Jolan, looking quite concerned.

'That's a very generous offer,' says Mum before I can elaborate on how I intend on getting them a goose. 'We'd like to take you up on that.'

They smile and the deal is struck for them to caretake over Christmas.

A couple of months later, I'm still pondering the problem of how to get a goose for Jack and Jolan. The island has an abundance of Cape Barren geese, but they're impossible to shoot with a .22 because they tend to stay out of range. There is, however, another way. In spring, they nest in the tussock country.

Dad drives us out and, having found the nests, my siblings and I steal three goslings that are big enough to survive without their parents, but too young to fly. I tuck my gosling under my arm and I'm headed back to the tractor to find a sack to put it in when there's a commotion behind me. I turn in time to see an adult goose charging at me with wings flapping. Before I can react, Elsa rushes forward snarling. Seeing it's about to be mauled, the goose takes flight.

Back at the house, we place the goslings in the yard of the bottom house.

'You'll have to water them twice a day,' says Dad, rolling a cigarette.

I already spend an hour feeding and watering chooks and ducks each day; adding the goslings to the list is no burden. 'Will they need grain?' I ask.

Dad exhales smoke. 'A bit, but I think they mostly eat grass.'

Two weeks later, I decide the goslings are a good trade-off. They've settled into the house yard and they no longer cower when I change their water. Best of all, they're keeping the lawn so trim that I won't have to mow it.

By mid-December, they're ready to slaughter and we do them along with some ducks before Christmas. I can scarcely wait to tell Jolan that we've secured her a goose for Christmas dinner and I do so at the airstrip when they fly over to caretake. She stands there wide-eyed and speechless. I've never been prouder.

Christmas off the island is not what I'd hoped. It involves going from relative to relative, which I find boring and uncomfortable. Christmas lunch is held at Nan and Pop's and there are twenty guests. Dad has brought one of the slaughtered geese for Pop. At lunch, he likes it so much that he goes back for seconds.

Seeing as there are twenty people present, I don't bother with the goose preferring to eat turkey. Besides, I'm hoping there'll still be one left in the freezer when we get home.

We arrive home on the second of January. Jack and Jolan are well and there have been no problems while we were away except one. They'd been caught out by some kayakers who'd come ashore while they were getting around au naturel.

'How was the goose?' I ask.

'Goose and duck were superb,' replies Jolan.

I grin with joy, pleased that the caretakers enjoyed the bounty of the Island.

In due course, Mum cooks up the remaining goose. I await with eager anticipation as Mum serves it up with roast vegetables. When I finally get to taste it, I'm disappointed. It bears no resemblance to duck but instead tastes remarkably like muttonbird. Not worth the effort.

Libby Belle

Since Elsa is Maree's dog and Suzi-Wong is mine, Stephen decides he wants a dog of his own. Dad agrees that having a third dog will be no burden and makes enquiries. Mum mentions the fact to Uncle Ernie and it just so happens that his bitch has had a litter of pups and there's one bitch pup left. Do we want it?

Given the Shetland pony Cheeky turned out to be a lemon, and the goats he'd recommended were way older than they were supposed to be, we're cautious. Ernie, however, arrives the next day in a Cessna that his mate has flown him down in. Since he's brought the pup with him, it seems rude to refuse to take it.

The pup is a kelpie and a sweet thing but horribly timid. Stephen names her Libby-Belle and he's given responsibility to train her, which includes toilet training. When next I see her making to squat in the house, I hurry to take her out. Libby rolls onto her back and wets herself with fear.

'You need to be gentler with her,' says Mum, as I mop up the mess.

I agree to show some patience and as the weeks go by Libby learns to go outside and she settles in with the other two dogs. In doing so, she becomes a part of the family.

On a cold wet day, we are all hauled up inside. Elsa is under the school desk; Suzi is on the mat by the fire. I wonder where Libby is but since she's Stephen's dog I'm not overly concerned. A moment later, Libby starts making a strange noise which is neither a bark nor a growl. Before I can discern what's happening, she runs past at full speed.

At first, I think she's just being a pup charging around letting off steam. Then it occurs to me that Libby doesn't really know how to play, so it can't be that. She shoots past me again, this time heading for the French door. Stephen, who's been trying to put her out, opens the door and she runs outside.

The dog is now charging around the house yard like she's possessed. I move towards the door to go investigate.

'Stay inside!' barks Dad.

'What the hell's wrong with Libby?' I ask.

He gives no reply as he disappears through the door.

Ten minutes later, Maree, who's also gone out, comes back inside crying. 'Libby's dead.'

I've heard no gunshot, so I know Dad hasn't shot her. I go outside. Elsa and Suzi are caged and Dad is fastening a padlock to the sliding bolt. I think that queer, but my immediate concern is for Libby.

Conducting a quick search, I find her lying dead on the grass. There's foam around her mouth and she's urinated on herself.

'Don't touch her,' says Dad.

I've seen death before. It's a fact of life on the island and I never feel anything for the animals I slaughter. But seeing Libby dead, I begin to sob. I have never felt so emotionally wounded before. It's like having my insides ripped out. I look back at Elsa and Suzi.

'You are not to go near the dogs. Do you understand?' says Dad.

I feel heartsick that we might lose the other two as well. All I can do is nod.

Dad places a hand on my shoulder. 'I'm going to phone the flying vet. He can examine Libby and hopefully get to the bottom of this.'

I've recently watched the movie *Old Yeller* on television. It's about a dog who contracts rabies, turns rabid and has to be put down. 'It wouldn't be rabies, would it?'

'I don't know. The vet will get to the bottom of it.'

Dad puts on heavy rubber gloves before placing Libby in a heavy garbage bag and then into an empty grain sack. He fastens it shut with rope and writes CAUTION POSSIBLE DISEASE on the bag with a felt pen.

The vet lands in his Cessna and Dad meets him at the airstrip.

The next day, the veterinary pathologist phones through the autopsy results. The good news is Libby didn't have rabies nor any other disease. She died from snakebite and apparently her behaviour isn't unusual. We're saddened by the loss, but at least it means Elsa and Suzi aren't going to die.

Rescued Crayfish

When boats come into the bay, I like to look at them through Dad's binoculars. Not in a peeping tom sort of way; I'm just curious. Dad also likes us to get the boat names, which Mum records in the daybook for the records. Today, a large two-masted yacht has sailed in and anchored.

'Looks like they're coming ashore,' I report from my position on the veranda.

Their dinghy lands on the beach and two men and two women walk up to the house. They baulked at the electric fence, so Dad wanders down to greet them. While Dad enjoys living on the Island, he misses adult company and tends to welcome visitors readily.

The sailors are two couples in their late twenties who are sailing around the world. They're accompanied by two Doberman pups who are only about half grown.

Knowing how much Elsa and Suzi eat, I say, 'Those pups would take a bit of feeding.'

One of the women, Freya, nods. 'We've run out of dog food.'

The pups don't look hungry so they're obviously eating something. 'Then what are you feeding them?' I ask.

'Oh, Bjorn went diving and got some crayfish, but we don't like it so we're feeding it to the dogs.'

Dad's face turns a shade of purple and for a moment I fear he'll pass out. 'You're doing what?'

Freya casually repeats herself before saying, 'Do you have any dog food to trade?'

'We'll get you as much wallaby meat as you want,' stammers Dad.

Freya glances at Bjorn. 'What about meat for us?'

'Steak, roasts, strips, mince, what do you want?'

'Some steak would be good,' replies Bjorn. 'Would you mind if we lit a small fire on the beach to heat a barbecue plate?'

'Not at all,' replies Dad. 'Joy, can you please grab some steak out of the freezer.'

Mum gets a strange look in her eyes. 'We'll bring the steak to the beach and exchange it for the cray.'

'Sounds good,' says Freya. 'Would the children like to see our yacht?'

We would indeed and so we all head to the beach. Bjorn ferries us out in his dinghy, while his three companions explore the beach with their pups and our dogs. The yacht is incredible. Opulent and very comfortable. When we finish exploring the sailors' mobile home, Bjorn opens an ice chest to reveal two large crayfish about four kilograms each in weight.

'Your mother seems a little unsure of the trade,' says Bjorn as he puts the pair of them into a sack.

Stephen explains what happened with the scallop fisherman.

Shaking his head, Bjorn replies, 'That's appalling.'

We're wary of visitors, but these people are clearly honourable.

'Do you need any vegies, eggs or fresh goat's milk?' I ask, knowing we have a surplus of those items.

'Only if you have it to spare.'

Seeing the crayfish, Dad has us put together a large box of vegies from the garden. It's accompanied by a carton of eggs, a litre bottle of goat's milk, a tub of yogurt and several bags of beef meat, including the asked-for steak.

'This is too much,' says Freya when the food is offered.

Dad waves her protest away.

That evening, we go shooting and bone out ten kilograms of wallaby meat which we pack into kilogram lots and place in freezer bags. The exchange takes place on the beach, where the sailors are sitting around their campfire.

'We're wondering if we could climb the hill tomorrow,' asks Freya.

'I can drive you up most of the way if you want,' says Dad.

'No, we'd like to walk,' she replies.

Dad doesn't understand bushwalking and neither do my siblings, but I do. 'I know the way, I've been up there before. I can guide you if you want.'

'Tomorrow's a weekday. Don't you have school?' asks Freya.

'I do my lessons by correspondence. I can catch up another day.'

She glances at Dad, who nods permission. 'In that case, we'll meet you here in the morning at eight.'

I return the next day with a small rucksack containing lunch, a drink, the hand-held UHF and Dad's binoculars. I lead them up the dunes where the 8430 had to be towed up by the dozer and then follow the track the vehicles made en route to the beach. At the foot of Home Hill, I lead them up a gully. The last bit is quite steep and we emerge onto large flat stones. The height affords a panoramic view in all directions.

I glance towards Cape Barren. 'Did you climb any of the mountains over there?' I ask.

'We climbed Mount Munro,' says Freya.

I feel jealous. I want to go over there. I want to climb the mountains and not just the biggest one they'd climbed.

'You like to climb,' says Bjorn.

It's not a question but a statement and I nod.

'Shame we don't have more time,' says Freya. 'We have to be in Hobart in a few days, else we'd take you over there walking.'

It is a shame. We rest for an hour before I lead them back to the beach. Freya kisses my cheek before getting into the dinghy, which I help shove off the sand. I wait on the beach until they set sail and wave as they disappear around the point. I know I'll never see them again, but it's okay. Friends are like ships that pass in the night or, in this case, a yacht that calls upon an island. There's no stress, just a memory to cherish.

Arrival of the Bees

Douglas is down on his hands and knees crawling across the new pasture. Dad is waiting by the tractor, his expression revealing he thinks the boss an idiot.

'The clover isn't seeding due to a lack of bees,' says Douglas.

'Could it be also why certain plants won't fruit in our garden?' I ask.

We've grown great vines of pumpkin and zucchini, but despite an abundance of flowers they haven't fruited.

He stands up. 'I would think so.'

When next Howard flies over, his plane contains beehives. In two trips, he brings ten. Dad is allergic to bees, as am I, although not as severely. We stay away from the hives, leaving Stephen and Maree to transport them into the interior and find a place to put them.

A few weeks later the apiarist who'd supplied the hives flies over. Stephen takes him out to look at them and they report the bees are doing well. So well that they'll have plenty of honey to sustain them through the winter.

It is a day like any other when Mum opens the linen cupboard. It has been built into the kitchen side of the brick chimney in the centre of the house. Three bees fly out of it. A single bee flying out of the linen cupboard is cause for alarm; three almost causes a panic. Dad exits his chair at speed and is across the room faster than I thought possible.

Stephen, who finds bees fascinating, moves in to investigate. Placing his ear against the bricks he says, 'There's a swarm in there. I can hear them buzzing.'

The colour drains from Dad's face. There's no question that the bees have to go, the question is how. Dad goes to the phone and calls Douglas. I can't hear what's said, but when he hangs up he calls Howard.

'Howard will be over directly with some smoke bombs,' says Dad. 'I'll be in the bottom house.'

As promised, Howard arrives an hour later, carrying a paper bag with four smoke bomb cans in it. While waiting for him to arrive, Mum's emptied the linen cupboard and Stephen has drilled some holes through the top so the smoke will better penetrate.

'Shame to waste a good swarm,' says Stephen.

Howard is gazing towards the generator shed. 'If I'm not mistaken, there's another one moving in over there.'

From where I'm standing, I can't be sure it's bees but there is definitely a black shape moving against the sky.

'It's a shame to kill them but I don't recall bringing over any empty hives, so even if we capture them, we'll have nowhere to put them,' says Howard.

Howard heads inside, where he removes a smoke can from the bag, peels off the top and lights the fuse. Acrid smoke curls out the top, filling not just the chimney but the entire house.

Stephen drives Howard back up to his plane. When he returns, Stephen reports that the bees have also taken over an old grader that's parked in the bush next to the airstrip. Without further ado, he heads over to the generator shed to deal with the swarm.

Mum opens all the doors and windows. Thankfully, there are enough cracks in the ceiling boards that the updraft moves the smoke into the attic. A secondary consequence is that the black house spiders that Mum has tried in vain to evict begin dropping dead from their webs. We have to check our beds carefully before getting into them that evening.

The next day, I help Dad in the workshop. Douglas has phoned back and instructed him to make some bee homes by cutting a slit in a fuel drum and peeling it open before placing a piece of plywood on top.

'That's not going to work,' says Stephen. 'Bees won't go near anything chemical, especially not diesel. That's why you have to use natural paint on the frames.'

Dad rubs the bridge of his nose. He finishes making the one he's started but doesn't bother making any more. Having placed a little honey in it, he takes it out to the hives just because Douglas has said to.

At the weekend, Douglas's father ED lands in his plane. He's brought with him a man from Leverington called Neil, along with the equipment we'll need to extract the honey, including an extractor and empty food-grade buckets to put the honey in.

Stephen goes with them and they return on the David Brown with the top box off each of the hives. The boxes are placed in the kitchen of the bottom house. Now they begin the extraction process by removing the ten frames from one of the boxes and removing the wax seals with a hot knife.

When they've uncapped four frames, ED loads them into the extractor. 'Who wants to turn the handle first?' he asks.

Always eager to be in the thick of it, I step up and begin turning the handle. Five minutes later, both my arms are killing me, but honey is still flying out of the frames. I stop to mop the sweat off my brow.

'We're not going to be able to hand-spin all these frames,' says Neil. 'There's a hundred of them and they're double-sided. We need to attach some kind of motor.'

'Did you bring one with you?' I ask, resuming spinning.

Neil blinks. 'No.'

'You're on an island. If you didn't bring it with you, then you won't find it here.'

ED chuckles at my logic.

Dad gets a silly grin on his face and disappears out the door. He returns a moment later carrying a variable-speed electric drill and an extension cord. Having removed the handle from the spinning mechanism, Dad fits the chuck of the drill to it. Neil now has his engine.

ED scoops up some honey with a teaspoon, which he puts in his mouth. 'This is heath honey. You won't find better than that anywhere in the world.'

Having tasted it, I agree. 'Perhaps the island should host bees rather than sheep.'

Stephen nods. 'The island could supply a unique product, and honey never spoils.'

Dad shoots us both a look that says be careful what you say. ED doesn't comment. I'm confused as to why. Surely keeping bees would be better than smashing machinery creating pasture.

The extraction of the honey continues for several days. The honey is placed into the buckets with the lids pressed tight. Once the honey is removed, ED and Neil fly off with a bucket of honey. Stephen spends the rest of the week removing the wax from the frames and rewiring them with a blank wax sheet. Having loaded the frames back into the boxes, he takes them back out to the hives.

My idea of further investing in hives and honey production is never mentioned again.

Stranded Kayakers

The next summer, I see a kayaker paddling across the Channel. Having seen the size of the swell a westerly can produce in that stretch of sea, I find his arrival quite disconcerting. Who in their right mind would traverse these waters in such a small craft?

As Dad has again taken Stephen and Maree off the island, I meet the kayaker at the wharf beach.

'Where'd you come from?' I ask after I've established his name is Garry.

'Wynyard,' he replies. 'My party headed for Wilsons Promontory, but I got sick halfway up the side of Flinders Island. They had to go on without me. I'm headed back, but I don't want to cross Bank Strait on my own. We're to rendezvous at Preservation Island but they're overdue.'

I blink as I try to take in what he's just said. I point to his kayak. 'You were planning to cross Bass Strait in that?'

'Yes, you island hop all the way across.'

'Sure, if you say so. This is Clarke Island, but I'm guessing you know that.'

'Yes, I was wondering if you had a telephone I could use.'

'We do. It's at the house and you're welcome to use it.'

While Garry is using the phone, I break out Dad's map of the Eastern Bass Strait Islands which Clarke Island is a part of. Now I can see what Garry was talking about. The kayakers have come across the face of northern Tasmania to Cape Portland, and crossed Bank Strait to Clarke Island before crossing Armstrong Channel to Cape Barren Island. From there, they've crossed Franklin Sound, which is dotted with islands, to Flinders Island. At the top of Flinders Island, things become a little more difficult as the islands are much further spaced. A continued journey to Wilsons Promontory would likely take them to Craggy Island, the Kent Group, the Hogan Group, East Moncoeur Island and finally to Victoria.

It's not a journey I would even contemplate in a vessel smaller than a fishing boat. Still, it's the same route the Tasmanian Aborigines are thought to have made in canoes many years ago.

Mum, having made Garry a sandwich and cup of tea, asks, 'So what's your plan of action?'

Garry sits down at the kitchen table. 'I've just let my boss know that I'm delayed. All I can do is paddle back and wait a bit longer for my party.'

'You're welcome to stay here if you want,' says Mum.

'Can't risk it, because there's no way to let my party know where I am. If they get to Preservation Island and discover I'm not there, they may continue without me and I'll have lost the opportunity.'

'Have you got enough provisions?' asks Mum.

'I've enough for a week.'

That doesn't seem long to me. I've known westerlies to blow for a fortnight without letting up. 'Do you supplement your rations with seafood?' I ask.

Garry shakes his head. 'I can't, I'm allergic to all forms of it.'

It's all I can do to not laugh at the irony of it. These waters have an abundance of seafood for the taking and he can't eat any of it. It just seems so wrong.

Garry finishes his sandwich and drains his mug. 'I'd best be getting back.'

I escort him to back to his canoe and watch him set off across the shark breeding ground in his kayak.

A few days later, he's back to use the phone again. As it's his birthday, Mum insists on cooking him a roast duck meal, which he agrees to. By the time he's eaten, I can see the beginnings of a westerly picking up. The Channel is dotted with white caps. If it sets in, the poor guy will be stranded on Preservation Island until it quits.

'You sure you don't want to stop here?' I ask.

He pauses as if to consider his options.

'You could leave your kayak here and catch a plane to Launceston on Munro Airlines.'

'Then my kayak would be stuck here.'

'True, but it'll be safe here until we can get it on a boat for you.'

Garry winced. 'Nah, it'll be right.'

He sets off into a significant chop and I hope he'll make it safely back across the Channel.

It's a week later that the phone rings. Mum answers it.

'That was Garry. He managed to thumb a ride on a fishing boat and both he and his kayak are home safe. Apparently, his party made it across to Wilsons Promontory, but didn't want to risk the return journey. So they flew back and had their kayaks freighted home.

I sigh. So he waited all that time for nothing. If he'd known, he could have put his kayak on the *Flinders Trader* or one of its sister boats, the *Lady Jillian* or the *Katika 1* and had it shipped to Launceston. Then he could have flown home. But he had no way of knowing.

Teeth and Claws

I stare at the little ball of orange fluff that's in the bottom on the box. We're not supposed to have a cat, but we're overrun with mice and hoping she might help. Besides, the Island is already well-established with feral cats, so what's one more.

By week's end, everyone is ready to kill the kitten. She's gotten into Mum's sewing boxes and shredded dozens of patterns. She's gotten into the stationery cupboard and made a hell of a mess. Her favourite trick is getting up onto the school desk, destroying schoolwork and tossing things onto the floor. Worst of all, there's no evidence that she's the slightest bit interested in hunting mice. The kitten, who is yet to be given a proper name, is dubbed Catastrophe.

A while later, Catastrophe, having gotten pregnant to a feral cat, births a litter of three kittens. One is stillborn, leaving a boy and a girl. Dad gets rid of the girl, leaving just the boy. He's a big kitten, too big for Catastrophe to pick up, but every time she tries and fails, Elsa rushes over to assist.

Two months later, Catastrophe destroys Dad's monthly fuel record. It's the final straw. He takes her for a walk with his rifle and returns without her. Elsa now assumes full responsibility for the kitten and that evening she lifts him onto the old couch in the lounge and goes to sleep with him between her front paws.

The kitten wakes Elsa because he's chewing on her front paw. Lifting her head, Elsa yawns, dangling her big pink tongue. The kitten latches hold of each side of it. Elsa yelps in distress and I detach the kitten. Elsa hurries away with a bleeding tongue.

As the days pass, the orange and black striped cat grows enormous.

He's always hungry, but we've been told not to feed him more than twice a day. I've gotten into the habit of saving him wallaby livers, kidneys and hearts, which he devours with relish. One evening after I've fed him, the cat is still looking at his bowl demanding more.

'That's all there is,' I say, showing him the empty tub.

The cat glares at me, but he's seen a mouse sneaking along the side of the wall the same as I have. He waits until it's within striking range before lashing out. Hit by an enormous paw with attached razors, the mouse doesn't stand a chance. I watch in awe as he tears it to pieces and eats it.

The next morning, there are half a dozen dead mice on the kitchen floor left behind as offerings.

'That cat's all teeth and claws,' says Dad as I pick up and dispose of the dead mice.

From that day forth, the cat is called TC.

When next Leverington's head stockman Joe comes over with Scott, Dad brings up the subject of castrating the cat.

Sitting at the kitchen table, Joe looks thoughtful. 'I've never cut a cat before, but I've done plenty of lambs and calves. I can't see how it would be any different.'

Since lambs and calves don't have sharp teeth and claws, I disagree, but keep my thoughts to myself. Mum retrieves a scalpel from the medical chest and Dad picked up the cat and takes him outside. TC is not a cat to be handled and I hurry out to see just how badly this is going to end.

Dad holds TC's front half while Scott holds his lower half, including his tail. Joe moves in with the scalpel in hand. A moment later, TC emits a spine-chilling hiss and Dad hollers from pain. TC has bitten Dad's thumb and it's now dripping blood profusely.

'Got one. I've just got to extract the other one,' says Joe.

'Be quick about it,' replies Dad.

'Got it,' says Joe a moment later, wiping the cuts with gauze dipped in disinfectant.

At that moment, TC starts peeing. The stream hits Joe in the side of his face and runs down his cheek beneath his shirt. Scott lets go; Dad tries to do the same, only to find the cat still has hold of his thumb. The cat is not only refusing to let go, he's now attacking with the claws of his front paws. Scott grabs TC's head and somehow manages to pry his mouth open. Once detached, the cat runs off.

When next both Dad and TC are in the kitchen together, the cat lies on the mat in front of the combustion stove flicking his tail while glaring. During the operation, he's managed to sink two of his canine teeth right through Dad's thumb and out the other side. Dad's thumb is now slathered in antiseptic ointment and heavily bandaged.

Come summer, Mum's sister Cynthia decides to visit with her toddler Reba and her baby Jake. Stephen has again moved out to the sleepout with Maree and I've agreed to move out of my bedroom and sleep on the night-day couch in the lounge room.

'We head out to milk and feed the kids around seven,' says Mum after dinner. 'If TC wanders in, he'll want feeding.'

Cynthia returns an angry look. 'If the cat thinks he's going to get fed before I've fed my own children, he can think again.'

Nothing more is said about the cat.

The next morning, I come in from the miking stand carrying two buckets of milk. Jake and Reba are crying, as is Cynthia. I follow a trail of blood across the kitchen floor to Cynthia, who is sitting on a kitchen chair. There's blood oozing around a wad of tissues from her big toe.

TC is on a mat in front of the stove flicking his tail and examining his claws.

I immediately feed him before heading back out to find Mum. 'Cynthia's injured and the babies are upset,' I say.

'What do you mean, she's injured?' asks Mum.

'She refused to feed TC so he's slashed open her big toe. Going to need stitches, I reckon.'

Mum stands up to go inside and I take over milking the last goat. When I finish, I go inside. Cynthia's toe is heavily bandaged like Dad's thumb had been previously. She needs stitches but there's no one qualified to administer them and she doesn't want to pay Munro to fly her to Flinders Island and back, so she's forgoing them.

She's stopped crying; now she's seething. The kitchen is quiet. Mum is feeding Jake a bottle of milk and Stephen has Reba seated at the kitchen table, trying to get her to eat porridge. Clearly, it's a food she's never eaten before.

Having ladled porridge into a bowl, I sit down to eat. Strangely, I don't feel for Cynthia. Mum tried to tell her that TC didn't do requests nor did he like to be kept waiting. She'd refused to listen and in doing so she'd gone against the natural order of the island. She paid dearly for doing so.

Dad comes in with a cheeping box of ducklings. Opening the warming oven door, he sits the box of ducklings in it. The mother has obviously abandoned them and he's trying to warm them up. If they survive the next twenty-four hours, we'll hand-rear them.

'Great, not only will the kitchen have a savage beast, but the floor will be covered in duck shit. Not for long, though. That cat will rip them to shreds,' says Cynthia.

Elsa sits herself on the kitchen mat and begins licking the ducklings.

'Cat won't get near them,' replies Dad. 'Elsa mothers anything little, regardless of the species.'

Cynthia screws up her face. 'You're all mad here. The bloody lot of you.'

It might be true, but that's how we have to be to live here. We've had to adjust to the rhythms of the island and that includes keeping a feral cat to keep the mice in check. It's just the way it is.

Orphan Calf

When Dad pulls up on the David Brown with a grin on his face, I can tell something is up. I peer onto the trailer and amid the fencing gear is a Hereford bull calf. He doesn't look old enough to be weaned.

'Found him in the tussock country standing beside his dead mother. She'd been shot by fishermen.'

The cow wasn't the first one that we'd found shot. Rogue fishermen and other unwelcome visitors would sneak ashore and shoot the cattle. Dad theorised that they wanted the meat for themselves as well as for their craypots. It was unsavoury and criminal.

'What you going to do with him?' asks Mum.

'I'll have to put him down. He's too young to survive on his own,' replies Dad.

'Can't we hand feed him?' I say. 'I mean, we have to feed the kids by hand. What's one more animal?'

'You can try, I suppose,' says Dad. 'We'll have to get some powdered milk. It'll cost a bit to feed him.'

I sigh, because there's no point paying for milk powder to raise a bull calf who's only going to be slaughtered. We can slaughter cattle for free, so there's no point bothering with the expense.

'Douglas is on the phone,' says Stephen, emerging from the back porch.

Dad heads inside to take the call and Stephen comes over to examine the calf. He might be an unaffordable expense, but with roan and white fur, he's a handsome lad.

Dad returns shaking his head. 'The man's queer. He's agreed to pay for the milk powder.'

I prick my ears. Dad has a low opinion of the boss, but I've come to realise he never does anything without a reason.

'Did he say why?' asks Mum.

'He's planning on using him as a Judas.'

I wouldn't have known who Judas was nor what he did, but my teacher had been slipping Bible parables into my lessons. She'd gotten into considerable trouble when Mum queried the fact. Still, it wasn't all bad. At least now I understood the reference. The calf was to be raised on the premise that he might one day lead his wild brethren to the wharf to be shipped off. Dad thought the plan stupid. I didn't care. At least we'd get to keep the calf.

Stephen carries the calf into the house yard. Mum walks off and returns in a bit with a bucket of powdered milk. We always keep some powdered stockfeed milk on hand for emergencies. Taking the bucket, she dips her fingers in the milk before putting them in the calf's mouth. He sucks eagerly. She repeats the process, but this time she lowers her finger into the milk. The calf, realising the finger is not the source of the milk, starts drinking heartily.

'Do we just leave him wandering around?' I ask when he's emptied the bucket.

'I guess so,' replies Mum.

Stephen carries the calf over to the trees, where there's shade. Sitting him down, he returns to the house yard. Seeing a foreign invader near her milking stand, Mandy comes strutting over to investigate. The calf is as large as she is, but that's no deterrent. She circles him before butting him. The calf responds by butting back. Mandy butts once more before letting up. She was never serious; she was just testing the calf's mettle. She begins heading off, only to glance back. The calf gives a quiet moo and hurries after her. When the other goats try to challenge him, Mandy defends him.

Dad shakes his head again. 'You wouldn't read about it. She won't feed her own kids, but she takes pity on a calf and invites him to join her herd.'

Having watched a lot of David Attenborough, I know the behaviour is unusual but not unheard of. Animals of another species will sometimes invite an orphan to join their herd.

At milking, I put a collar on the calf, whom we've named Chris. Having given him another bucket of milk, I begin scratching his back. He lays his head back and arches into it.

Mum shakes her head. 'You do realise he's going to grow into a big bull, don't you?'

I do, but I also know he'll be my bull.

Night Raid

I'm bludging on the veranda when I'm supposed to be doing school, and Bryce comes wandering up from the direction of the wharf. He has a man with him, whom he introduces as Teddy once they're in the kitchen.

'Teddy's interested in checking out the lagoons,' says Bryce.

'Ah yeah,' says Dad. 'After some ducks, is he?'

'Be interested to see what's there,' Teddy replies.

All the freshwater lagoons are on the reserve on the eastern side of the island. In the time we've lived here, we've never once gone into it.

Dad takes a sip of his coffee. 'Can drive you out there, I suppose.'

'Can I come?' I ask. It's a school day, but I'm good at catching up when I have to.

'I suppose,' says Dad.

On the way out, I collect the four-ten from the shelf along with a box of shells. Teddy is armed with a double-barrel twelve-gauge. I assume we'll take the David Brown, but Dad climbs into the 8430 and hooks up the truck trailer. We climb aboard and hang onto the front.

An hour later, Dad is barrelling across metre-high scrub making his way towards the closest lagoon. The country out here is different again to other parts. The vegetation is dotted with plants called kangaroo tails which for some reason don't grow in the interior. The lagoons are surrounded by lush bluegum trees and a different taller river sheoak which grows right up to the water's edge.

Dad pulls up about a half a kilometre from the lagoon. Teddy and I get off to make our approach on foot. We're about three-quarters of the way when we spot two hundred wild ducks floating on the surface. Teddy indicates for me to go left while he goes around to the right.

I creep towards the lagoon, mindful that snakes would make their home here feasting on duck eggs and later ducklings. I keep low for the last section and I have to peel back the rushes to see. The ducks are still here, but they're on the other side and way out of range.

I go to sneak along the bank, when suddenly it caves in. I find myself standing in chest-high water. The bottom is mud which threatens to suck off my boots.

Two shots ring out and the entire flock of ducks take to the wing and fly off. The chance to shoot a duck is gone. Tossing the gun onto the bank, I haul myself out and head back in the direction of the tractor. Teddy catches up with me and I note he's not carrying a duck.

'Did you miss?' I ask.

'No, it's unsportsmanlike to shoot at ducks on the water. I thought you'd shoot one as they flew off.'

I hadn't even raised my gun, let alone fired off a shot. 'They were too far away.'

'Pity,' he replies.

At the tractor, Dad is leaning against the tyre rolling a cigarette. 'Decide to go for a swim?'

'Bank gave way and the bottom was muddy as,' I reply.

Bryce is sitting on the mudguard. It's clear he's only come to humour Teddy. We climb back onto the trailer. With wet clothing, I'm cold and the idea of travelling all this way to shoot ducks is no longer appealing. I won't bother with it again.

Back at the house, I shower and change before walking into the kitchen.

'Maree's finished high school. She's in Launceston at college doing year eleven,' Dad's saying.

Bryce has obviously asked about her whereabouts.

Dad turns to me. 'Bryce wants to know if you want to slip across to Preservation Island and grab some muttonbirds.'

The memory of our day birding is still fresh. It was something different to do, but a lot of work. 'Can't afford to take tomorrow off as well,' I reply.

'Not tomorrow. Now,' says Dad.

I glance out the window. It will be dark within the hour. He wasn't going birding. This was a night raid. 'Yeah, okay.'

After dinner, we all head down to the wharf. I expect to see the *Bimny*, but tied up is the *Sea Fairer*.

'This is my own boat,' says Bryce.

I nod. 'Have you still got the lease on Preservation?'

'No,' he replies. 'It came up for renewal, but the government wanted too much. I let it go because the lease on East Kangaroo Island was cheaper.'

If I remember my self-taught geography lessons correctly, East Kangaroo is off the west coast of Flinders Island across from the town of Whitemark. I've never been up that way and I wouldn't mind going, but I know Mum won't agree to let me have a week off school, so I don't bother asking.

Rather than taking us around to the bay where we went last time, Bryce cheekily pulls into the wharf and ties up. By torchlight, he takes us to a different rookery from last time.

'How many do you want?' I ask.

'A dozen.'

Strange. If he only wants a dozen, why does he need me when he has Teddy? Still trying to think it through, I don't bother to ask if we're poaching. The moon is quite large and I have good night vision, so I don't bother turning my torch on. Instead, I steal away into the night to murder some muttonbird chicks.

'Where's Dion?' asks Mum when Bryce returns without me.

'Over there,' he replies.

I look up and realise that only Bryce and I have come onto the rookery, the others have waited at the edge. I do a rough count. Deciding I have enough, I pick my way around the holes as I make my way back.

Mum gives a startled cry.

'What?' I ask as I emerge soundlessly out of the darkness.

'You scared me. I thought you were a ghost.'

The graves on this island are countless. I wonder if any of the dead haunt. Do spectres glide across the rookeries at night? I don't know, but living in a haunted place, I've come to realise the dead cannot hurt the living.

'Where'd you get to?' Mum asks. 'I was worried.'

'I was getting birds,' I reply.

'Well, why weren't you using your torch?'

'I can see better without it.'

Mum wears thick glasses and she's chronically night blind. She can't comprehend that I can see well enough in the moonlight. Heading back to the wharf, I let Dad, Mum and Stephen take the lead as Dad lights the way with his big-beamed dolphin torch.

Teddy, who has been waiting by a bank, falls in beside me. 'Aren't you worried about snakes?'

I don't bother to try and explain my intuition which offers me some protection. 'Worrying only means you suffer twice.'

He gives a nervous laugh and appears to stumble slightly. 'Snake!'

He flees down the track, leaving me standing there. I stand statue-still. If he's stepped on a tiger snake, it'll be upset. It won't distinguish between the one who trespassed against it and the innocent bystander. I peer at the ground beneath my feet. There's a dark shape against the pale sand, but there's nothing writhing.

I gently nudge the dark shape with the toe of my boot and realise it's a cowpat. Teddy is terrified of snakes? It doesn't make any sense. Why would a man who's terrified of snakes go hunting ducks? It's queer.

'Dion!' cries Mum.

I'm standing in the centre of the track, but I realise she can't see me. 'I'm here.'

'Are you bitten?' asks Dad, who's coming towards me with a length of wood ready to bash it to death.

'No. There's no snake. Teddy stood on a cowpat.'

Bryce is the first to start laughing. A moment later, everyone is, including me.

'Snakes are thick as hairs on a cat's back around the rookeries,' says Teddy in his own defence.

'Like they would be around a lagoon,' I reply. 'I mean, duck eggs, ducklings, frogs… I can scarcely imagine how big and fat snakes would grow feasting on them.'

Teddy sways on his feet. 'Nah, snakes don't like water.'

'Who told you that load of shit?' I question. 'Snakes float and swim rather well. They don't care about water and they need to drink same as everything else.'

Teddy swallows. I leave him standing there and we head back to the boat. Between the two of us, we've taken twenty birds.

'You want to pluck up here?' I ask.

'No, we'll skin them,' replies Bryce.

I reach for my pocketknife, but Stephen says. 'I got it, mate.'

He's way better at dressing birds than I am, so I leave him to it. Thirty minutes later, it's all over and the birds are in two clean buckets. Bryce's dozen and eight for ourselves. Not a bad raid.

The Drovers

'What's wrong?' asks Mum when Dad steps away from the phone, where he's been talking to Douglas.

'Joe's hurt his back and Scott has quit.'

The Trader is due in next week which means there should be a muster this week.

'Has the muster been called off?' asks Mum.

'No. Douglas has had a phone around his neighbouring properties and he's recruited six men who fancy themselves as drovers.'

Mum stares incredulously. 'What are we going to do with six cowboys for a week?'

'We'll have to feed them night and morning as well as cut sandwiches for their lunches.'

The 'we' wouldn't include Dad: he never lifted a finger in the kitchen. Fair enough in some ways, since he worked hard at his job.

'Is this a paying job?' asks Mum.

'No. He's sold the men on the challenge of mustering the island's wild cattle. I don't think he intends to pay the drovers, just cover their expenses.'

A challenge and a working holiday. I could see how Douglas had sold that.

'I meant me,' says Mum with steel in her voice.

Dad winces. 'Douglas has promised to send over some grain for the chooks and ducks.'

'Grain? I'll have to cook and clean up after three meals a day for a few bags of grain!'

'Feel free to call him back, but they're on their way. Howard will be flying them over tomorrow.'

'And what are we supposed to feed them on?'

'You'll need to phone through a grocery order to Scottsdale supermarket. If Websters' truck isn't coming up today, we'll have to organise a courier. Douglas will have to pay for the order and the freight.'

Mum looks doubtful. 'Has he agreed to that?'

'He'll have to. There's no other way we can feed six men for a week.'

Mum gets up and goes outside. At first I think she's stormed out, but she has just walked over to the garden to see what's ready to harvest. When she comes back, she starts making a shopping list.

'Stephen, do you want to take your brother fishing?'

Stephen grins. This isn't just to get us out of the house. Mum needs the fish to feed the men with. We're being entrusted to go and get food. It makes me feel important.

When we get back, Dad is down at the bottom house calling for a hand. 'Where have you two been?' he asks.

'Mum sent us fishing for fish to feed the men with.'

Dad's anger subsides. 'How'd you go?'

'Eight decent-sized parrotfish and a couple of leatherjackets which we've cleaned and filleted.'

Dad looks proud. He's fond of telling people how capable we are. He gestures at the old burnt-out combustion stove. 'We need to get that out of the way.'

'What for?' asks Stephen.

'The hot water cylinder still works. It just needs a fire to heat it. If we can get the stove out of the way, we can probably utilise the open fireplace.'

I'm not convinced Dad's plan will work. However, with our combined strength, we manage to move the stove out of the fireplace and across the room. With the aid of the loader bucket, Dad's able to get it out of the house.

With the stove out of the way, I can see that he's right. The installers had simply put the stove into the fireplace and now the stove is out of the way the fireplace is again useable.

Dad sets to work with the arc and gas welders. He builds a new grate and extends the copper pipe which he runs down the side of one of the log brackets. Over the copper pipe, he welds a piece of heavy angle iron so that the hot water pipe won't be damaged by someone throwing a log in.

A fire having been lit, three hours later hot water is coming out of the tap over the sink.

On cue, Mum appears at the door with a mop and bucket. She pauses when she sees the fire now burning in the kitchen. It's timely, because it means the men won't need to use our bathroom. They can now shower here.

'Well done,' says Mum.

Howard flies four loads the next day to bring over the six men and their luggage, which includes saddles and the provisions. Dad ferries them down after each load straight to the bottom house, where they'll be staying. The men will still have to come up night and morning for meals, as Mum doesn't want to carry hot meals down to the other house.

There'll be no school this week. Stephen and I will have to manage the milking and feeding of the chooks and ducks on our own. We'll also be needed to help cook and wash up after the meals as well as help Dad whenever he needs a hand, which is most of the time.

That evening, a new issue arises. Mum literally does not have enough plates to serve everyone at once. So she serves six meals for the drovers, we wash up and then she serves four more meals for us, plus a fifth for the young stockman, Shane, whom Douglas has sent over from Leverington.

The next morning, we're up at five. Mum has to make eight cut lunches: six for the drovers and one each for Dad and Shane. She then cooks a hot breakfast of bacon, sausages, eggs and toast, which she serves to Dad, Shane and the drovers. Dad and Shane have to be served on entrée plates. We have time to help wash up and eat before going out to do the milking. We then have to set about baking bread, because not enough has been sent over. Mum also bakes biscuits, cakes and desserts to feed the horde with.

Despite the work, the first day is fun. It feels good to be genuinely contributing to the work of the island. By the third day, we're all over it. There isn't even the promise of a pay cheque at the end of it to look forward to. To make matters worse, the drovers, who spent the first evening bragging about how many cattle they would bring in, are failing dismally.

By the end of the week, everyone is exhausted. The drovers have managed to bring in only a paltry twenty-five head of cattle – a fifth of what was hoped for. Still, any cattle are better than none.

On Saturday, the day of departure for the drovers, Howard phones to say he won't be able to fly them off until the afternoon.

At mid-morning, Shane comes up to the house. 'The men are wondering if they can go out and shoot a sick cow they saw while mustering. She has a cancer on her face.'

'I don't have time to take them out and I don't have a high-powered rifle,' says Dad.

'I brought over my three-hundred Willoughby rifle and I'm happy to drive them out,' says Shane.

Dad looks torn. After Phil, he doesn't trust this young man to handle the drovers on his own, but he doesn't have time to accompany them. Still, the cow does need to be put down and it is best done with a high-powered rifle, which Dad doesn't possess. The stockmen have always brought a high-powered rifle over with them to shoot a beast in order to take some of the meat back to Leverington.

'Yeah, all right, but make sure they're back in time to catch the plane. Howard could arrive at any time after lunch and he doesn't like to be kept waiting.'

Howard arrives around two and ED arrives between Howard's second and third loads. ED has brought two extra men with him to help unload the *Trader*.

'The weather's forecast to be fine for the next few days,' says Dad that evening at dinner. 'ED spoke to the *Trader*'s captain before arriving and he's agreed to sit the *Trader* on her bottom as long as she's empty. When she's floating again, we'll load the cattle.'

Mum pauses as if searching for an explanation. 'By the time the *Trader*'s floating again, it'll be dark. There are no lights at the wharf.'

'ED's brought two flood lights with him. We'll be able to power them from the welder,' Dad replies.

A night load. That sounds exciting.

The next day, the unloading of the *Trader* goes more smoothly than ever. We are now deft hands at it and Dad has more men at his disposal than he's ever had before. Best of all, the *Trader* has brought with her a new tractor: a Massey Ferguson of similar size to the David Brown, with a loading bucket and backhoe. She's old, but she still works and she is much needed.

By four, the *Trader* is empty. Dad fits the welder to the three-point linkage of the David Brown and drives her down onto the wharf. While he does this, Shane and the other two men saddle horses and round up the cattle that the drovers have spent all week mustering. They manage to get them all onto the wharf and locked into the yards without losing any of them. It's a first.

A quiet stillness descends on the island. We're all tired and we slip away for a nap before dinner. At nine, we all head to the wharf for the night load. In the dark, the cattle are subdued. They can't see what lies before them, so they walk down the race and onto the *Trader* as if they're tame. After so many failures, it's a surreal sight to behold.

We all sleep late the next day. ED flies out at ten, taking the two men he'd brought with him. Shane is left behind to help Dad sort out the supplies from the *Trader*. Howard will come and get him in due course.

After lunch Stephen, who loves riding motorbikes, takes a joyride to the creek crossing. When he returns, he pulls up outside the workshop where Shane and I are helping Dad sort the new supplies.

'That cancerous cow is wounded, but she's still alive. I saw her on the creek bank up from the crossing.'

Dad sighs heavily and turned to Shane. 'How is it that you were all gone for hours yet only managed to wound the cow?'

'We shot her on the way back. We thought she was dead,' he replies.

'She's not,' says Stephen angrily.

'Back from where?' asks Dad.

'We went out across the pasture and the drovers shot six bulls – one each.'

Dad removes his tobacco from his top pocket. 'Best show me where, and bring that rifle of yours.'

'It's not here any more. My brother needs it, so I sent it back with ED.'

Dad rubs the bridge of his nose. From the house, he grabs his .22 along with his camera and a spare roll of film. A different situation but still a déjà vu moment. When we get to the creek crossing, the cow is where Stephen said it was. Dad shoots at her with the .22. Aiming behind the ear, he manages to bring her down and he walks over and fires another shot into her head at close range.

Lying where they'd been shot were six dead bulls. Dad photographs each one of them before returning to the house.

That evening, he phones Douglas. 'It's a gaolable offence to shoot livestock,' says Dad when he gets off the phone.

'What's going to happen?' I ask.

'Douglas intends to confront them about it. If they deny it, he plans to take the matter to the authorities. Shane will be called as a witness and I may be as well.'

It's serious.

The next evening, Douglas phones to say that each of the men admitted guilt and have agreed to pay compensation. I don't ask how much, but I figure their working holiday has turned into an expensive jaunt.

The Slaughtering of a Beast

Since the drovers have all but eaten us out of house and home, Dad arranges for Jack and Jolan to come over so we can go off the island and do some shopping. First chance he gets, Dad goes into a firearm shop.

'After something in particular?' asks the store owner.

'Yeah, have you got any army surplus .303s?'

The store owner shakes his head. 'No, the only military rifle I have is a 6.5x55. It's slightly smaller than a .303 but, in my opinion, it packs just as much punch. What do you need it for?'

'Shooting wild cattle,' says Dad.

'It'll do fine,' says the store owner.

The rifle, being army surplus, is much cheaper than any of the modern firearms, as is the ammunition. The only drawback is that the full wood stock makes the rifle heavy and it's not fitted with a scope. Dad thinks it over, but decides to buy it.

Maree is having some issues attending college, so Mum decides she'll stay in Launceston for a few days and fly home on Munro. Dad drives us boys to Cape Portland and we fly back with Howard.

'Any issues?' Dad asks Jack at the airstrip.

'No, except there's a giant bull making itself at home in front of the dunes near the home beach.'

It's odd, because the wild cattle tend not to come within kilometres of the house. Once we've unpacked, Dad makes a cup of tea and takes it onto the veranda. A short while later, the bull comes moseying along the base of the dunes. He's black, horned and very mean-looking. Using his horns as a digging tool, he tosses sand into the air as he enlarges his bull hole.

I grab the binoculars for a better look. 'He's in good condition. I reckon he's a breakaway from the muster.'

Dad takes a look through the binoculars. 'Best place for him is the freezer.'

The next day, Dad spends most of his time sharpening all the knives. In the late afternoon, he loads his new high-powered rifle and we head down to confront the bull. We stop at the fence because if Dad misses we both know the bull will charge. The fence won't stop him, but it will slow him down. Hopefully enough for us to make a run for it.

Dad takes aim. There's a loud boom and the bull falls onto his side. We're through the fence in a moment and jogging towards the kill. When we reach him, Dad shoots him in the head again for good measure. Handing me the rifle, he cuts the bull's throat and blood gushes out. I can't believe how much there is. Litres and litres of the stuff.

'Hold his back leg, can you?'

I do and Dad cuts off the bull's penis and testicles. His reasoning is that he doesn't want them to taint the meat.

He starts skinning out the back leg. 'Go and get the loader.'

I head up to the workshop and grab the recently arrived Fergie. By the time I get back, Dad has skinned out all four legs. He hooks a gambrel through the back legs and I hoist the bull up a bit by raising the bucket. When Dad has skinned down to waist height, I hoist a bit more.

At the halfway point, it's time to remove the guts. There's no easy way to do this. Dad has to reach inside all the way to his shoulders, grab hold as best he can and reef out the guts. They come bit by bit and then out with a rush and go thump on the ground. Removing the liver, heart and lungs is even harder because they're attached by membrane. They have to be cut away carefully, and each organ is very heavy.

I raise the bucket a bit more and Dad finishes removing the hide. He then takes an axe and chops the bull's head off. I drive slowly back.

As I pass by the milking stand, I see Stephen milking. Damn, the hour's later than I thought.

When Dad appears, Stephen starts yelling. 'What's the meaning of leaving me to do the milking on my own while you two go off and slaughter a beast!'

Dad baulks. He looks like he's been slapped across the face by a wet dishcloth. It suddenly occurs to me that Mum manages the milking with the help of us kids. Because he rarely does it, Dad has completely forgotten it needs to be done.

'Best help your brother while I sort this,' he says.

I do just that. When we're done, the light is fading. We find Dad atop a stepladder working a meat saw in an effort to cut the carcass in half. When he sees us, he stops – his brow is glistening with sweat.

'Fetch me the chainsaw,' he says.

I hurry off. Why he's trying to cut it in half is puzzling, because Dad normally just hangs beasts from the big limb of the pine tree. Still, Dad always has a plan, so I grab the saw. When I hand it to him, Dad drains the chain lubricant oil out and replaces it with cooking oil. Having done so, he starts it and proceeds to cut the beast in half. Shards of bone and mincemeat fly out the back as he does so.

'What are you doing?' asks Stephen when Dad switches off the saw and he can finally be heard.

'We need to get it into the meat safe and the only way we can do that is to quarter it.'

Stephen's face reddens. 'Bulls weigh half a tonne. Deduct a hundred kilograms for guts, skin and head, and each quarter still weighs a hundred kilograms. How are you going to carry a hundred kilograms of meat and bone into the meat safe?'

Dad blinks. Maths isn't his strong point. Normally, we only kill yearlings. This is the biggest beast we've ever killed. Its size is intimidating and Stephen is right. Even quartered, it's too big and heavy to get into the meat safe. Pop intended it for wallabies, goats and maybe, one day, sheep.

'Look at the frigging mess you've made,' says Stephen. He storms off, leaving us to it.

Taking Stephen's point, Dad hangs the two halves from the pine tree limb and we cover the carcass with old sheets.

Mum arrives the next day on Munro. Upon examining the beast, she shakes her head. 'Even though it's empty, I doubt all of him is going to fit in the freezer.'

Whether it will or not is a moot point. We still have to process as much as we can. The only place to do it is on the kitchen table. We've done it before of course, but never one this big, and we still don't really know what we are doing. Dad bolts a hand mincer to the end of the table and we take turns cranking it. We slice and dice all day long. By late afternoon, there's still an entire back leg left but the freezer is full.

'Shame to waste all that meat,' says Stephen.

'Couldn't we salt some of it?' I say. 'I mean, they sailed out from England with salt meat in barrels.'

'We've got brine, but I don't know if we've got enough salt,' says Mum.

We've made silverside before, but only on a small scale; never this much at once.

'What if we used seawater?' I ask.

'Don't be daft,' says Stephen. 'It'll have sand in it, which will get all through the meat.'

Dad takes a moment to consider. 'We could strain the sand out.'

The next day, Dad and I go to the beach to collect seawater. Every time I dip a bucket in, the surge from the waves washes sand in. I fear Stephen is correct. Dad, however, has the idea of hauling up buckets from the wharf and so we drive there on the David Brown. When he lowers the bucket suspended on a rope, the handle comes free and he loses the bucket.

I've had enough. I jump clean off the end of the wharf into twelve hundred centimetres of seawater. As I wade through it, the cold water's no longer as freezing as it was that first time I went into the sea here.

Not because the temperature of it has changed, but because I have hardened up.

I retrieve the bucket and walk over to the rocks alongside the wharf. I fill it and pass it to Dad. He takes it and pours it through a fine-weave cloth stretched over a funnel into a clean twenty-five-litre drum. To collect fifty litres of seawater is labour-intensive, but what isn't on this island?

Back at the house, Mum is scrubbing out a large plastic vat that washed up on the beach a few years ago. When she's happy with the cleanliness, Dad manages to get it through the meat safe door by turning it on its side. Once he's poured the water in, Mum drops a peeled potato in.

'It has to float for it to be salty enough,' says Mum. She walks over to the house and returns with a five-kilogram bag of salt. While Dad is stirring with a large wooden spoon, she pours in four kilograms before the potato floats. Once it does, she adds the powdered brine.

Normally, when there's anything happening with meat, Stephen is always present. His absence is conspicuous.

'Stephen's upset that you didn't consult with him before shooting the bull,' says Mum quietly.

Now that Mum's mentioned it, it does seem odd that Dad took me with him to slaughter the bull rather than Stephen. He's the far better slaughterman and butcher. I doubt it was deliberate on Dad's part. He'd just been so keen to try out his new rifle that he hadn't thought it through. Hadn't thought any of it through.

Mum and I hold back while Dad goes over to apologise to Stephen. When we wander into the kitchen, they're both carving up the last of the meat which we intend to salt down. We finish off and collapse in the lounge room. It's all well and good to say the meat is free, but it takes a lot of effort to process it.

The Grader

Mum looks deeply concerned when she hangs up the phone. 'That was Munro Airlines. They're officially complaining about the rough surface of our airstrip. Unless it's smoothed, they'll discontinue servicing us.'

Dad regularly slashes the airstrip to keep the vegetation down; not that he needs to, because the wallabies do the bulk of the work for him. He can't, however, do anything about the surface, which has in recent times become quite bumpy. We can live without Munro's service, but it would be a nuisance. With Maree now living in Launceston, Mum and Dad take it in turns to fly there and see her every month or so. With the service discontinued, they wouldn't be able to fly directly to Launceston.

'Will the 8430's blade be able to fix it?' asks Mum, looking hopeful.

Dad rubs his chin. 'A bit, but we really need a grader.'

Mum snorts. 'Fat chance of Douglas shipping one of those over.'

Dad takes Stephen and me with him to help put the blade back on the 8430. Up at the airstrip, Dad takes some test cuts. When it's only skimming the surface, it seems to work okay. A while later, he pulls up and walks over to the old grader. If I have to guess, I'd say she hasn't moved in over a decade. Upon closer inspection, I realise there are bits missing from the motor.

Dad seems undeterred by this fact. He's more interested in the rest of her. He stares at her while smoking a cigarette and a smirk appears on his face. He has a plan for getting her going but, short of an expensive rebuild, I have no idea what he has in mind.

'You're not quite understanding me,' says Dad through the phone to Douglas. 'We don't need to get the motor going. We just need to get the hydraulics line fixed, then we can power them through the 8430.'

There's a redness in Dad's cheeks and his rate of sighing indicates he's starting to lose his cool. When he hangs up, he shakes his head and mumbles something that sounds like 'imbecile'.

The next day, Dad drives the 8430 up to the grader. He attaches a tow chain. Turning to Stephen, he says, 'Right, jump in the 8430 and take it steady – and I mean steady.'

'Can I safely assume we're taking her to the workshop?'

Dad nods.

Stephen tows the grader down to the workshop, where he pulls up. Having unhooked the tow chain, he drives the 8430 out of the way. Dad drives the David Brown over and positions her bucket over the top of the front wheels. Using the bucket to lift the wheels off the ground, Dad unbolts them and moves them out of the way. A few hours later, he has fashioned a drawbar out of heavy steel and welded it on the front of the grader so she can now be towed. Next, he removes the drive chains from the twin back wheels so they're freewheeling, before dismantling the hydraulics.

A few days later, ED lands. His arrival tells me that having had no luck convincing Douglas of his idea, Dad's gone to ED. It won't sit well long-term, although I doubt Dad cares.

Dad removes all manner of hydraulic fittings and takes them down to the grader. Later that afternoon, he summons us to take a look. The grader is now hooked up to the drawbar of the 8430 and two hoses are plugged into her hydraulics. Climbing into the cab, Dad demonstrates that the grader blade now moves freely. I can't believe he's managed to resurrect her.

The next day, the grader is towed up to the airstrip. Dad drives the 8430, while ED operates the grader. By week's end, Dad is rolling the airstrip with the towable rollers and the airstrip is as good as new.

Before climbing back into his plane, ED promises to return and help build some new roads.

Wallaby Cull

The population of wallabies is still an issue. Although there are no immediate plans to bring over sheep, Douglas is still concerned that they're eating too much grass. He's again threatening to lay 1080 poison.

'We're not poisoning again,' says Dad. 'It didn't work last time, it won't work this time.'

'Well, what else can we do?' asks Mum. 'Douglas is determined to lower the population.'

'Howard has a professional shooter to deal with his kangaroo problem. He's going to ask him if he wants to come over here and deal with ours.'

On the next new moon, Howard flies over the professional shooter. His name is Rex and he brings his wife Shae with him along with their two curly-coated retrievers. They settle into the bottom house and Dad and Rex spend the day welding a frame for the carry-all and fitting the top with foam. When it's built, it allows Rex to take a resting shot from the carry-all.

That evening, Dad, Stephen and I take Rex out to the interior, where the new pasture is growing. Dad has connected a hand-held spotlight to the David Brown. From the illumination, we get our first glance at the sheer number of wallabies there are. There are literally hundreds of them.

For the next three hours, Rex shoots wallaby and, for the first time ever, we don't bother to pick them up. We simply leave them where they fall. The official tally is two hundred and twenty-six.

'Seems a shame to waste all that meat, not to mention the pelts,' I say the next morning at breakfast.

'There's nothing to be done, lad. It's too expensive to fly off the meat. Even if we chartered a plane to fly it direct to Launceston, unless it's fitted with a cool room, the meat will be rotten on arrival. As for the pelts, the Greenies have put an end to the fur trade.'

I grit my teeth. I hate the use of the word Greenie, which Dad is fond of using. 'According to Bryce, these islands once survived on the fur from seals and wallabies.'

'That's true,' says Mum, 'but they hunted the seals, not to mention the whales, almost to extinction.'

I consider this and see her point. 'But the wallabies have come back with a vengeance and the fur is just being wasted.'

'Try telling that to the Greenies,' says Dad.

I sigh. 'What about the meat? Couldn't we preserve it by smoking or salting it?'

Dad's growing impatient. I can see it in his eyes. 'Who's going to want smoked or salted wallaby? The meat's only good for dog tucker. Besides, Douglas would never go for it.'

I wonder if he might if it was suggested, but there's no point pressing the matter. Dad isn't going to suggest it and there's no way he's going to want to skin several hundred wallabies after every cull.

I'm still deep in thought when Rex and Shae come in to ask if they can do some quail shooting. Dad says it's okay, so I drive them and their retrievers out to the tussock country on the David Brown. I've never been quail shooting before so I'm not sure what's involved. I hold back and watch as the retrievers flush out the quail.

The first shot is fired and I expect to see the birds fly away but to my surprise a bird falls. Rex's retriever brings the bird to him, which I'm also impressed by. They shoot a dozen between them and that night we dine on slow-cooked quail. I like the meat and consider how I might shoot some myself. It won't be easy, because I don't have access to a twelve-gauge nor a hunting dog.

We do have the four-ten, however, and I've become quite proficient at using it. The first morning after Rex and Shae leave, I get up at first light. On the bank live some small birds which I'm sure are a species of quail. By sneaking up on them, I'm able to shoot three.

'They're not quail, mate, they're bronze-winged pigeons,' says Stephen.

My heart sinks.

'They should still be all right eating, though.'

He helps me to clean the birds and Mum cooks them up for dinner. Dad's not impressed. There are limits to his culinary tastes and pigeon is out of scope. Stephen and I are swinging the other way and are keen to try other bush meats.

'What's that?' says Mum when I drop something into the sink the next day.

'Tiger snake,' I reply.

Having chopped off the shot head, allowing for a decent margin of error, Stephen and I have removed the skin and guts. He's intent on making himself a new belt; I'm more interested in the meat. I set about frying a chunk in hot dripping the way I would have cooked a piece of fish. The meat is tough and stringy and nothing short of disgusting.

The snake is followed up by a blue-tongued lizard, which was worse than the snake. Next a cockatoo, which might have been better if it'd been cooked for three more days. Ditto for the currawong. After the eels, which we caught using handlines in the creek, Mum says no more.

'So, we can't deep-fry some witchetty grubs?' asks Stephen. 'I was thinking of doing them in batter.'

Mum lets out a groan of anguish which we decide means no.

A while later, one of the workers from Leverington, Mack, flies over. He's only a few years younger than Dad and dead keen on hunting and fishing, which is why he's happy to come over.

As soon as Mack is settled in the bottom house, Dad calls Stephen and me into the lounge room. He reveals two new .22 rifles which Mack has purchased for him. 'I'm gifting these to you boys on the proviso that you use them safely and responsibly.'

We both know he means that if we don't, he'll confiscate them, but it's all good. Stephen and I both know how to safely handle firearms.

'What about Maree?' asks Stephen.

Dad's expression turns stern. 'She's been given more than just her allowance while she's been away, so she doesn't get one.'

I shrug; that's between Dad and Maree. Both rifles are fitted with a scope, but they're not identical. One has a tubular magazine which runs through the stock; the other has two ten-shot detachable magazines, with the spare taped to the butt.

Stephen picks up the one with the tubular magazine. 'I'll take this one.'

I'm pleased, because I know reloading on the fly will be difficult. I don't tell him this, however.

In a safe area in the paddock, we shoot at a box which has a professional shooting target on it. Mack has bought over a stack and he's showing us how to 'sight' the rifles. Apparently, if the scopes are bumped hard enough, they need to be resighted. On the side of the scopes are two calibration dials which correspond with the targets, so there's less guesswork.

That night, Stephen and I go out with Mack and Dad to try out the new rifles. With two shooters, one on each side of the tractor, a bigger arc can be covered. It's more efficient. We shoot three hundred and nine wallabies and set a new record.

Mack stays for a fortnight and vows to come back during the summer to do some serious hunting and fishing. It's something to look forward to.

That evening, after I've gone to bed, I overhear Mum and Dad having a heated conversation in the kitchen.

'If she's not going to knuckle down and study, then she can bloody well look for a job. I'm not paying for her to live in Launceston so she can spend her time partying!' There is finality in Dad's voice.

Maree arrives home a few days later and Stephen vacates the sleepout so our sister can have it back. Even at the airstrip, I can tell Maree has changed. She's always been strong-willed, but now she has serious attitude. In the kitchen, she lights a cigarette and proceeds to smoke it without the slightest concern for what Dad and Mum think.

Neither of us boys says anything, but Stephen raises an eyebrow. If Maree has started smoking, then she has also, no doubt, been under-age drinking. Two guesses who's been paying for it. No wonder Dad refused to gift her a rifle.

When next Rex and Shae fly over, they seem a little cool.

'What's up with them?' I ask Dad.

'I made the mistake of telling Rex that Mack came over shooting. He's feeling insecure.'

I can't reason this. 'Why? It's not as if it's a paid job, or is it?'

Dad shakes his head. 'Nah, he hasn't been paid wages, but Douglas has allowed him to order a few things from Websters on the Island's account. No great amount, just bits and bobs.'

Being paid in kind is fairly common on farms. I know Dad from time to time would charge certain items from Websters to the Island account. Things like tools he needs for the workshop as well as a new spotlight for the wallaby cull. I also know that Douglas has at times queried the items. If Rex exceeds what Douglas considers a fair thing, he'll be let go. Much as his efforts are appreciated, he's no longer needed. We can handle the wallaby cull on our own, especially now we have two decent rifles.

Stephen comes walking in from where he's been visiting at the bottom house. 'Rex wants to know if you want to go out shooting Cape Barren geese.'

It's one thing to steal a few chicks, but to kill them en masse is another matter entirely. 'They're a protected species, aren't they?'

Stephen shrugs. 'Apparently, there's a season on them.'

I don't bother to grab my rifle as I head out. Cape Barren geese know if you're armed and will keep a distance of a least half a kilometre between the one armed and themselves. A .22 is only accurate up to a hundred metres and I never shoot at anything over fifty. It doesn't matter, because Rex has bought his .222 (aka triple-two) with him, which is fitted with a bipod.

Stephen drives the David Brown out to the tussock country where

I brought Rex and Shae to shoot quail. He pulls up half a kilometre from two geese who are grazing on a tiny patch of green between the tussocks.

'I doubt you'll get any closer,' says Stephen, switching off the tractor.

Rex jumps off the carry-all and takes up a position lying on the ground, his rifle supported by the bipod. He takes his time sighting his target and when he shoots, to my astonishment one of the geese falls over. The second goose doesn't fly off, but looks at his mate unsure what's happened. Hastily reloading, Rex fires a second shot. The second goose also falls over.

Impressed, Stephen raises an eyebrow. We collect the geese and take them home with us, where we dress them out for meat.

That evening, I go out shooting wallaby with Dad, Rex and Maree. Maree uses my rifle; Rex has his own. I'm official counter. My job is also to reload the spare magazines on the go so there's no need to stop.

'How many?' says Rex when we return home.

'Two hundred and seventy,' I say.

Rex snorts. 'You can't count. It had to be at least four hundred.'

I'm not prepared to swear before a judge that my count is exact, but I'm confident of my estimate. 'I didn't miscount.'

Dad nods. 'Be about right. It's about what we normally shoot.'

Rex storms off. He's angry because the night's shoot didn't break the record. That doesn't matter to us. Culling is just a job; it's not a competition.

The Commercial Pilot

The telephone rings and since I'm the only one around, I answer it.
'Hello.'
'Dion, it's Howard.'
'Mr Miles,' I say.
'There's been an accident with my plane. Everyone's all right but the plane's damaged and we're stranded on Outer Sister Island.'
My mind reels. Outer Sister Island is north of Flinders Island and Howard doesn't normally do charter work. I recall, however, Rex saying Howard was going to fly him, his wife and dogs there so they could do some quail shooting. The flight was in lieu of some money that Howard owed Rex for work he'd done at Cape Portland.
'How can I help?' I ask.
'I need you to phone Swan Island. Evan Moore lives there with his wife and they have their own plane. Ask him if he'll fly up and get us.'
'Okay, I'll see if I can find his number.'
'I know the number.' He reels it off. 'But the phone here, the one I'm talking to you on, is restricted to local calls.'
This is common for islands that don't have permanent residences. The phones are distance-restricted so fishermen can't come ashore, kick in the door of the dwelling and run up a bill making long-distance calls.
He gives me the number of the phone he's using before hanging up. Thankfully, Dad walks in and I explain what's happened. He takes over proceedings, calls Swan Island and arranges the rescue.
That night, Howard phones to say he got home safely. Unfortunately, while taxiing off, the front wheel had dropped into a rabbit hole. The propeller hit the ground and it damaged the casing among

other things. An aircraft mechanic will be flown over to remove the damaged parts, but new ones would have to be ordered and shipped from the United States. In short, the plane will be stuck on Outer Sister Island for some time and thus out of action. It's a serious blow.

'What are we going to do for a plane in the meantime?' I ask.

'Evan Moore from Swan Island has agreed to take over, but he only has a Cessna.'

That means Evan's plane won't have the cargo space nor the carrying capacity. Still, it could be worse. There might not have been a plane or pilot to take over and we'd have had to rely on Munro Airlines. The island would not have been able to stand the expense.

When next I'm to fly off, I climb into Evan's green and white Cessna and sit beside him in the front. I put my seatbelt on and examine the dash. It's similar, but different, to the one in Howard's plane. More modern, I believe.

Evan reaches down beside his seat and retrieves a laminated safety card. Pointing at a picture, he says, 'In the unlikely event that something happens to the plane, this is the brace position. Your life jacket is under your seat.'

I nod. Not even on the commercial airline Munro have I ever been given a safety briefing. I return to looking at the dash, but Evan isn't finished.

'Behind the back seats is the life raft. It's very important to know the raft, when inflated, is larger than the inside of this plane. So make sure it's outside before you begin inflating. To inflate, you have to pull a forty-foot cord. At some point, you're going to think it's never going to inflate, but just keep pulling. If I'm injured, promise you'll do your best to get me out.'

I nod again.

'Don't be tempted to jump out into the sea as we come into crash. The impact will maim or kill you. Wait until the plane has come to rest and get the raft outside and inflated. I'll radio for help before we crash, so know that help will be on the way.'

Okay, great. 'But you know how to fly, right?'

He's taken back. 'I spent forty years flying for Qantas. I've never had a single incident.'

He finally starts the plane and flies us to Cape Portland. There are no problems and I disembark. When it comes time to return, I climb back into the plane and again sit in the front. Evan again reaches for his safety card.

'You briefed me on the way over.'

'And I'll be briefing you every time you fly with me. Now, if I can just have your attention for just a few minutes.'

I look sharp. After all, safety is paramount.

Leverington

Dad drops his packed bag of clothes in the hallway before coming into the kitchen. Maree has a job interview on Flinders Island, but Dad's unsure whether the job's suitable for his teenage daughter. Thus they're flying up to spend a few days with Uncle Ernie to check it out. Rather than pay fares on Munro Airlines, Uncle Ernie has arranged for a mate with a plane to fly down and get them.

An hour later, the plane is late arriving but that's nothing unusual. People tend to do things in their own time in this part of the world.

When the plane does arrive, it's a black and white 172 Cessna. Dad and Maree climb in and it takes off heading for Flinders Island. When they return five days later, it's in a red and white Cessna with a different pilot. It leads me to wonder just how many mates with planes Uncle Ernie has.

At the airstrip, Dad hands me a box with six enormous frozen turkeys in it.

'Where'd you get these?' I ask.

'They run feral on the property Uncle Ernie manages,' replies Dad.

We return to the house and Stephen takes one look at the turkeys and goes and grabs the meat saw. As they are, there's no way they're going to fit in the oven, they're just too big. With my help, he saws them in half and we manage to get them into the deep freezer.

I don't need to ask about the job, as Maree is looking crestfallen. She has, however, obtained a Saturday newspaper from the Whitemark shop and is now sitting at the kitchen table searching for jobs.

Staring intently, she says, 'This looks like a job vacancy for Leverington.'

Dad leans over Maree's shoulder. 'Yep, that's Douglas's number.'

'You'd have thought someone would have let us know,' says Mum.

Maree's been doing some casual paid work for Douglas. Since she hates doing mechanical repairs with Dad, it's been mostly riding a horse around the fence lines looking for damage or anything else that's noteworthy. The work is only tokenism and it pays a paltry $2.50 an hour.

Maree gets up and, to my surprise, phones Douglas there and then. When she's finished, she says, 'He's agreed to give me a trial run.'

'When?' asks Mum.

'As soon as I can get there.'

Howard's plane is still out of action. Rather than phone Evan Moore on Swan Island, Dad instead phones ED.

'Well, ED's excited about you working at Leverington even if Douglas isn't. He said he'd be over in a few days and he'll take Maree back with him.'

According to Dad, ED has a high opinion of all of us. Personally, I've found ED to be a little gruff and intimidating, but Dad assured me that's just ED's ex-army style. Apparently, he'd been a Light Horseman and had served in Gallipoli during World War I.

ED kept his word and Maree left us yet again, about a week later.

Three months later, when the spring school holidays are approaching, Dad mentions casually if I'd like to spend a week with Maree at Leverington.

'What's the catch?' I ask. Maree and I have always had a topsy-turvy relationship. She being the eldest; me being the youngest. It's a sibling thing.

'They're shearing at Leverington and could use a hand.'

I'm not under any illusions that I'll be paid for working from dawn till dusk, but it will be an adventure and a chance to experience working with sheep. 'Why's she asked me rather than Stephen?'

'She's asked both of you,' says Mum, 'but we can't afford to send you both at once. You'll fly off with your Dad and he'll drive you down. Then he'll hang around for a week and bring you back before driving Stephen down.'

It seems like a lot of toing and froing to me. 'Wouldn't it be easier to get ED to fly me down?' I've never flown with ED but I've heard stories that he likes to do aerial acrobatics, which sounds like fun.

'ED's flown up to Queensland,' says Dad.

I'm disappointed about not getting to fly with ED, but I'm excited about going to Leverington, so I go and start packing. Howard has his plane back and he arrives that afternoon. Dad drives me to Leverington in the Kombi.

When we arrive, I'm surprised to learn that Maree is living with the new head stockman and his family. Joe has left and his replacement is called Pluto. He has a large family still living at home and his youngest son is sixteen. The farmhouse they're living in is therefore crowded and I'm left wondering why I'm needed. I'm shown to a room that has two others already sleeping in it and I'm allocated a bed. I feel awkward because I'm not used to being in a house that has this many people I don't know in it. There's nothing to be done except make the best of it.

The next morning, I'm roused out of bed at five and fed a bowl of porridge along with a mug of tea. After breakfast, Maree, Pluto's youngest son, whom she calls Pud, and I climb into a Toyota Landcruiser flat tray and she drives us down across the property to where some ewes are lambing.

'We need to drift off,' says Maree as we enter the paddock with the lambing ewes.

I don't know what 'drift off' means. I can't ask, because both Maree and Pud have walked away. All I can do is watch what they do. They're walking across the paddock so I do the same. A few minutes later, I realise that the ewes that haven't lambed are drifting away from those that have. Maree and Pud are deliberately leaving behind the ones that have lambed. Now I get what drift off means and I'm able to help.

The ewes that haven't lambed are moved into an adjoining paddock.

'What are we doing?' I ask. Maree is like Dad in that she hates to explain anything about a job she wants help with. I'm just expected to know as if the information has come to me through osmosis in sleep.

'These are registered stud Merinos. We have to ear tag the lambs and record the tag numbers in a book,' says Pud.

Okay. 'That will require catching the lambs.'

'Yep,' says Maree, looking grim.

The lambs are only newborns, but there are some who are still quite lively on their feet. By the time we've caught and tagged them all, I'm puffed out. A bit of an issue, since it's not yet nine o'clock.

Maree drives us to the shearing shed. I recognise the same shearers I saw the day Mum brought us here. The difference is they're not shearing, they're only crutching and wigging – removing the wool from around the sheep's face so they don't become wool blind.

'Keep away from the board 'cause you'll just be in the way,' says Maree. She leads Pud and me into the yards. 'We need to back up the shed.'

This is a term for bringing the sheep forward towards the board – the place where the sheep's wool is removed. The shed is a series of yards that get progressively larger the further out you go. Sheep need to be dry to be shorn and in theory the shed can hold a day's sheep. Crutching is three times faster and so we're dealing with three times the sheep. Added to this, Pluto is drenching them before letting them back out. Not even during the unloading of the *Trader* have I ever seen such chaos.

I help backup the shed all the way through to outside. On the way back in, Pluto commandeers me to help drench. There's nothing difficult about it. I just have to put a nozzle, attached to a container knapsack, into the sheep's mouth and squirt the dose.

'Don't miss any,' says Pluto, 'or that one can re-infest the entire herd.'

The moment I'm done, I'm called to back up the shed again. This time when I get back inside, I find myself at the edge of the board.

Pluto's got Pud drenching and Maree is counting sheep out of the shorn pens.

'Oi, get your hands out of your pockets and look sharp on a broom!'

I know the head shearer, who's known as the ringer, is yelling at me, but I'm under orders to stay away from the board. However, one of the two board workers, whose job it is to sweep the wool aside, has dashed off to the toilet. The one remaining is trying to cover all four shearers but isn't keeping up. There's no time to argue or even think. I grab the straw broom and head out onto the board, sweeping as fast as I can. There's wool everywhere, but I just have to sweep it into the hoppers. The wool pressers take it from there.

'I thought I told you to stay off the board!' yells Maree.

'And I told him to sweep,' retorts the ringer, coming to my defence.

The official sweeper returns and I'm relieved of my broom. I look around for Maree, but she's backing up the shed again. I go to help her, but I'm tapped on the shoulder.

'Use those long arms of yours to grab an armful of wool.'

I realise it's the wool presser. I do as asked, and carry an armful of wool into the sorting and press room, where I dump the wool on a large sorting table. I spend the next fifteen minutes carrying wool. Then the other sweeper needs a toilet break, so I'm back on the board. Maree is yelling at me for not helping her back up the shed. Pluto, however, wants me drenching.

At noon, a bell rings and the entire shed comes to a standstill. I follow Maree out to the Landcruiser and she drives Pud and me back to Pluto's place for lunch. An hour later, we're back at it.

At five, the shearers stop, but we still have to back up the shed ready for tomorrow, bring more sheep in from the paddocks and take the others away.

At seven, we arrive back at Pluto's house. I'd hoped we'd finished but now Maree has me chopping up a sheep carcass with a half axe to feed the sheep dogs. Having worked all day, they're ravenous. It's seven-thirty before we're finally finished for the day and I'm allowed to peel off putrid clothing and have a shower. I'm nodding off over dinner and go to bed straight afterwards.

The next day, I get up and do it all again. Thankfully, on Saturday, the sixth day, there's no crutching, so all we have to do is tag the lambs. While we're doing it, Pluto moves sheep around. We're all done by ten.

'Did Dad say what time he's coming?' I ask Maree.

'He's not. Pluto's driving up to Scottsdale and Dad will collect you from there.'

At Scottsdale, Dad's there to meet me. Instead of driving me to Cape Portland, he takes me to Little Musselrow Bay. He's been staying there with a mate who has a shack near the beach. Shack is a general term because the place is very palatial. Much nicer than the house we live in. The moment I arrive, I have to take a shower because, apparently, I stink of sheep manure, even though I showered earlier and I'm wearing my good clothes. The bathroom is separate from the shack and has a gas hot water service.

Inside, I'm shown the upstairs section that's glassed on all four sides like a lighthouse. It affords a view of the bay and across to Swan Island.

'How'd you go?' asks Dad.

I move my hand from side to side to indicate my performance was only fair. I explain the long hours.

'I hope you got paid,' says Dad's mate Gerry.

'Fifty dollars,' I show them the cheque Pluto handed to me before we left Leverington.

Gerry's eyes darken. 'Highway robbery.'

'Mr Miles wasn't going to pay me at all, but Pluto insisted I get something.'

'He's only just started paying them a pittance for the work they do on the island,' says Dad. 'It's not right, because we couldn't manage without them.'

I keep quiet. Fifty dollars is still more than I thought I'd get. It's better than nothing.

Dad and Gerry had had plans to take me out fishing in Gerry's boat but I'm too tired to do more than simply stroll along the bay's beach.

The next morning, Dad drives me around the short trip to Cape Portland. Howard flies me home and takes Stephen back with him.

All I want to do is rest, but it's just Mum and me to do the milking and feed all the animals. Thankfully, I have the second week of the holidays to rest up. I need it.

Cape Portland

A month after we return from Leverington, Howard flies over to deliver supplies. Unusually, he has his daughter Louise with him. At a guess, I'd say she's about fourteen. She speaks very properly with a refined upper-class accent when she says hello.

Once the plane is unloaded, for the first time ever, Howard doesn't immediately fly back. Instead, he leads his daughter over to the carry-all and they climb on. At the house, Mum flies into a mild panic as she tries to find something suitable for morning tea for such distinguished guests.

Howard is nonplussed that we only have goat's milk for his coffee and Louise is happy drinking water rather than the offered cordial.

Addressing Stephen and me, Howard says, 'I hear you both did well at Leverington.'

I screw up my face. 'I'm not convinced of that. I got yelled at a lot.'

Howard takes a calculated sip of coffee. 'You didn't give up, though, and you were prepared to have a go at everything. I've employed men who've walked before lunch on their first day.'

Okay, interesting.

'We'll be lamb marking at Cape Portland beginning in about two weeks. I'd like to employ both of you for about three weeks.'

I suck air through my teeth. It would be a great learning opportunity, but I'm sure Mum won't allow us to have that much time off school.

'Will we be paid the hourly rate?' asks Stephen.

Howard's taken back. 'Didn't Douglas pay you?'

'He gave us both a cheque, but the amount on it was a little small,' replies Stephen.

Howard mutters something rude. 'You'll both be paid the award. You can stay in the shearers' quarters. I know you're both capable of taking care of yourselves, but there'll be adults around if you have any problems.'

Mum's looking unsure.

Dad says, 'It would be a great opportunity for the boys, but if it doesn't work out, you'll bring them straight back, yes?'

'I give my word, but they'll be given a proper go,' says Howard.

'What about school?' Mum questions.

Howard nods thoughtfully. 'They'd have to catch up at a later date. I think Stephen can plod along and finish with correspondence, but I think Dion needs to go to a proper school. He should think about that seriously.'

I find a spot on the floor and keep my eyes on it. Howard has questioned me a few times about school during the flights over and back. I know he's right; I'm just not quite ready to agree with him.

'I think a couple of weeks' work would give them a better idea of what working on a farm is really like. After that, they can both make informed career choices while there's still time.'

Mum sighs. 'I'll let them go, but it's their choice.'

There's no question that we'll be going. We both pack and Howard flies us both over to Cape Portland two weeks later. When we arrive, we choose a room each and spend some time sprucing them up. In the kitchen of the shearer's quarters is a box of groceries that Mum has ordered from Scottsdale supermarket. Stephen sorts it out and packs it away.

Despite the fact that we've come here to work, I've brought schoolwork with me. I set myself up at the far end of one of the long tables in the dining room, where my lessons won't be in the way. I'm about to make a start when the head stockman, Dale, walks in.

'So you've come over for the lamb marking, have you?' says Dale.

It's not a question, so I just nod by way of response.

'I've heard you both know your way around the killing yards, so how about you both come with me and we'll slaughter some sheep for meat.'

There's no meat in the box of groceries from Scottsdale. Mum couldn't order any as it would have gone off in transit. So we'll be needing a dressed sheep.

We walk with Dale over to the killing yards. Penned up are six sheep awaiting slaughter. Dale gestures to them, but doesn't say anything.

I enter the pen and ask, 'Have you got a rifle handy?'

'Why would you need a rifle?' he replies.

'When we do goats, we shoot them first,' says Stephen.

'These aren't goats and all you need to do is slit their throats,' says Dale.

I'm not sure if he's taking the piss or not. It is, however, a moot point, because we neglected to bring a rifle with us, so we don't have one at our disposal. Shrugging, I grab a sheep, throw it and stick my knee between her ribs and hip the way I've seen the shearers hold the sheep they're shearing. The sheep struggles but I have her pinned. Grabbing her under the chin, I hold the back of her neck against my shin so her throat is exposed.

Drawing my hunting knife from its sheath on my right hip, I hold it firmly. I know to kill her by bleeding her out; I need to cut the jugulars which are at the sides. Slashing the trachea and oesophagus will only injure her. Knowing this, I slash around in a wide arc. As her heart is still beating, blood sprays two metres in the air. I expected a lot of blood, but not for it to come out the way it did. I cop it across the side of the face. When I'm sure she's dead, I make my way over to a nearby tap, where I wash the worst of the blood off. Stephen kills his with more finesse and we start dressing them out. Dale stands there and watches us. In time, he gives us a hand, but six is no small number and it takes us several hours.

That evening and the next day, I get into my schoolwork and manage to do two days' worth. At three, Dale returns. We climb into a tiny Suzuki four-wheel drive and go with him across the farm to a paddock. Dale is towing a set of portable yards, so obviously they need to be set up, but he doesn't explain what he wants us to do.

I soon discover that I'm more of a hindrance than a help. Stephen fares a little better but he's still yelled at incessantly. When the yards are up, Dale rounds up a mob of ewes and lambs and puts them in the yards. We're taken back to the shearer's quarters and Dale tells us to be ready tomorrow at seven.

'Will we be coming back for lunch?' asks Stephen.

'No, we'll be there until we finish the mob, hopefully before six.'

That means we'll be needing a cut lunch. We only have three loaves of bread. Enough for this week, but it's not going to last us three weeks. As neither of us has a driver's licence, we can't drive the Kombi to Gladstone for more. We'll have to find a way to order more, else we'll have to make it. Stephen has foreseen the same issue and is now baking a slice so we won't need as many sandwiches.

We get up at six and we're ready and waiting by seven. Dale drives us out to the yards. Howard has already arrived and he has two other men with him along with his daughter Louise.

'This is Bruce and Peter,' says Dale by way of introduction. 'Dion, you can help Bruce pick up, and Stephen can cut tails. Peter's going to help Howard.'

Picking up is straight forward. It involves picking up a lamb and placing it in one of four cradles that are mounted at table height on a stand. Once in the cradle, the lamb is locked in in such a way that its backside is facing the sky and they can't move. Dale steps up with a set of shears. The first lamb is a ram and he snips the top clean off the scrotum and pulls out the testicles. Having done so, he removes two chunks of skin from either side of the anus.

'Why are we cutting chunks out of them?' I ask.

'It's called mulesing,' replies Dale, moving onto the next lamb. 'Wool won't grow on the scar tissue, which reduces the likelihood of flystrike.'

It's barbaric as far as I'm concerned but I keep my opinions to myself. Stephen steps up, grabs the tail of the first lamb and, with one swift cut, slices the tail clean off. He's squirted with blood but ignores it. Having cut off the tail, he uses a paintbrush to smear an iodine solution on the lamb's wounds.

In no time at all, I'm into a rhythm. Dump a lamb out, put a lamb in. Leapfrog a cradle, which Bruce has just serviced, and repeat. Behind me, Howard and Peter have the ewes in a race.

'What's happening with the ewes?' I ask.

'We're checking to see whether they have milk. If they're dry we notch an ear,' says Howard.

Louise suddenly spray-paints DD on one of the ewe's backs. 'That one was dry two years running, so she's done.'

By done, Louise means the ewe is headed for the killing yards to be slaughtered as mutton.

The next lamb I grab is unusually large. I shove him into the cradle, but despite repeated efforts to lock it, it keeps springing open.

'Hurry up!' yells Dale.

I'm holding up the production line, so I leave the lamb as is and move on.

Dale suddenly lets out a yowl of pain. 'You useless f—. Blind Freddie could see that lamb wasn't locked in!'

He's cut the tip off his left thumb and blood is going everywhere. Stephen has gone for the first aid kit and everyone has stopped working.

'The cradle wouldn't lock,' I reply.

'Well, why didn't you stop there and hold it closed!' he shouts.

'Because you told me to move on.'

He glares at me angrily.

'Dion's got a point. You did say that,' says Howard, coming over. 'You should have explained about big lambs and you should have been able to tell it was a big lamb.'

'I'm sorry,' I say.

'Useless c—!' says Dale. 'I shouldn't have to explain things to you.'

I'm suddenly angry. 'I'm doing the best I can. I'm only twelve.'

Dale's mouth drops open and he just stares. 'I'd taken you for sixteen.'

'I've only just turned fifteen,' says Stephen.

'I'd taken you for eighteen.'

Dale's finger looks painful, but once it's taped up, we resume. He's still cranky, but I can sense a shift in his attitude. The next time I ask a question, he provides the answer in great detail.

At morning tea, we wash our faces and hands from a drum of water, using a piece of soap that's been brought along. Stephen pours tea from a Thermos he's borrowed from the shearer's quarters before breaking out his slice.

'Where'd you get that?' asks Bruce, rubbing his belly.

'Baked it last night.'

'Baked?' The way he says the word it's as if baking is some secret knowledge that is unobtainable.

Stephen offers the slice around, which seems to ease the tension from earlier.

The break is only fifteen minutes. Before we can start again, we have to count and bag the lamb tails and rake up and bag the cut off skin. While Dale and I are doing this, the others back up the yards. When we start back, I slice tails while Stephen picks up.

It's getting on towards five when we finally finish the mob. By the time we've brought the new mob in, it's five-thirty and it's almost six when we arrive back at the shearers' quarters.

'When are you planning to cut up those sheep?' asks Stephen.

Dale swears. 'Forgot about them. We'd best do them tonight. I'll come back about seven-thirty.'

We've already made a start by the time Dale arrives. We're used to chopping up with knifes, meat saw and cleaver. Dale, however, starts the bandsaw and makes short work of it. I bag and label the meat and we're done inside an hour.

For the next seven days, we work through wind, rain and sun, often all in the same day. We're tired and cranky and our clothes are putrid. The evening of the seventh day a serious storm rolls in and Dale tells us there'll be no work tomorrow.

I try to sleep in the next morning but I can't, as my body clock is set for early. Instead, I commandeer an old washing machine, dump my clothes into it and set it going. After breakfast, I know I should get on with school but I seriously can't be bothered. The storm has cleared, so I peg my washing out and go exploring. There's nothing much to see, just sheds with machinery in them. I wish Howard had brought our motorbikes over. Then we could have gone for a ride, maybe even found a beach.

As I walk past the workshop, I discover a man inside wrestling with a tractor tyre that's larger than him. He spots me and I hurry over.

'You one of the Clarke Island boys?' he asks in a friendly manner.

'Yeah, I'm Dion.'

He goes to offer a greasy hand but changes his mind. 'I'm Paul.' He has the wheel suspended on an overhead crane. He repositions it so it's lying flat. 'How you getting on with Dale?'

I shrug.

'He's a prick. Him and I don't see eye to eye.' He unchains the wheel and rolls a new tyre down ready to fit. 'No sheep work today?'

'Nah, Dale wasn't sure how long the storm was going to last.'

Paul nods. 'I could use a hand if you've got the time.'

Dale could turn up at any time and tell us we're starting again. Then again, I might sit around all day and be bored.

'Yeah, no worries. You'll have to explain things, though.'

Paul looks taken back. 'Hasn't that prick been showing you what to do?'

I suppress a wince and don't answer him. Paul gets that I don't want to talk about Dale and drops it. I help him change the tractor wheels and after lunch we do some repairs to other machinery. Like my father, I prefer mechanical work to stock work.

Howard pulls up and he's surprised to see me in the workshop. He speaks to Paul but I don't eavesdrop; I just continue with my work.

That evening I don't know whether to add today's hours to my time sheet. Howard didn't ask me to help Paul and I could have refused. I ask Stephen but he just shrugs. I decide not to.

The lamb marking continues the next day. For the next two weeks when I'm not lamb marking, I'm in the workshop with Paul. If he's not there, I help the builder, Joel.

On the twenty-second day since arriving, I dump the last lamb out of the cradle. We pack up the yards and head back. That evening, Dale dumps his blood-soaked lamb marking clothes in a cut-in-half diesel drum and invites us to do the same. He pours diesel on the clothes and sets them ablaze. It's a ceremonial burning that officially marks the end.

The next morning dawns fine. Howard hands us both an envelope with a cheque in it before flying us back. I'm exhausted but it was worth it. Not for the cheque, which is smaller than anticipated, but for the experience.

'So what did you learn?' asks Howard.

'I'd do it again,' I reply carefully.

'But?'

'But I think I'd prefer to get an apprenticeship as a mechanic or builder.'

Howard nods. 'You wouldn't consider university?'

My eyes widen. I don't know anyone from my extended family who's been to uni. 'That'd be beyond me.'

He leans closer. 'Don't sell yourself short. You've got an inquisitive mind and you're not frightened of hard work. Think about it.'

I'll need to. I also know it's time to go to a proper school. I'll miss the island, but the adventure was never meant to be forever. It's time to consider the future.

Swan Island

Stephen and I have barely gotten back from Cape Portland when the phone rings. Dad gets up to answer it.

'Evan's been talking to Howard. He wants to know whether you'd both be interested in going over to Swan Island for a few days,' says Dad.

'I take it he needs a hand,' replies Stephen.

'Yeah, they have a wind generator. He needs to lower it so he can do the annual service. It's nothing technical, he just can't manage it on his own.'

'How long are they going to be away this time?' asks Mum.

Dad waves off her concern. 'It'll just be for two nights.' He smiles, obviously proud that his boys now have a reputation as hard-working responsible lads.

'It would be a one-off opportunity to see another island,' says Stephen.

'I know that,' replies Mum, 'but just don't forget you have three weeks' schoolwork to catch up.'

Stephen wrinkles his nose. I know he has no intention of playing catch up.

'Will Evan come and get us in his Cessna?' I ask.

Dad shakes his head. 'No, Howard is bringing Douglas over for two nights next weekend. Evan has arranged for Howard to drop you on Swan Island as he flies back and then he'll bring you back when he comes back for Douglas.'

'Is Douglas aware of this?' asks Mum.

'No idea, but if he's got issues with the arrangement he can take it up with Evan and Howard.'

A week later, when Howard arrives with Douglas and another man I've not seen before, he doesn't appear to have any concerns about the arrangements. We climb in and Howard takes off. When we reach Swan Island, Howard flies low over the settlement, before heading out to sea.

'Not much of an airstrip,' I say.

Howard grins, banks around in an arc and lines up his plane. Rather than dropping at an angle like normal, he flies in low, just a few metres above the sea. The moment his plane is over the rabbit-proof fence around the perimeter of the airstrip, Howard sits the plane down and hits the brakes hard. The plane pulls up at the other end of the short five-hundred-metre airstrip just in front of the fence.

My face splits into a grin.

'There's only a few pilots who'll land here,' says Howard.

Obviously, Munro Airlines couldn't land their twin-engine aircraft here. Clarke Island's main runway is a kilometre in length and only just long enough. But what Howard is saying is that even the charter planes won't land here unless they have the right pilot.

Howard spins the plane around and powers down. On such a short airstrip, there's no point taxiing. Evan is waiting in an old yellow Land Rover. We put our things in the back and watch as Howard takes off. The plane's wheels, which don't retract, only just miss the fence.

We climb in and Evan drives along the side of the airstrip. His own plane is tucked into a cleared area in the scrub. There's no hangar, but the plane has a pull-on cover to protect it from the worst of the salt air.

'I'll give you the grand tour,' says Evan.

He drives along a sandy track that has been slashed and onto a beach on the northern side. It's a nice beach with white sand and aqua water, but it's quite exposed to the Roaring Forties that rush through Bass Strait on their way to New Zealand. At the end of the beach, Evan exits and takes a track which leads to the eastern end of the island. Here there's a view across to Cape Portland and Little Musselrow Bay. On the southern side is another nice beach, but again it's not very sheltered. As we head back, we pass a muttonbird rookery.

'Do you have many people come over for the mutton bird season?' I ask.

'None. Swan Island's rookery is permanently closed. The island's part of the Waterhouse Island group which, along with a section of Cape Portland, form a bird sanctuary.'

I nod. I've heard Howard talk about the reserve on Cape Portland, but Stephen and I had no way to get over and see it while we were working there.

The Land Rover scoots along and I can't help but be jealous that our island doesn't have a four-wheel drive. We emerge through the low scrub into a cleared area. There are three houses and the lighthouse. One of the houses looks very grand, the other looks similar to our house on Clarke Island and the third is in dire need of some maintenance.

Glancing around, I see no wharf, just the foundations where one once was.

'The wharf and boatshed burned down in 1982,' says Evan.

'How do you get bulk supplies,' I ask.

'By barge,' he replies.

I wince as I remember the debacle we had the day the barge arrived.

'Do you have anything to do with the lighthouse?' asks Stephen.

'No, it's fully automated. We do, however, get paid for the four weather reports we do each day.'

Evan pulls up beside the second-best house. 'We also rent out the best house as a holiday cottage. We offer package deals where I fly them on and off.'

The advantages of being a pilot with a plane when few pilots will land here.

We get out and notice rabbits scurrying every which way.

'Yes, they're a considerable problem. I have to walk the boundary fence of the airstrip each day to make sure there are no breaches.'

I know that if they weren't fenced out, they'd quickly destroy the airstrip. Thankfully, our island doesn't have many due to the feral cats.

We go inside and we're shown to a room where we'll be sleeping.

After morning tea, Evan takes us out so we can work on the wind generator. It sits atop a long pole held in place by guide wires. Attached to it is also a length of rope.

'Does your tractor have a bucket?' asks Stephen.

'No,' replies Evan. 'The generator isn't heavy, it's just awkward.

As Evan slacks the guide wires, Stephen and I hold the rope. Once there's enough slack, we lower it gently to the ground.

'Is it 240 volts?' I ask.

'No, it's an American-made one and only 110 volts. We use an inverter to convert it to 240 volts,' says Evan.

'That sounds complex. How efficient is it?' I ask.

'The fridge and freezers are on timers, so they run about half the time and it'll power the lights. We have a diesel generator, but we try not to use it.'

'What about stove and hot water?'

'Gas,' he replies. 'Howard flies us over bottles, because they're too big for my plane. There's a coal stove, but it's too hard to get coal and there's not enough trees to cut firewood.'

Evan grabs some spanners. He unbolts the wind generator's blades and proceeds to open the casing. I can see now that he needs to replace the bearings for the shaft and regrease it.

'What do you do for water?' I ask.

'We make do with the rainwater we catch off the roofs.'

Back before the lighthouse became automated, this island supported three families. There had to have been a well or spring. Given time, I knew I could find it, but we were only here for two days, so I don't mention it.

'Do you run any stock or fowl?'

'No. We were thinking of getting some goats, but haven't got around to it.'

'We have milking goats. They're a lot of work, but they're worth it.'

He shakes his head. 'No, we don't want them for milking. We just thought they'd keep the weeds back which the rabbits won't eat.'

'Well, Dad would probably sell you some. We've got heaps.'

He nods thoughtfully. 'I'll ask him about them, then.'

Evan finishes the generator and we help stand it back up.

'What else do you need doing?' asks Stephen.

'There's plenty to do, but you boys should go exploring. I wouldn't want you to say you came here and didn't get to see the place.'

Stephen nods and we head off for a walk. Initially, we intend only to go as far as the rookery, but we end up walking the entire perimeter of the island which takes about four hours. This island is not unlike our own, but it's different in that it doesn't have the same style of rocks. The rocks here are squarish and black.

As we're approaching the settlement on our way back, I pause to take a look. Evan and his wife have made no attempt to live the semi-self-sufficient lifestyle that we're living. They have no animals, not even chooks or ducks. They have no garden and without water having one would be difficult. I wonder whether they even hunt or fish.

There's something else. They're not just managers like ourselves, they're the owners. That means they're not paid a salary and they're responsible for every expense. In that regard, we have it easy. Douglas has to pay the bills and I'm under no illusion about how considerable they are.

We get back just as Evan's starting a weather report and so we tag along. He notes cloud cover, checks to see if there has been any precipitation, checks wind speed, humidity, temperature and barometric pressure. All this he records on a clipboard. Back in his office, the data is transferred to a logbook and his record sheet is faxed to the Bureau of Meteorology in Hobart.

'Interesting that they kept the weather station,' I say.

'Yes, each lighthouse also has a weather station. Eventually they'll be automated too, but for now it keeps us in work.'

'You ever lose track of time and forget to do them?' asks Stephen.

Evan lifts his sleeve to reveal an expensive-looking digital watch. 'We set reminder alarms. We're both trained to do them, so if I'm off in the plane or across the island, Margo does them.'

Having to do them four times a day would be a tie down, but I could see how the income they provide would be necessary.

The next day, we help Evan to build a paling fence. Their backyard is very exposed to wind and he's hoping it will provide a little shelter. I explain how Mum planted creepers which eventually grew into living fences, but Evan doesn't appear to be much of a gardener. I don't think he'd be that interested even if he had water.

That evening, Stephen and I borrow Evan's .22 and go out and shoot a dozen rabbits, which we dress for meat. Evan takes four and we'll take the rest back with us. Howard arrives the next day and flies us home. I would like to have stayed longer, but it's good that we got to go.

Major Decision

Over the next weeks, I complete schoolwork as I never have before. Starting at eight instead of nine, I work until four instead of three. I also do an additional three hours in the evening. The pace is unsustainable, but it's just so I can catch up. Stephen, as I predicted, continues to amble along at his slow pace. He barely completes his lessons each day, so there's no hope that he'll catch up.

'Why are you so determined to get it done?' asks Mum. 'You hate school.'

'I hate this sort of school,' I reply, 'but I need to finish this year before school ends.'

'And after that?'

'Howard was right. I need to go to a proper school, beginning next year.'

Mum looks shocked.

'You don't approve?' I ask.

She glances away for a moment before returning her gaze to me. 'I knew this day would come, but now it has, I have reservations. You do a power of work around here, both you and your brother. Your father and I didn't realise how much until you were away at Cape Portland and again on Swan Island. You'll be missed.'

It's comforting to know I'm appreciated but it's not enough.

'Are you sick of this place?' asks Mum. 'I mean, you were born on the road and this is the longest you've ever lived in one place.'

'It's not that.' I look away. 'I don't want to end up like Maree.'

Maree had left Leverington and was now working at Cape Portland for Howard but she was still unsettled.

'Maree's different from you. She's made her own choices.'

'Sure, but farm work is hard for low pay. I don't mind that so much, but I know I'll never get ahead doing it. I know I'll never be in Douglas and Howard's class, but I want a decent education and that's not possible here. That's what Howard was trying to show us. It wasn't about lamb marking – he could have got older, more experienced people for the same price. It was about showing us what our future will become if we just let it unfold.'

Mum is close to tears but she holds them back.

'That man who came over with Douglas. He was a real estate agent, wasn't he?'

'Yes.'

'Which means the island's lease is going to be sold, isn't it?'

'Yes, but we might be able to stay on with the new leaseholders.'

I shake my head. 'You know that I'm slightly psychic. I have a bad feeling about it. I think our time is coming to an end.'

Mum stands up and paces. 'Don't say that. I don't want to leave.'

'I don't have a choice. I have to go. I know I'll regret it if I stay.'

Mum walks away, leaving me to get on with my studies.

A few days later, Dad calls me to come and sit at the kitchen table with Mum so we can discuss what I've decided.

'So you have made the decision to go to a proper school?' he asks.

It's more of a statement than a question but I nod.

'I phoned the headmistress in Hobart. She's suggesting that we send you to Sheffield,' says Mum.

'Why Sheffield? I just assumed I'd go to Ulverstone and live with Nanna Doris.'

'Yes, that's an option, but Sheffield school has its own farm. Your teachers think you'd make the transition better if you go to school there.'

'But where would I stay?'

'We'd have to find somewhere for you to board,' says Mum.

'That'll be expensive,' I say.

Dad lights a smoke. 'We paid for Maree to go and she misbehaved. We'll pay for you to go, but we expect better behaviour.'

I feel insulted that my behaviour is even being questioned, but I remain silent.

'In any case, we'd still have to pay your board even if you lived with Nan. But the government will pay us an allowance because of where we live.'

Right, so some of the expenses would be covered.

'The thing is,' says Dad, 'I don't think you realise what you're getting yourself into. It'll be more structured, compulsory sports, lots of other kids…'

I haven't forgotten any of that, especially not the bullying, but I'm older now. I survived Leverington. I survived Cape Portland. I'll survive returning to a proper school. 'I'll manage.'

Dad tapped the ash off his cigarette. 'Will you?'

I nod. 'I will.'

'Your teachers have arranged for you to spend a day at Sheffield before school ends this year,' says Mum. 'Your dad will take you off and drive you down and back again.'

I nod and head back to my desk.

Stephen looks at me and shakes his head. 'You'll be back within a month.'

No, I wouldn't. I'm tougher than you know. I'm tougher than all of you know.

Ironically, at the airstrip, Howard glances at me with a deep look of approval in his eyes. During the flight he reassures me that he'll fly me back for each of the school holidays. I'm still not sure what he sees in me, but I know I have to succeed.

We arrive in Sheffield that afternoon. Thirty minutes from Devonport, the town is located under the lee of Mount Roland. The town itself is small, but the school services a big area, with many of the students being from farms.

We arrive early before school starts the next morning and take a seat in the principal's office.

'I've put you in with a small class of grade sevens. All the teachers have been briefed and I've found someone who will show you the ropes today.'

On cue, a blond-haired boy appears at the door with his school bag slung over his shoulder.

'And here he is now.'

The boy introduces himself as Zeke. After a brief stop at his locker, he takes me to homegroup.

'So, we have a new student with us today,' says the teacher when everyone is seated. 'Dion is from Clarke Island and he's never been to a proper school before.'

Not true, I have, but it was five years ago.

Fifteen sets of eyes turn to me as if I'm a circus exhibit.

'I want you all to make him feel welcome.'

I feel my cheeks turn scarlet. I'd have preferred it if she hadn't done that. Thankfully, she doesn't ask me to give an impromptu speech, but instead got on with other announcements. The first class is social science, which is my best subject. I'm fascinated at how the teacher actually explains things rather than just expecting people to make sense of the lesson from poorly written notes printed in a workbook. School might actually be fun.

At recess, I follow Zeke as he leads me to a courtyard where people are playing handball. I don't know how to play, so I just hang about. Seeing me on my own, a girl walks over. Her tunic is ridiculously short, there's not a centimetre of her face that isn't caked in make-up and she's chewing a piece of bright pink bubblegum.

'So, island boy, eh.' She blows a bubble and it snaps loudly on her face.

There's four other girls with her, which means she's the leader of a clique. Aside from Maree and Howard's daughter Louise, whom I never had a conversation with, I've never spoken to a teenage girl before. Still, I know her *modus operandi* is to make a fool of me. I also know that regardless of what I say she's likely to succeed. Afterwards, I'll have to suck it up. I brace myself. This isn't going to be pleasant.

'Looks like a dork to me,' says one of the others.

'Like a tall streak of pelican shit,' adds a third girl.

They laugh hysterically, which is of course mandatory if you want to be in the clique.

Bubblegum steps closer. 'I filched a ciggie off my dad this morning. You want to share it with me?'

The laughter is now conspiratorial giggling.

They can laugh all they want, but I'm not going to be busted for smoking on my trial day or any other day. 'I don't smoke.'

'What, you've never had a smoke before?' asks Bubblegum. She goes to take my hand, but I shake it off.

'I bet he's never been kissed before either,' sniggers a blonde girl.

That is true, but it isn't my fault. Who the hell was I going to kiss? Elsa, the dog?

'Come on, you can tick off two things today.'

She tries again to take my hand, but again I shake it off.

'What are you, frigid?'

I blink because I have no idea what the word means.

'Perhaps he's gay.'

'Or prefers sheep.'

They all laugh again.

Okay, now they're getting nasty. Time to fight back.

'How much does your dad spend on Spakfilla for your ugly face?'

They stop laughing but some nearby boys start.

'F— you,' says Bubblegum. In a huff, she marches her gang away.

The bell rings and Zeke comes over. 'What'd you say to Clare?' he asks.

'I just suggested she uses too much make-up. That was after she got nasty.'

'How so?'

I brief him and he gets a strange look on his face.

'I doubt she'd have lit a cigarette at school, but she might have given you a kiss.'

'You're a braver boy than me if you'd kiss her,' I say.

'Beggars can't be choosers, mate, and we all have to start low. Plus, a word of advice. Hell hath no fury like a girl scorned and Clare's a nasty piece of work. She'll get you for that. Best to just ignore her and her snooty friends.'

Fair enough, but why so sensitive? The women who work on farms cop more crap than that day in, day out. These girls are different, but I have no frame of reference for how much.

I manage to get through lunch without Clare hassling me, but I do notice she's with her gang and they keep casting a look of daggers my way. I wonder if I should just go and apologise, but I don't have the courage. Besides, it's five against one and they have better social skills than I'll ever have. I'll end up a laughing stock again.

The day comes to an end. I survive, but I've made an enemy who I'll have to face next year. Ah well, it could have been worse. Dad peppers me with questions the entire drive back to the Cape but I provide only short answers. There's nothing to discuss. What happens at school stays at school.

Kangaroo Bay

After Christmas, Mack returns as promised to do some fishing and shooting. Maree is also on leave from Cape Portland and is home for a few weeks. The weather is fine and calm so Dad, Mack and I take the dinghy out.

Dad has made up a glass-bottom box and we're floating just out from the rocks between the wharf and the beach. Dad's eyes are wide and he's pointing to something below us which only he can see.

'What you looking at?' asks Mack.

'Crayfish. Flipping crayfish, he's right there!'

When I finally get a look through the glass-bottom box, I can see him for myself. He's in about three to four metres of water and there's no way I'm diving to get the spiky critter. Dad can talk Maree or Stephen into it, but I'm not doing it.

When the boat has drifted over sand, Mack switches from bait to a silver wobbler. I watch with great interest as he drops the wobbler to the sand before lifting it off hurriedly. On about the sixth lift, a fish grabs it and Mack hauls in a flathead. We've never caught any flathead before; we normally just go after the parrotfish.

We both switch to wobblers and we catch several more.

'You do much floundering?' asks Mack.

'I bought a flounder light years ago, but I've never used it,' replies Dad.

Mack glances at his watch and then the beach. 'Tide'll be full tonight and if the weather stays like this, it'll be perfect for it.'

We head back. Stephen's been wanting to go floundering for years. He's even built some spears from tea tree poles whittled smooth and fitted with high-tensile wire with barbs cut in.

That evening, we go floundering for the first time. Mack holds the light while Stephen has the spear. He spears one flounder, a cocky salmon and a flathead.

'The beach has got too much slant on it,' says Mack. 'The best place to flounder is on tidal flats where the water's shallow a long way out.'

'Like Kangaroo Bay,' I say. 'You can wade out a hundred metres or more and the water's still only waist-deep and warm as.'

Mack cocks his head. 'Where's this?'

'North-east corner of the island. It's a bitch to get to because you have to cross the reserve. The original track is still there, though. We found it a couple of years ago. Mum found a sign and everything.'

Mack glances around to gauge opinions. 'Is he taking the piss?'

'No, I found the sign,' says Mum. 'It was a relic of the days when the nudist colony was here.'

'I meant about the beach.'

'It's there all right,' says Stephen, 'but I don't fancy driving back in the dark across the reserve. One wrong turn and you'd end up in a lagoon.'

'Don't you have tents?' asks Mack.

'Two of them,' I reply, 'but we've never used them.'

'Then we'll head over there tomorrow and camp the night,' says Mack.

'Camp?' says Dad as if the word is anathema. Dad's idea of roughing it is to watch black and white television.

'Right, well, that's settled,' I say. 'Camping trip to Kangaroo Bay, leaving tomorrow.'

Mum smirks at how we've roped Dad into a camping trip without him having a say in the matter.

The next day, I half expect Dad to tell Mack he can take us his blooming self, but instead I find him pouring boiling water on the gas bottle of his little barbecue. The metal around the gas stays colder than the empty space, showing the level. Mum can't go because someone has to stay behind and milk the goats, but she's happily organising food along with bedding and the two barely used tents.

'I was thinking,' says Dad once he's wrestled his barbecue into a sack. 'We ought to take the dinghy.'

The dinghy isn't like these modern ones cast out of aluminium. It's tin plate with wooden seats and very heavy. Still, there's enough of us to lift it on.

'I'll toss some old tyres onto the back of the truck trailer and we'll tie her on. I just don't like the idea of walking around Kangaroo Bay in the dark. The Channel is a shark breeding ground after all.'

I'd heard that since we'd arrived on the Island, but I'd never actually seen a shark. Still, I'd seen plenty of stingrays and they were just as deadly. 'Sure, okay.'

A couple of hours later, we're all loaded up and heading for Kangaroo Bay. It's only the third time I've been on the reserve and each time it feels forbidden. That's why we never go onto it. Still, we're not looking to do any harm. Just spear a few flounder.

Dad finds the old track and the 8430 powers across to Kangaroo Bay in an hour. The bay itself isn't much of a beach. The sand is coarser than everywhere else and up the western end is a bed of native mussels. Still, it's the best swimming on the Island because the water's shallow and warm. So productive that Douglas had looked into aquaculture, but nothing ever came of it.

'Oh, yes,' says Mack as if he's just received a seductive smile from a pixie. Clearly, he's happy to be here.

My siblings and I pitch the tents and fuss with bedding, while Dad sets up his barbecue and puts water on to boil for a cup of tea.

After a barbecue lunch, I head off along the beach in an easterly direction with Stephen. At the far end is Seal Point, which juts out. On this piece of land, it's the closest I can get to Cape Barren Island, while still being on our island. It looks to be only about a kilometre across, although it's probably further. Close enough to swim or to slip across in the dinghy.

'You want to go over there, don't you?' says Stephen.

I do. Something is calling me to go across and climb in the

rock-faced mountains. Something from an ancient time long past. I can't explain it. 'Can't get across even if we wanted to. This is where the Channel is narrowest, which means there'll be strong currents.'

Stephen nods and we head back. Having lifted the dinghy off the trailer, the five of us squeeze in and we motor along to the far end, where we drift fish for a while until it gets dark. Once it is, Mack and Stephen get in the front, Maree and I get in the back and Dad sits in the middle and takes the oars.

Dad rows at the gentlest pace, Mack shines the light and Stephen holds the spear. There's fish everywhere, but they're either out of range of the spear or slipping under the boat before Stephen can take a shot at them. After a few missed attempts' Stephen gets his eye in. Now he's getting flounder, flathead, cocky salmon and squid.

'How we going?' asks Dad.

'We've probably got enough,' replies Mack. 'No point being greedy.'

Dad wipes his brow on his sleeve. 'I meant how far along the beach are we?'

Mack lifts the light and shines it on the beach. We can see that the 8430's about a hundred metres along. Dad lifts the oars and proceeds to roll a cigarette.

With my superb night vision, I can see that something's breaking the water. 'There's something big over there.'

'Big stingray,' says Mack, shining the light in completely the opposite direction to where I'm looking.

'No, to the starboard side. It's coming this way.'

Mack redirects the light and suddenly recoils from shock, causing the boat to rock violently.

'Steady on,' says Dad.

'We're only in about fifteen hundred centimetres of water, but the dry sand of the beach is about ten metres away. If we fall out, there's no danger of drowning, but we'll be exposed to whatever's in the water.

'Shark,' I say as the exposed fin becomes visible. I can't see what sort it is, but it's about two metres long.

'Should have brought a rifle,' says Dad. 'We could have got some flake.'

I'm not sure if he's taking the piss. The shark is just curious. It has a quick look, decides we're boring and heads back out into deeper water. Still, we're keen to head off in case he decides to come back with larger mates.

Alongside camp, we haul the dinghy high up onto the beach, where she won't float away. While Dad is boiling water for a cup of tea, Stephen lights the gaslight and takes it down to the water's edge. Mack and I go with him and we clean the fish before placing them into the cooler.

'I've never seen a beach quite like this one,' says Mack.

I nod. 'I doubt many people fish here. It's too shallow for the fishing boats. A few might anchor further out and motor in in a dinghy, but I've heard the fishermen complain about shifting sandbars.'

Mack nods. 'I'd love to bring my eighteen-foot runabout over. I'd fish and camp all along here.' He wrinkles his nose. 'Be a bit risky crossing Bank Strait, though, and then there's the risk of not being able to get her back.'

I nod.

The next morning, we check out the mussels. There's plenty of them but they're small and difficult to dislodge from the rocks without damaging them. We decide not to bother with them and go beach-combing instead.

Having had a successful trip, we pack up after lunch and head home. Already we're making plans to come back.

Sheffield

All too soon, the school holidays come to an end and it's time for me to pack my bags for Sheffield. Mum intends to get me two uniforms plus some additional new clothes for the weekends, so I don't have that much to pack. I decide at the last moment I'll take my tape player and a dozen tapes, which have been recorded from Maree's pop music records.

As Mum and Dad both want to see me settled in school at Sheffield, Howard agrees to bring Maree over to stay with Stephen for a week while Mum and Dad take me off the Island. I'm a little nervous about starting school, but that's not my biggest concern. They still haven't found anywhere definite for me to stay, although we have been told there's a man setting up a hostel for students like me who'll be living away from home. The man's name is Hans and he lives on the edge of Sheffield in a two-storey concrete house with a flat roof. It looks like a squat castle which the lord is too poor to renovate. Hans greets us at the door and we're led into a rustic kitchen, where we're invited to sit at the table. En route, I pass a picture of Jesus hanging from his cross, with blood dribbling down his side. Aside from that, the place is Spartan and has an eerie feel about it.

'You're a practising Christian?' asks Mum.

'Gospel Hall,' replies Hans, lighting a cigarette. 'We read the Bible three nights a week. Dion will be more than welcome to join in once he's done his homework.'

Dad's face darkens. Except when Nan and Pop stay, religion is never spoken of.

'What will the board be?' asks Mum.

'Seventy dollars a week full board, but Dion will be expected to do chores, including his own washing and ironing.'

I'm not fussed about that, but I don't like the look of this bloke nor his house. However, I remain silent.

Hans slides his chair back and stands up. 'I'll show you the room.' He leads us upstairs to one giant room. There's no furniture, not even beds, just old mattresses on the floor.

Mum grimaces. 'Are you going to build some walls and get beds and new mattresses?'

Hans looks affronted. 'No, living austere is the way to Christ.'

Dad's seen enough. He's already heading back down the stairs. We follow him as he heads right on out the front door.

'Not what we're looking for,' says Mum to Hans before retreating to the Kombi.

Dad motors down the street and round to the caravan park where we stayed last time.

'You're from that island,' says the caravan manageress. 'Weren't you checking out the school last time?'

'Yes,' says Dad. 'Dion will be attending the school this year. He was supposed to live with Hans…'

The woman is shaking her head violently. 'No, he can't stay there. I have it on good authority that he interferes. Police know, but can't prove it.'

'Oh,' says Mum looking white.

'Do you know anyone else who might be looking for a boarder?' asks Dad.

The woman squints as she hands Dad a set of keys to one of the caravans. 'I'll phone around and let you know.'

Inside our rented caravan, we sit sombrely around the tiny table sipping tea. Today's Saturday and I'm supposed to start school on Monday. Mum and Dad had been assured by someone at the school that I'd be able to stay at Hans's place, so they hadn't bothered to investigate anywhere else. In other words, there's no back-up plan.

Unless the caravan park manageress can find me somewhere to stay, I won't be able to attend school in Sheffield.

'I could always go and live with Nana Doris in Ulverstone,' I say.

'But Ulverstone's school has no farm. Sheffield's does, that's why you're enrolling here.'

That's true but I have the distinct impression I won't be spending much time at the school farm anyway, so it probably doesn't matter.

There's a knock at the door and Mum opens it to reveal the caravan park manageress.

'You need to go to this address and talk to a woman named Diane. She's the one who's supposed to be handling the accommodation for the out-of-town kids.'

Mum thanks the lady and we all pile into the Kombi and drive to the address. I wait in the car, but I see a short plump woman open the door. Out of my earshot, Mum and Dad talk to her in low voices. Ten minutes later, I'm summoned.

'This is Diane and she's agreed to board you for the first term or so.'

I'm led inside. The house is a compact three-bedroom house which is tidy.

'I have three boys, but they're never around of a weekend,' says Diane.

'How old are they?' asks Mum.

'Sixteen, eighteen and twenty. The youngest finished high school last year and he'll be catching the bus to Devonport to attend year eleven at Don College this year. The middle one has a green-keeping apprenticeship in Burnie and only comes home of a weekend. The eldest has a job at the local sawmill.'

Mum looks concerned but Dad doesn't. I'm shown the bedroom where I'll be sleeping. The room has two single beds, so obviously I'll be sharing the room with one of Diane's boys.

'How much will the board be?' asks Mum.

'Sixty dollars a week full board. I'll charge him only half price for Saturday and Sunday as we're all away at football during the day and he'll have to fend for himself.'

That's not an issue. I am, however, concerned about living in a house with three older boys. If they decide I'm imposing and making work for their mum, or they don't like me for other reasons, then it'll be a living hell.

We step out onto the front lawn for a huddle.

'What do you think?' whispers Dad.

'Can I have some time to think about it?' I ask.

Dad narrows his eyes. 'What's to think about?'

'Just overnight,' says Mum. 'You'll need to have an answer by morning.'

I understand we're short of time, but that's hardly my fault. I'm not the one who left it all to the last minute. They had all summer to sort this out. We return to the caravan park and the lady walks back over to enquire how we got on. She's also decided that the caravan's too small for three and has brought the keys to the one next door for us to use at no extra charge. It's generous and I retreat from Dad, who keeps probing for an answer, so I can think things over.

I know this is a major three-way intersection in the road of life. I can return home defeated without even having had a go. I can go to Ulverstone and impose on Nana Doris, who's not expecting me and is thus not prepared. Or I can roll the dice. If things turn bad, the first two options will still be available, but I'll be seen as a failure. So, while I appear to have three choices, I really don't. I have to roll the dice, be strong and stick to my resolve of making it when no one thinks I can.

When Mum comes over to tell me dinner's ready, I follow her back to the other caravan.

'I've made a decision. I'll stay with Diane.'

Dad looks shocked rather than pleased. Then it occurs to me that he was expecting me to choose the first option of returning to the island. Knowing that, I'm even more determined.

I move in with Diane the next morning and Mum and Dad drive away. They aren't even going to hang around a single night to see how things pan out. I'm truly on my own and I've never felt so alone. But this is my choice and my decision and I can get through it.

Diane's boys tumble through the door around four. I try to sink further into my armchair in the hope they won't notice me, but it's silly. Of course they'll notice me: I'm the tallest in the room.

'This is Sam, Leo and Mouse,' says Diane.

I shake hands with every one and they slump onto the couch and remaining armchair while Diane returns to the kitchen.

'So, you're from where exactly?' asks Leo.

'Clarke Island,' I mumble.

'Where in the blazes is that?' asks Sam.

I explain where it is, that we're the only permanent residents, and the basics of what we're doing there.

They're not really interested, which is a good thing. It means they'll stop interrogating me in a bit.

Mouse glances towards the kitchen to check on his Mum's whereabouts before saying, 'So what do you do for gash?'

Coming from social isolation, I'm not sure what he means.

'Right, you three, that's enough of such filth,' says Diane storming into the room. 'Dion's only turning thirteen and I won't have you three leading him astray.'

'Thirteen,' exclaims Mouse. 'I'd taken him for at least sixteen.'

Diane gives them all the frost eye before leaving. The boys have decided it's boring here and they're heading back out again.

Sam turns to me before leaving. 'Two things. If you do get yourself a girlfriend, don't filch our condoms, and stay away from Katren. She's gorgeous, but trouble.'

I swallow, but nod.

The next morning, I put on my new uniform. Brown corduroy trousers and a yellow shirt. It's warm, so I put the green jumper into my new backpack. It already contains my new school stationery. Diane hands me a brown paper bag with a cut lunch in it, which I also add to my backpack, and we set off to walk to school.

Diane is a teacher's aide, but she also works part-time for the *Kentish Times*, which is the local paper. She assures me that I won't see her at school because her office is in the printery.

We arrive early and I'm told my homegroup will be in the library and I'll be given everything I need to know there, including a timetable of classes, so I head straight over. Having found a suitable book, I begin flicking through it.

Zeke comes hurrying in about ten minutes later. Before he's even said hello, he snatches the book off me and shoves it on a random shelf. 'That was so uncool. We're never seen reading the books, mate.'

A sinking feeling descends through my stomach. I'm mostly self-taught. If I can't read the books, how else am I going to learn?

Zeke slips away to talk to his mates and I'm again left alone. A short while later, Bubblegum Clare comes hurrying in. She's got another girl with her, but not one of the four from her gang.

'Katren thinks you're a hunk,' says Clare louder than she needs to before blowing a bubble and having it snap on her face.

The sickening feeling gets worse, but I chance a look at Katren. Everything in the room falls away. It's just me and her. She has long black hair and a dark complexion and is perfect from head to toe. She's tall, slim and wearing only her school tunic, and I can't even blink. Instead, I rest my eyes on her bare legs. There's something about her that takes my breath away. I don't believe in love at first sight, but I do believe in reincarnation. I've been with this girl in another life and we have a deep connection.

'Well, are you going to say hello or just gawk at her?' stammers Clare.

I want to talk, I really do, but not a single intelligible word will come to mind. My tongue feels thick in my mouth and I've broken into a sweat. I mumble something indiscernible.

Katren doesn't say anything either. She just stands there looking right back at me. She's wearing no make-up, earrings or other jewellery. She doesn't need those things. She's completely and utterly comfortable in her body. She's like no one I've ever seen before.

'Well,' says Clare.

I swallow again. I still can't talk to Katren, so I turn to Clare. 'She's way out of my league.'

Katren turns and slowly glides away, holding her head high like a proud princess. I watch her leave. I don't try to stop her and I know I'll regret not doing so for the rest of my life. I also remember Sam's warning to stay away from Katren because she's trouble. It's not her, but the fact that every boy at school will be prepared to fight for just the opportunity to talk to her. I can't risk being beaten up.

Clare harrumphs before storming away.

Zeke's across the room in a flash. 'Dude, what the frig?'

'I know. I panicked.'

He nods in understanding and takes a seat. Others are rolling in and Zeke introduces me to his mate Akki, a red-haired boy with freckles. We shake hands and I get the impression Zeke and Akki have been asked to look out for me. If that is the case, they don't seem to mind.

Homegroup drags on till recess and we're given our timetables, told who our teachers will be and assigned lockers. At recess, I go to my locker to examine what's in the brown paper bag Diane handed me.

'Oi!'

A big lump of a lad comes swaggering towards me. He's pissed about something he's blaming me for and I don't need to ask what grade he's in. Obviously, he's in grade ten.

'What the f— do you think you're doing?'

I'm trying to decide whether I want a banana or potato chips for morning tea, but I'm pretty sure that's not what he's asking. I turn to face him. He's pimply-faced, ugly and looks mean. I remain silent.

He comes right up to me and just smashes me in the face repeatedly. I'm too shocked to consider ducking or blocking. I don't even think to fight back. I just sway on my feet clutching a bloody nose. Unfortunately, he's not done and he wrestles me to the floor.

The initial shock passes. I forget about my nose, use all of my considerable strength to roll him over so I'm on top and draw my fist back to punch him. Before I can, someone grabs my arm. I try to shake it off, but the arm is strong and a moment later I'm being hauled off. I round on this new boy.

'Cool it, mate. I've got no beef with ya,' he says.

I glare at him, but I come to the conclusion he's speaking the truth. He was just breaking up the fight. But I'm angry.

'He hit me. He…'

'I know, I saw it all.'

I take a deep breath and I'm let go. Several teachers are hurrying towards us. The boy who attacked me is taken to the principal's office; I'm taken to the first aid room. I'm okay, but by the time I'm let go, I'm late for my next class. I take a seat on my own. Thankfully, the English class isn't taxing; the teacher is just outlining the work for the term to come.

At lunch, Humphrey, the boy who attacked me, is waiting for round two. It's all very familiar. I remember this from the last time I attended a proper school. I know that if I don't fight back, I'll be beaten up every day for the rest of my schooldays.

Humphrey comes charging at me, head down like an angry ram. I treat him exactly like an angry ram. I wait until he's committed to the charge before stepping off the line of attack at the last possible moment. Humphrey keeps going and I help him on his way by giving him a good shove. His head slams into an already cracked window that's awaiting replacement. It shatters into a million pieces and he keeps going through the window and outside.

I hadn't intended to throw him through a window, only shove him out of the way. Fearing he might be seriously hurt, I hurry over and peer through. He's sprawled over a hedge and not moving. Damn, is he seriously hurt? Has he cut his face or damaged his eyes? I look for a way to get to him, but the doors are a long way down the corridor. There's no time to use one of them, so I clamber through the now glassless window after him.

Humphrey, mistaking my intentions as hostile, now tries to flee. His feet become tangled in the hedge and he comes a gutser on the paved path. I suck air through my teeth. Damn, that had to hurt.

'Break it up!' yells the principal, who's running towards us.

I raise my hands and back away. Humphrey scrambles to his feet. He's grazed the skin off his nose, but otherwise he seems unhurt. There's not even any cuts from the glass, but there is a wet patch around his groin. He must have pissed himself.

We're frogmarched away and placed in separate offices. I'm left alone, only for ten minutes, but it seems like an hour. Finally, I'm taken into the principal's office and asked to sit on the opposite side of his desk.

'Right, I've heard Humphrey's version, now tell me yours.'

I give him a rundown of what happened.

'So why did you jump through the window after him?'

'I thought he might have been seriously hurt. I was trying to get to him fast.'

The principal blinks. 'But why would you go to his rescue rather than call for a teacher?'

I consider for a moment. 'I didn't really think about it, sir, I just reacted. Where I live on Clarke Island, there is no help. There's just who you're with at the time.'

He rubs his chin. 'So you didn't jump through to beat him some more.'

'No, sir.'

'He thinks you did.'

'Sir, I wasn't even wanting to fight with him. I was just defending myself.'

'By throwing him through a window?'

I explain the move I use with angry rams.

He places a hand over his mouth to cover a smile. 'Why was he fighting with you?'

I try to explain about Katren, but I make a mess of it. It doesn't matter, because he has the gist.

Sighing, he sits back in his chair. 'That poor girl. She's not even flirtatious, but everyone still fights over her. Doesn't even matter if she's interested in the boys or not.'

I remain silent.

'Look, Humphrey's on his second warning. One more incident and he'll be suspended or even expelled. I'd prefer not to get the police involved. What do you want to do?'

'Get on with school, but I don't want to be bullied. I came here to learn.'

The principal nods.

'What about the window, sir? Will we have to pay for it?'

'Ordinarily yes, but in this case the window was already damaged from a ball that went astray. So, no, you won't have to pay for it.'

I'm dismissed to finish out what's left of the lunch break. There are no more incidents for the rest of the day. When I get home, I'm chastised by Diane and Sam for fighting at school but, as I explain, I never started either fight. Still, they tell me that if there's any more trouble, I won't be able to stay here. It all seems terribly unfair.

Still angry at the injustice, I change into work clothes and hurry to the school farm dairy, which is about a kilometre up the road.

The school farm manager, Kerry, is in the dairy getting ready to milk. He scrutinises me with hard eyes. 'So you're that island boy.'

I feel a chill run down my spine. Kerry doesn't want me here; he's just humouring his boss, who is probably the school principal.

I nod.

He tosses me a vinyl apron. 'They said you know how to milk.'

I remain silent as I put it on. The dairy has a pit which can stand ten cows on a platform on each side. Hanging from a centre rail are ten sets of suction cups, water hoses and iodine sprayers. Kerry gets the first batch of cows in. I stand there waiting for instructions and a demonstration.

'They told me you knew how to milk.'

'There's been a misunderstanding. I can milk goats by hand. I've never been in a dairy before.'

He grunts angrily as he hoses off teats before shoving on suction cups, working fast and making his way down the row. Once he has, there's just enough time for him to hose off the other ten cows' teats before removing the cups from the finished cow and shoving them on the next one ready to go on the platform opposite. There's no time for error or slowness.

Pulling a lever allows the ten milked cows to file out, and ten new ones to file in. The cows know the drill, they don't need to be roused.

'Right, you'll do this lot.'

I feel a sense of panic. It will take me days if not weeks to build up the kind of speed and proficiency this man has obtained over years. Still, I have a go, and I make a mess of it. It's not as easy as it looks getting the cups on, and the cows take umbrage at my incompetence.

'You're slow as a wet week and you're all arms and legs.'

It's true. I still can't fully coordinate my large gangly body.

When the milking's done, Kerry says, 'There's not much point you coming back. You're not suitable for the weekend milking job.'

I'm taken aback. No one had said anything about this being a job trial. I thought it was just after-schoolwork experience. I walk back to Diane's house. I'm covered in cow shit and had all I can take for one day.

The next morning, Katren is waiting for me beside the locker bank. As I walk to school with Diane, I'm in quite early. Thus, Katren and I are alone in the corridor.

I glance at her and swallow. I want to talk to her but I really can't afford to.

'So sorry about what happened yesterday. I thought you were older than you are.'

'Yeah, I get that a lot,' I mumble.

She waits a moment to see if I'm going to talk to her. When I don't, she ambles away. I curse myself for being craven. I really do want to be friends or even something more, but I just can't afford any more trouble. It sucks, but that's the way life is. Life isn't fair and I know it.

At recess, I make myself go out and play football. I've never even touched a football before, let alone handballed or kicked one. All the boys have a good laugh but I take it on the chin. Zeke and Akki do their best to teach me. The handball is simple enough but I can't master the kick. I go out again at lunch. I don't improve much but I feel a shift in the boys' attitudes towards me. I'm prepared to have a go, and that matters.

The next morning, a red-haired girl takes a seat beside me in homegroup. There's plenty of spare seats, so I know she's not sitting where she is because she's forced to. The question is, what does she want?

'I'm Kay,' she says warmly, 'and I've decided you need my help.'

I sigh. 'How so?'

'At first, I thought you were nasty, then I thought you were stupid, but having asked around I now know that you're neither of those things. You're simply ignorant of social norms as a result of severe social isolation.'

'And I take it you eat alphabet cereal for breakfast while treating *Webster's Dictionary* as a bit of light reading.'

'And you try to hide your social inadequacies behind sharp remarks, but you really don't have the wit to pull it off.'

She has me, so I remain silent.

'I can help you if you'll let me.'

'Why do you want to? It will seriously damage your cool status.'

She glances at me sideways. 'Do I look like I'm cool enough to be in a clique?'

I remain silent.

'See, you're already learning, because that was a trick question.'

I roll my eyes. 'Answer my question.'

She nods thoughtfully. 'Let's just say there's something about you that piqued my interest in a non-romantic sense. It's the way you ask questions in class. It's led me to wonder if there isn't a brilliant mind behind the facade you present. Someone I could learn from if there was a mutually agreeable friendship.'

Howard had seen the same thing, but I still don't know what that thing is. After yesterday, especially at the dairy, I feel like a complete failure. Still, I don't have enough friends to shun this one. 'Do I have to sign a contract?'

She giggles. 'No.'

I nod. 'What can I ask you?'

'Anything, as long as it's not personal.'

'How do I get Clare to stop preying on me? I'm sure she had a hand in yesterday's fights.'

'Whoa, straight to the top. Clare saw you as an easy laugh, but she was mistaken. When she pushed you into a corner, not only did you come out swinging, but you hit with a killing blow. You seriously hurt her, when a wing clip would have sufficed.'

'Now she sees me as a challenge?'

'Not quite. Now she's hurting because she really wants to be friends, but at the same time she can't afford to risk her cool status. Thus, she thought she'd feel better by getting you into a fight, but given how that panned out, I suspect she's actually feeling like a complete bitch.'

'So what do I do?'

'You have to apologise, but not in public. You need to look for the opportune moment.'

My eyes bulge. 'I'm not going to apologise.'

'Then suffer your pride.'

I grit my teeth in frustration. Homegroup is starting so there's no further opportunity to talk to Kay.

That afternoon as I'm leaving the school to walk home, a summer squall blows in. Thinking it will pass quickly, I decide to hang about under the roof near the front door. The rain soon eases, as I predicted it might, when Clare comes stomping out. She's almost reached the concrete footpath when she slips on the wet pavers and comes a gutser.

I suck air through my teeth. That had to hurt. She'd been getting something out of her bag at the moment she'd slipped, and consequently her things have scattered everywhere. I'm hesitant to help, but there aren't many people about and she's not moving.

I mosey over and pick up some of her things. She's still on the ground and she's crying. Damn it. I put her things down, straddle her, reach down, put my hands under her armpits and lift her up. She's way lighter than I imagine her to be and I lift her clean off the ground. Her feet are swinging high and dry and I have to sit her down.

Rather than thank me, she shrieks at me to let her go, which I immediately do. Snatching up her bag, she hurries over to where a car has just pulled up and gets in slamming the door after herself. She's neglected to pick up some of her things, so I do it for her. Thankfully a woman, who I assume is her mother, gets out of the car and comes over. I hand the things over.

'Thanks for helping Clare.' She glances back at the car. 'So sorry about this. She's not angry at you, she's angry at her father and me for separating.'

I'm momentarily stunned. I've read somewhere that behind every bully is a person in pain.

I go home. No matter what I do, I can't stop reliving the scene. I tried to be nice and she'd just shrieked at me. Had I embarrassed her? Of course I had, but what else was I supposed to have done?

The next morning, I spy Clare at the lockers early. It's an anomaly because Clare prefers to get to school at the last moment. I'm thinking her mother has given her a lift in and that's why she's here early. She's not with her gang and this is, as Kay put it, the opportune moment.

I approach carefully. Clare glances left and right and realises she's alone with me. She looks scared.

I try to lean casually against the wall the way I've seen the cool boys do it. I can't pull it off, but I do it anyway. 'So sorry I embarrassed you yesterday. I know better than to approach. I know I'm not cool enough, I just didn't think.'

Clare is taken back. She goes to speak, but for the first time ever nothing smart comes out of her mouth.

'Sorry I called you ugly the first day we met. I was cruel and there was no excuse for it.'

She looks at me with deep suspicion in her eyes.

'Sucks about your parents. I'm living away from home so I know what it's like to not have them around.'

She closes her locker.

'I know we can't be friends, me being so uncool and all that, but I don't know, could we be civil?'

She still hasn't said anything. Ah well, it was worth a try. I turn to go, when Clare grabs my sleeve. I turn back and a moment later she's buried her face into my chest. Her arms have also found their way around my waist.

I feel panicked. Crap, what have I done? I awkwardly touch her back. Thankfully, she lets go.

She finally speaks. 'Thanks for getting me up yesterday.'

I can hear people approaching. Clare has as well, but quick as a flash she plants a kiss on my lips. It's over in half a second and she's hurrying away, leaving me panic-stricken. What the hell was that about?

At homegroup, I can't wait to quiz Kay.

'Nice of you to help Clare up yesterday, but you should have been gentler. The way you reefed her onto her feet it was as if you were pulling a stuck sheep out of a bog.'

I wince. I can see that now.

'Next time, just offer your hand and wait for the damsel in distress to take it or not.'

Makes sense. 'I spoke to her alone this morning.'

'And?'

'I apologised like you said to.'

'And?'

'She sort of thanked me for helping her up, but it was very awkward.'

'Of course it was. And?'

'And nothing.'

'So there was no contact or kiss?'

My cheeks flush red. 'Who told you about that?'

'You just did.'

Bitch. 'But what does it mean?'

'Describe the kiss.'

'Kay…'

'Just do it.'

I describe the entire scene.

Kay looks thoughtful. 'She's definitely forgiven you, so well done. Lips, as opposed to cheek, mean thank you and I like you.'

I feel panicked. 'But she won't expect more? I mean, I don't "like her" like her.'

'No, she won't expect more, but you can talk to her now when she's not with her gang.'

I breathe a sigh of relief.

Things get easier after that. I get on at school and don't bother with the farm outside of agriculture class. Zeke and Akki become my mates, along with Kay. It's incredibly nice to have a friend who's a girl, without her being my girlfriend. I realise I can talk to her about things I can't talk to Zeke and Akki about. Because we're only friends, we're able to dance together at the school social without feeling awkward.

When I finish dancing with Kay, Clare wants to dance with me and we're able to without me feeling stupid. I realise since the day we spoke at the lockers she's subtly changed. She's stopped wearing quite so much make-up, she's lost the bubblegum and her new tunics are the standard length rather than being shortened.

As the year comes to an end, I reflect fondly and realise I'm proud of myself. I won a thousand-dollar scholarship for best student living away from home. I've played a full season of football. I've always been the worst on ground, but I've never given up and I've turned up for every training session and played in every game. There has been no cricket team to play in, but I've learned to bat and bowl in a fashion and played in a few social games. My grades are good in every subject and while I know I'll always be socially awkward, I'm feeling much more confident around people.

On the last day of school, when I'm packing up my locker, Zeke and Akki are punching me on the arm as a way of saying goodbye. It's a boy thing.

I approach Kay. 'Help you with your things, miss?'

She grins, 'Nah, I've got it, mate.'

'I just want to say thanks for being a friend. I wouldn't have made it without you.'

She closes her locker and zips up her bag. 'I know you wouldn't have, but don't go getting all mushy on me, big boy.'

She jabs a finger into my stomach and I recoil as a reflex action. My face is now level with hers and she plants a kiss on my lips. It's quick, the same as Clare's was, and she walks away.

It's okay, I don't need to ask what that was about; she's trained me well. I look for Clare and see her further down the corridor. She gives me a girly hip and shoulder and I gently tug her ponytail. Apparently, I'm now cool enough to be seen with.

'See ya next year?' she says smiling genuinely.

'I hope so.' I put my arm around her shoulder and give her a gentle squeeze and she leans her head into my arm.

Next year, we'll both be a year older and I'll consider asking her out.

It's time to go and something occurs to me. I'm going back to the island for the summer, but I'll never be going back to live. I have two more years of high school and after that I'll go on to do year eleven and twelve at college or I'll get an apprenticeship. It feels good because I know the decision to roll the dice was the right one.

The Last Summer

I rub the ball back and forth on my trousers as I walk to the end of my run-up. Stephen is the batsman and he's notoriously difficult to get out. The fielders, who consist of my family plus Dale and his wife, are spread out. None of them is paying attention or taking this seriously.

Stephen knows how to guard his wickets and since it's backyard rules there's no LBW. There is, however, the fence behind him and if the ball hits the bat's edge before the fence, it's considered caught behind or in the slips. But Stephen's never been gotten out this way. There's another fielder. She's white, has four legs and has positioned herself at silly mid-on. She's hunched and ready. When I don't run in to bowl, she chances a quick glance my way. I give her a quick nod. She's my best hope, but can I bowl to her as my field?

I grip the ball the way I've been taught and come in off a ten-pace run. I bowl it as fast as I can, pitched on middle stump. The ball swings just enough to move it across to leg stump. Stephen is caught off guard by the pace and swing and clouts it to stop it thundering into his unpadded legs. He hits it in the air and it speeds towards Elsa like a shot out of a gun, but she still catches it in her mouth and doesn't drop it.

I let out a hoot and begin punching the air. Stephen blinks and realises he's been caught out. He can't believe it. One of Elsa's teeth has been knocked out and there's blood dribbling everywhere but she's barely noticed. She's still holding the ball around a massive grin.

'Take it easy. It wasn't that good a delivery, mate,' says Dale.

'Piss off! Merv Hughes couldn't have done better.'

Maree's trying to see whether Elsa's all right. 'Who's Merv Hughes?'

I'm not a Christian, but I make the sign of the cross at her.

'He's arguably Australia's best bowler,' says Dale.

I take the bat. Stephen takes the ball. He doesn't bowl, he pitches it in at tremendous speed. But the ball is short and I throw everything I have behind the bat. It sails back over his head and lands far enough away to be a six on every oval I've ever played on.

Dale shoos some flies away from his face. 'Six is out and enough for today. I think it's stubby time.'

There are nods. Stephen jumps on the motorbike and rides away to get the ball. I'm too young to drink beer, but there's a viable alternative. I'm just about to slide the padbolt back on the store room when there's a boom. Damn, the ginger beer bottles are exploding. I don safety goggles and use the lid off the steel garbage can as a shield. Chancing it, I manage to grab a glass litre-sized bottle of homemade ginger beer.

It's so fizzy that the only way to get the contents out without wearing it is to turn the bottle upside down in a clean bucket. It fizzes violently, but I catch most of the liquid in the bucket and pour it over ice.

'So I've come up with a new way to fish,' says Stephen, helping himself to a glass of ginger beer.

'How's that?' I ask.

'By spearing.'

I'm not quite following him, but the next morning we head down to the rocks at the other end of the beach. We don't normally fish here, but I trust Stephen knows what he's doing. We've brought only one handline with us and Stephen has his spear.

He threads a limpet onto the hook of my handline. 'So the idea is you toss the bait out and slowly bring it in.'

I don't understand but do what he asks. It's not until I see a dozen fish trailing the bait that I realise what the go is. Stephen thrusts. He's speared a cocky salmon. We move along a bit and this time when Stephen thrusts there's a mass of black ink. He lifts a squid from the water.

'Hooley-dooley,' I say.

'I know, right. Mum and I have been getting all sorts of fish since

Mack was here and I started spear fishing. Dad and I have even been out trawling for pike. They're not at all wormy.'

'What about flounder and flathead?'

'Nah, Mum and Dad won't go.'

'Want to go tonight?' I ask.

'Sure.'

It's not quite calm enough but we go anyway. However, the ripples on the water's surface reduce visibility to such a degree that we can't continue. We're disappointed and decide to head back.

'What about at the wharf beach?' I ask.

Stephen shrugs. 'Might as well take a look.'

We're halfway around when I see that there's now a dam where Pop and I found water all those years ago. There's also a pump shelter.

'What's going on here?'

'Oh, didn't we tell you? Dad used the Fergie's backhoe to dig out the spring and then moved the pump. We've finally got decent water.'

I feel vindicated. I knew it would work. Shame to have not dug a dam here from the outset, but better late than never.

'I'll tell you what else is new. ED sent over a dozen fruit trees along with some grape cuttings last April. They've all survived, so the island now has an orchard.'

It's a good thing but a shame we didn't establish one when we first arrived. If we had, some of the trees might be fruiting by now. Hindsight's a wonderful thing.

At the wharf beach, the water is much calmer. We wade in to our waists and I shine the light back and forth. There are no fish.

'I thought they'd come in here,' I say.

'They would,' says Stephen. 'There's something here that's stopping them.'

Remembering that shark from Kangaroo Bay, I tense and use my good night vision to search for a protruding fin. I don't see one. A shadow moves at the edge of the light. We watch it closely. It moves around to block our return to the beach.

'What is it?' I ask.

'Frigging great octopus,' replies Stephen.

I consider our options. If we can't get past it to the beach or rocks, we'll have to swim out deeper and head for the wharf. The problem is that the battery for the light can't be submerged and I really don't want to damage it. However, if that thing grabs us, it will pull us under and we'll be drowned.

Before we have time to consider our options, it darts towards us. Stephen picks his moment and thrusts his spear with all his might. There's a flailing of limbs which seem to come from everywhere. They've got large suckers on them. A tentacle tries to wrap around my leg but I somehow manage to dodge it. It's got Stephen, but he's strong and taken a wide legged stance while leaning heavily on his spear.

I reach for my hunting knife and consider moving in to stab when I realise the thrashing is subsiding. Stephen has driven his spear into the octopus's head and pushed it right through. Not only can it not get away, but it's rapidly dying.

I wade back to the beach and offload the battery and light, but angle it on the sand so we can still see. Wading back in, I grab a limb in each hand. Stephen removes his spear and I'm able to drag the octopus backwards to the water's edge. At this point, gravity kicks in fully and I can't move it any further.

Stephen tosses his spear up the beach and gives me a hand. Together we drag it clear of the high-water mark. I retrieve the light so we can have a decent look. It's mostly grey in colour, with each limb a metre and a half long.

'That could have gone either way,' says Stephen.

'Didn't know who it was messing with,' I reply, giving Stephen a high five.

It's too heavy to carry back to the house, so I run off to get the tractor. I'm jogging up on the dam when I see something big and yellow tucked into the scrub. Realising Dad has simply parked the Fergie in the nearest shelter close to where he was last using it, I jump on and start it.

At the wharf beach, I scoop the octopus up into the bucket before driving back to the house.

'What do you think you're doing bombing around on the tractor after dark without any lights?'

I've left the flounder light with Stephen and he's still bringing up the rear. 'The catch was too big to carry.'

Dad cocks his head, walks closer and finally spots the octopus in the bucket. 'How the blazes did you get that?'

'Bloody thing attacked us, but Stephen got him.'

Mum's comes out, takes one look at the octopus and says, 'Right, that's it. No more floundering.'

I grit my teeth. We should have left the stupid thing where we killed it.

Stephen arrives, takes his knife and slices off a limb. He peels the skin off the same way he would an eel. Inside, he slices off wafer-thin strips and fries it like abalone. It has a flavour similar to squid but it's a lot more chewy.

'What if we minced it up?' I say.

Dad's rolling his eyes, but Stephen retrieves the mincer from the pantry and we mince up the remainder of the limb. Stephen then makes octopus patties. They're nice but very rich.

We skin and dice up the rest of the meat and freeze it. Dale wants to take some back with him, which is fine. The rest we can use as bait or cook up at a later date.

It seems strange to me that it attacked. Even wild animals don't attack unless threatened or they consider you food. I go to the bookshelf and retrieve the *World Book Encyclopedia* O volume. Thumbing through it, I stop when I find octopus. I read the article, finally doing the research I was meant to do years ago.

'Says here that octopuses are territorial. That's why it attacked. It saw us as a threat moving into its patch.'

'Explains why we haven't been able to catch any fish off the wharf,' says Dad. 'Next time we go, we'll use the dinghy.'

I don't bother explaining that the article says that an octopus will come out of the water to take on a threat. If I do, Mum will never let us near the sea again.

The End of an Era

Now that we're older, Dad's given us permission to ride a bit further. Stephen and I have ridden to the edge of the tussock country and we're debating whether a bit further means we can continue to Spike Bay another kilometre and a half on.

Before we reach a conclusion, we hear the noise of a plane. It's ED in the Piper Comanche and he's coming in daringly low. We watch as he follows the contours of the land, making his way across the island.

'He's going to crash!' I exclaim.

In the tussock country there are massive house-sized boulders. ED is headed straight at two of them and there's no hope he'll fit between them. At the last moment, he tilts the plane sideways in order to fly through.

'Crazy old coot,' says Stephen restarting his bike. 'Come on, we'd best head back in case Dad needs us.'

By the time we get back, ED has landed and beaten us to the house. Through the kitchen window, I can see him and his passengers.

Mum meets us at the gate looking worried. 'Best not go in. The island's lease has been sold and your father's talking business.'

I grimace and we hang about until the new owner, his business partner and ED come out. We watch as they grab the David Brown and drive off.

Inside, Mum is doing some rough estimates on a sheet of paper with the aid of a calculator.

'Have they offered us a deal?' asks Stephen.

Mum drops her pen and shakes her head. 'The maths doesn't work.'

As he so often does, Dad proceeds to roll a cigarette.

Stephen folds his arms. 'What's the deal?'

Mum removes her glasses and rubs her eyes. 'They've offered a larger salary, but out of that we have to pay for our own flights, rent for the house, diesel for the generator and we'll no longer be able to shoot a beast for meat.'

I slide the piece of paper Mum's been scribbling on towards me. My year at Sheffield has improved my skills in mathematics and I rework the figures. 'I get similar results, but I don't think you're being conservative enough. We run the generator more than we're supposed to and fiddle the diesel records and without Howard and his plane there'll be no regular mail or supply plane. Not to mention that his Lockheed can carry loads the pissy Cessna planes can't.'

Stephen takes a look and, like me, reworks the figures. 'I agree.'

Dad nods. There's a look in his eye that's a mixture of anger and disappointment. When the owner and his business partner walk back into the kitchen, I go to leave, but Dad bids me wait. They look expectantly at Dad for an answer.

'The answer's no. Your deal is crap and you know it is.'

The owner smirks and I know instantly that he's a fully fledged prick. He reaches into the inside pocket of his jacket and pulls out a piece of paper. 'Try this deal.'

Dad slams his fist into the table so hard the coffee mugs bounce. 'I can work for a dickhead, but I won't be taken for a fool by a mongrel! No deals. We'll be leaving on or before settlement date.'

The owner is taken back. 'But...'

'No buts. Get out of our house. We need to pack. Oh, and all those tools in the workshop – they're mine, as are the saddles and bridles and a number of other things.'

The owner and his business partner scamper from the house. Probably because Stephen and I are ready to team up with Dad and beat the living crap out of the pair of them.

ED remains where he's seated. 'I don't know what deal they offered and quite frankly I'm appalled they tried to take you all for fools. But this place is more than a job to you all, else you wouldn't have put up with my son for as long as you have. My advice is to come up with your own deal. I'll assist with the cost of a lawyer and you can get it all in writing.' He stands up. 'We'll see ourselves to the airstrip and you can collect the tractor later.'

When ED has left, Mum says, 'That sounds like a plan.'

Dad shakes his head. 'No deal. I meant it.'

Mum gets up, calls the dogs and heads off in the direction of the wharf. The next day, Mum wants to hear our opinions.

'Well, I'd like to stay,' says Stephen, 'but the truth is I'm on my last year of school. After that, unless they offer me more than token work, I'll have to leave anyway.'

'Dion?' asks Mum.

I sigh. 'The truth is I've already left. It's nice to come back for the holidays, but I no longer live here.' I pause to collect my thoughts. 'There's something else. A man who lies to you or tries to pull a swiftie will always do it. Say what you will about Douglas and his strange ideas, but he's always been upfront and honourable. He gave us the run of the island and, to a point, we've done as we've pleased. Even with a better deal, this place is going to change and we'll be at the coalface. Even with a contract, I wouldn't trust the buyer or his partner. It's a long way to get justice when you're stranded on an island.'

Dad looks me directly in the eye. 'Well said.'

Mum starts crying. 'Am I the only one who'll fight for this place?'

'The working class don't fight against the cockies and win,' I say.

'If we leave, we'll be going to Leverington and there'll be no more Sheffield. You'll have to go to school in Cressy.'

It's like a punch to the stomach. I haven't thought of that. Still, I'm prepared to change schools and I have the benefit of a year's experience behind me. 'I'd prefer to continue at Sheffield, but it will be what it will be.'

For the next week, Dad begins to pack up his tools in the workshop. He's asked Stephen and me to sort out the chook problem.

I wasn't aware there was one until Stephen, carrying his rifle, leads me into the scrub behind the pens on dusk. Among the trees are dozens of roosting chooks.

'The numbers have got out of hand and there are breakaway groups. Now they're turning feral,' he whispers.

It didn't surprise me. With Maree and me gone, there've been fewer people to do the work. Not only haven't they kept an eye on the chooks, but the goats have also been breeding unchecked and are on the verge of going feral. Stephen has shot as many chooks as we could find. We've skinned the best of them for meat; the rest we've buried in a pit.

Mum is very sullen the next day. At dinner she says, 'I just wish we could all get back to the negotiating table.'

'It's over. I've phoned Bryce and he's agreed to ship our things back to Bridport on his boat. Howard has agreed to lend me his truck so I can transport it to Leverington.'

Mum starts crying again but there's nothing to be done except pack.

A few weeks later, I have to leave for Leverington in order to start school. Nana Doris has agreed to come and stay with me at the farmhouse while Mum, Dad and Stephen finish packing up. We've been given the same house we stayed in when we first arrived from Queensland.

Dad buys me a bicycle so I can ride to the farm gate to catch the school bus. He also gets me two new uniforms because the corduroy pants, shirts and jumper from Sheffield are the wrong colour for my new school.

My first week is a living hell. Last time, I had Zeke and Akki from the outset, as well as Kay. This time, there's no one and, try as I do, I can't seem to make friends.

Dad and Stephen turn up with Dale in an old Dodge truck loaded up with tools but not much furniture. I wonder where the fridge and washing machine and so forth are.

'Decided to let it go, lad. They did give us a cheque. It was a little small, but what can you do?'

I understand. The furniture can be replaced. 'Where's Mum?'

'They've negotiated with Douglas to have me stay on another few weeks and help them unload the *Trader*.'

I nod. The last days are dragging, but similar to when the caravan was sold and our days of travelling finished, the time at the island is over. I don't regret going there and I don't regret leaving. It's simply the end of an era.

Postscript

April 1996

The phone in my two-bedroom flat in George Town rings. I mute the television and reach down to answer it. It's Mum.

'Your dad has taken a caretaking job on Clarke Island.'

I sit up straighter, 'Doing what?'

Dad's health deteriorated rapidly within a year of him leaving the island. It was diabetes that he'd probably had for years before diagnosis. He'd been forced into early semi-retirement.

'It'll be just pottering around looking after the place, similar to what we had our caretakers doing.'

That sounds perfect for Dad and the salt air might do him some good. 'When's he going over?'

'Well, he's wondering if I bring him to Launceston whether you'll take him to Cape Portland on Saturday.'

I have a job at Rio Tinto's Comalco aluminium smelter at Bell Bay. I work shift work, but I have this weekend off. I was planning to go bushwalking but there'll be other walks. 'Can do. Is Howard servicing the island again?'

'No, but he still has a plane and he does a few flights here and there for the right people. Howard said he'd like to catch up with you both.'

'Okay, no worries.'

I hang up and take a serious trip down memory lane. I've had a hard time of it these past six years. Things didn't work out at Leverington and we moved to Ouse six months after leaving the island. I finished high school and tried twice to get into the army and failed both times. I also failed to get the apprenticeship I desperately wanted and was forced to spend a year at Elizabeth College in Hobart.

The following year, I took a three-year traineeship in pulp and paper making at Australian Newsprint Mills at Boyer. It wasn't what I wanted, but I gave it my all. However, when they failed to offer me a permanent position at the end of it, I quit and took a job at Comalco. Financially I was doing well, but I was completely unfulfilled and not knowing what I wanted to do with my life.

I tried to stay in touch with my friends in Sheffield, but keeping in touch was never my thing. Doing so also caused me to question whether I should have fought for the island so that I could have returned to Sheffield. Too late now; what was past was past. The year I ended high school, I received a single letter written by my four friends. Zeke had gone to agriculture school, Akki was to study accountancy, Kay was to study nursing and Clare hadn't said, which meant she was probably working in a dead-end job and living with her loser boyfriend. I shake it off; there's no point reminiscing. I can only look forward.

I collect Dad from Launceston on Friday and stay overnight in George Town. I drive him to Cape Portland early Saturday morning. We step out of my short-wheelbase Pajero and find Howard in the hangar.

'Ah, the Lockheed's gone!' I cry.

Howard gives us a warm smile and shakes hands with both of us.

'What this beast?' I say, referring to the plane.

'She's a Helio Courier H250. She was built for Papua New Guinea and will take off and land on a dime. Not an airstrip in the Furneaux Group she can't land on.'

I do a lap and look through the windows. She's a similar size to the Lockheed and also a six-seater, but she's a vastly different plane. Dad's travelling light. It's just his clothes, food and an electric bread maker.

'What are you doing these days?' asks Howard as he completes his pre-flight checks.

I give him the super-brief version.

He gets the gist and shakes his head. 'Go back to school. You're meant to be working with you brain not filling in time driving overhead cranes and sweating over an aluminium potline.'

I wince. I still don't know what he sees in me. Whatever it was or is, I've never found it.

I hang around until the plane disappears towards Clarke Island before heading back. Dad phones that night. He doesn't say much, just that some things are the same and some things have changed.

'Do you think we might be able to come over for a few days' visit in due course?'

'Yes, Trudi's keen to meet you all, but you'll have to pay your own way over.'

It's not a problem for me as I have a high-paying salary and plenty of savings. A few months later when Dad says it's time to come over, I phone Stephen.

'Already onto it, mate. Unfortunately, Howard's away, but he's happy for us to use the airstrip at Cape Portland. I've found a pilot on Flinders Island who'll fly us over, but he's only got a Cessna.'

That's not surprising, because they were a popular plane back in our time and things won't have changed much in five years.

'Carl and Michael want to come as well, so I've organised for the pilot to fly two trips.'

Carl is Maree's partner and the father of her daughter. She's currently five months pregnant with her second child. In her condition, there's no chance she'll be able to come. Carl is short-tempered and a bit of a risk. Still, if we refuse to take him, he'll take his anger out on Maree.

Michael is a farmer friend whom we've done a bit of work for. Mostly we fished and camped on his section of the Derwent River, as well as shot some of his kangaroos. In exchange we've helped him for free with his brushtail possum cull. He'll be fine.

'When?' I ask.

'Two weeks, and we're going for five days.'

Bugger. My longest break between shifts is only three and a half days, which means I'll need leave. A problem, given I've only been working there a few months. There's also the risk I mightn't get back, but that isn't such a concern. Even if they dock my pay, I'll manage.

When I explain to my supervisor where I want to go and why, he grants me leave straight up, saying he won't be responsible for me missing a trip like that.

Two weeks later, Stephen, Carl and Michael turn up at my flat in Stephen's Holden Rodeo.

'Slight change of plans,' says Stephen. 'There's been a lot of rain at Cape Portland and the pilot's worried about landing on the grass airstrip. He wants to fly out of Bridport.'

'What's the extra cost?' I ask.

'Fifty dollars each.'

It's nothing to me. 'Would it be better for him to fly us from George Town? Save us having to leave cars at the aerodrome in Bridport. I can get a mate to take us over.'

'Nah, it's all sorted now,' replies Stephen.

I know the three of them don't have the surplus cash I have, so I drop the subject. Stephen undoes the cover of his ute to reveal their gear.

'Even with two loads, all of that's not going to fit in a Cessna.' I doubt it would have all fitted in the Lockheed. 'You're going to have to sort out what you need from what you want.'

'Just how small is this frigging plane?' asks Carl.

'Imagine that someone's put wings on a small sedan. Then remember it doesn't just have space issues, but weight limits.'

Stephen rubs his chin. 'It'll be right.'

I disagree and head inside to trim back my own gear before phoning for pizza.

The next day, Michael rides with me, and Stephen and I drive to Bridport in separate vehicles. The plane arrives soon after and a man north of sixty gets out. Stephen shakes his hand and hands him an envelope full of cash as payment.

He tucks it into the inside pocket of his jacket and sizes us up. 'I'll take you three on the first load and come back for Stephen,' says the pilot, adding first our perishable food and then throwing my bag and sleeping bag on top.

I know without needing to ask that he's selecting what he thinks we can't do without. I wonder how much he'll get in on the next load and how much will be left behind.

The pilot points to me. 'You can get in the front seat beside me and the others can get in the back.'

I squeeze in. I'm not nervous, I've flown too many trips for that. I'm excited but also apprehensive about what I might discover. What has happened to our island since we left?

I note the direction the windsock is blowing. It's the wrong way for the main airstrip, which means he'll have to taxi along to the other one, or so I assume.

The pilot checks everyone has their seat belts on and that the doors are closed the same as Howard always did. 'You ready?' he asks.

I nod and the pilot opens the throttle fully and takes off on the access road, which is facing the right direction. Evidently, he couldn't see the point in all that taxiing when the access road will suffice. I grin manically. Damn, I've missed this.

I glance behind me. Michael is looking mildly concerned; Carl is white with fear. The plane banks round so it's in line with the coast and heading east.

Twenty-five minutes later, we're flying over Clarke Island. The tussock country has been burnt and is now grazing a mix of sheep and cattle. There are a lot of new fences and it looks like someone got busy with the 8430 and grader and built some decent roads.

We land on the main airstrip and get out. Neither Dad nor Mum, who flew over a month after Dad did, is here to meet us. We unpack the plane and the pilot takes off again.

Carl folds his arms. 'Where's your dad? He should be here to meet us.'

I would have expected so, but there could be a hundred reasons why not. Carl needs to chill out. I shoulder my rifle and bag.

'What's the plan?' asks Michael.

'The houses are just down the bank. We can walk.'

'What about the rest of the gear?' asks Carl. He's obviously still coming down from his fear of flying and trying to hide this behind gruffness.

'No one here to steal it. We'll head down and see about borrowing a tractor.'

Michael picks up his own bag, Carl refuses to carry anything and we set off. We've gone less than halfway when Dad rounds the corner driving the David Brown. We no longer have Elsa or Suzi, but Dad has a Jack Russell terrier named Jack, who's sitting on his lap.

'Sorry about the delay. Trudi's taken the Suzuki. She planned to be back, but she must have been delayed. I had to put the trailer on the tractor, hence the delay.'

Just as I thought, something simple and very typical Clarke Island.

'Good flight?' asks Dad.

'Top flight. He flies much lower than Munro, so we got a superb view of the coast on the way over.'

Dad nods, pulls out his tobacco and proceeds to roll a cigarette. It feels like old times all over again.

'Dump your gear on the trailer. You can come back up to the airstrip to wait for Stephen or you can keep going down to the bottom house.'

I dump my bag, but decide to carry my rifle rather than risk it getting damaged. 'I'll walk.'

Carl looks reluctant, but Michael falls in beside me.

'Much different?' asks Michael when we clear the bush and get a view of the settlement.

'A few things,' I reply. 'There's no goats grazing, so they're gone or turned out.'

I note as I pass our old house that our once lush gardens, including the flowers and the orchard, are gone. As are the chooks and ducks. It's more than a shame, it seems criminal. Neither the garden nor the fowl were just to fill in time: they were the food supply of the island. We pass the workshop, which looks the same, and we enter the porch of the bottom house.

'Knock, knock,' I say as I step inside.

Mum smiles. There's a little boy about four on the floor who's obviously Trudi's. He seems pretty content given his age.

'Good flight?' asks Mum, because it's the standard Island question.

I nod.

There's a low fire burning in the fireplace and a big cast-iron kettle simmering. Mum's already prepped a big teapot, so I pull on a leather welder's glove that's on the hearth and pour water into it from the kettle.

'The house looks all right,' says Michael. 'Stephen warned us that it was rustic, but this is okay.'

'Been renovated a bit since we left,' replies Mum. 'The gas stove is new, there's solar hot water and the house has been painted out and all the gaps sealed up.' She leads us into the bedroom, which is full of single beds, where we'll be sleeping.

Dad and Stephen arrive in due course on the David Brown and we go out to help bring in the gear.

'Where's the rest of it?' asks Carl.

'That's all he could fit in,' says Stephen.

The fishing rods are absent, as is Carl's beer and a big box of food.

'There's nothing perishable in the box of food, so he said he'd bring that over as a backload when he flies his second trip back to get us.'

I totally get it, but Carl is staring wide-eyed at where he thinks his beer should be. Carl gets aggressive when he drinks and Stephen may have deliberately left it behind.

'What about my swag?' says Michael.

'What you see is what there is.'

A concerned look comes over Michael's face. 'Is there going to be enough food? What about blankets?'

'It'll be fine,' says Dad. 'The pilot dropped a load of provisions off on his way down from Flinders and I'm sure the boys still remember how to hunt and fish,' says Dad.

We carry our things in. I knew to bring my bushwalking sleeping bag and Mum finds blankets for the others. It's a bit ad hoc, but no one is going to freeze.

'What's the plan?' says Dad when we've finished a top-up of tea.

'Are those old hand lines still here? Can we go fishing?' I ask.

Dad nods.

Having retrieved the handlines along with some other gear, we set off on a longer route to our favourite fishing spot. En route, Stephen disappears into the bush. He comes out carrying his fishing spear. Before he hid it, he oiled the handle and wrapped the prongs in plastic. The spear is in good condition and I high five Stephen.

'What the frig you going to do with that?' asks Carl.

'Watch and learn,' I reply.

At the rocks, I'm pleased to discover Stephen has lost none of his accuracy. He's soon spearing fish, including squid and cocky salmon. Wide-eyed, Michael is happy watching, but Carl seems put out. Stephen offers him a go on the spear, but he's too scared to go near the edge, so refuses. I remember now that he can't swim.

'You don't spear?' asks Michael.

I shake my head. 'It's harder than it looks, because the spear seems to bend in the water.'

He nods, satisfied with my answer.

Stephen and I clean the fish and we head back. Trudi has brought the Suzuki back, collected her son and gone back to her house. We help Dad lift an old two-seater couch into the back and he drives us over to Rebecca Bay. What used to take an hour on the David Brown and the rough track now takes only fifteen minutes in the Suzuki on the new road. That includes stops to open and shut gates.

The beach is still magnificent. I've brought with me a thirty-five-millimetre camera with interchangeable lenses and I endeavour to get some good photos.

'Can you take some for me?' asks Michael.

I pass him the camera. 'I brought four rolls of film with me. Knock yourself out.'

Taking the camera, he walks off with Dad, who's in his element telling stories from our time.

After a dinner of fish, Dad takes us out shooting. He heads straight up to the airstrip, which is odd because it was never where we used to shoot. When we arrive, I stare in disbelief. The airstrip is crawling with rabbits.

'What happened?' I ask.

'That dickhead I refused to work for got it into his head to poison all the feral cats. Now the rabbits are breeding unchecked.'

Michael cocks his head. 'There's no Tasmanian devils or quolls?'

'Nope. The feral cat was the top predator,' I say. 'Good news for the birdlife, but unless they do something about these burrowing sods, they'll have to install a rabbit-proof fence around the airstrip.'

'How long's the perimeter?' asks Michael.

'For all three runways, a shade under eight k,' replies Dad.

Michael sucks air through his teeth. 'That would cost twenty grand minimum, not including labour.'

The dog, Jack, is itching to get out, so Dad opens his door. Jack charges at the nearest rabbit, but to our amusement, leaps clean over it, runs at a wallaby and bites its backside. He's too small to kill it, but he gives it a dusting up. We hoot with laugher but Jack's happy to get back in the cab now he's re-established the pecking order.

'Trudi hoped you might help her out,' says Dad

He hands Trudi's rifle to Stephen, who nods. I wish I'd bought my .22 and a carton of ammo. As far as firearms go, I've only brought my .303 to have a go at the geese.

By the time Dad has driven down all three airstrips, we've given the rabbits a decent hammering. We bring back a selection of rabbits and wallaby. Stephen sets aside a selection of both for meat and we skin the rest out for Trudi's working dogs, which Dad is charged with feeding.

'If she wants to fly me over for a weekend, I'll bring my rifle and a carton of ammo and help her out some more,' I say.

Dad shakes his head. 'She can't afford the cost of the flights. Howard is the cheapest around but he doesn't want to fly every fortnight like he used to, and Munro isn't allowed to charge by the seat and island-hop any more.'

I wrinkle my nose and remember the trip Stephen and I had to Swan Island. Evan and his wife were in the same position even though he had his own plane. It's too bad, because I wouldn't mind flying over and spending more time here. Now I'm older, I can do more, but while I can afford it, I'm saving up to buy a house.

As I'm recovering from night shifts, I go to bed early. I'm also up early and I slip down to the beach on my own with an old towel over my shoulder. I head straight to the spot where the abalone were. They're still there and there's more than ever. I don't have my goggles and snorkel and the water's freezing, but I only have this one chance, so I take it. I dive in and manage to get six of them, which is more than enough. I wrap my catch in the towel and head back for a hot shower.

'Whoa,' says Michael who's up and pottering around making tea. 'Do you know what those things are worth?'

Abalone is often referred to as white gold. It can fetch up to four hundred dollars a kilogram to the right buyer. 'Yep, the perks of the island if you know how to get them.'

That day, Dad drives us out to the tussock country because he wants to show us something. He takes us to the one section he ploughed up. The tussocks are back lusher than ever, but that's not the worst of it. There's a sand blow large enough to bury a house and garage in.

'What happened?' I ask.

'Erosion,' says Dad.

Michael shakes his head. 'This country is too light to be ploughing. What was Douglas thinking?'

'Working for an idiot, that was the trouble. Controlled burning is the only way to manage this country. I tried to tell him,' says Dad.

By him, Dad means Douglas. 'The Aborigines called it firestick farming. Well, I should say that's what the academics called their methods of land management. I was thinking. Douglas had us spread all that fancy grass seed out here, but wouldn't we have done better with the kikuyu running grass?'

Michael scratches his chin. 'Well, yeah, it would certainly hold the sand down better, but how would you disperse it?'

'I spent six years digging the stuff out of the garden. You only need a centimetre of runner and it comes back. So, each time you weed instead of burning it, you bring it out here.'

'It would decimate the native grass, but so would any of the imported stuff. It would have stopped this, though,' says Michael.

Loading up my .303, I walk about a kilometre away, where I can take a long-distance shot at some Cape Barren geese without risking any of the stock. My first shot is right in line, but a metre too short. Taking aim again, my second shot is too high. I line up for a third shot but the opportunity's lost because the geese fly off.

'Never was a marksman,' I say when I get back to the Suzuki.

Dad drives us out across the interior.

'What happened to all the wild cattle?' I ask when he pulls up atop a knoll.

'The dickhead who took over from Douglas shot them all from a helicopter.'

It made sense to cull the wild rogue bulls but shooting from a helicopter seemed extreme.

'What does Trudi do for meat?'

'Eats rabbit and wallaby. She doesn't go fishing and she can't afford to sacrifice any of her stock.'

I shake my head. 'We used to live like kings here.'

Stephen's spied a goose and is asking for my rifle, which I hand to him. He takes a shot across the bonnet and kills it. He's a marksman.

'I don't know – seems to me we're doing okay,' says Michael.

We drive over and pick up the goose. I'm using military full metal jacket bullets. They're designed to punch a hole through rather than shatter on impact, so the damage to the goose isn't as bad as feared.

The interior now has heath growing again. Not as high as it once was, but it's on the way back.

'Am I disoriented, or is this where you ploughed and sowed grass?' I ask.

Dad smirks. 'The island's taking it back. All that time and money and busted machinery was for nothing. Trudi's husband nearly cried when I explained it to him.'

Trudi's husband has gone back to the Northern Territory, because they couldn't even make a living from the island. It doesn't help that they aren't prepared to live the semi-self-sufficient lifestyle. Not that it's all Trudi's fault. A young mum with a young son can't do the work that the five of us once did, but still she could do more than she was. Some farmers are just too proud to garden and run fowl for meat and eggs.

For our next few meals, we're spoilt for choice. Mum bakes a rabbit and cooks a wallaby stew. We also have the abalone, squid and fish to eat, along with the goose. As Michael said, we're eating pretty well.

That evening we break out the cards. It's just like old times before Dad got the television working properly.

On the morning that we're waiting for our plane, Trudi gives me her outgoing mail. She's embarrassed that she doesn't have enough stamps nor cash on her to pay for them. I'm not concerned. I'm happy with an IOU because I know how important sending mail is for people living on an island.

When the plane lands, he's again brought a load of provisions with him from Flinders Island. With the plane situation the way it is, Trudi, as well as Mum and Dad, must take advantage of every opportunity. On the way back, I'm again sitting in the front and Michael and Carl are in the back.

Once we're airborne, the pilot asks, 'Can you fly a plane?'

I shake my head.

He looks surprised. 'All those trips back and forth and you never learned to fly!'

'Nah, I was too young.'

'Take the yoke.'

I nervously reach out and take the yoke on my side while glancing at the compass on the dash. 'What bearing?'

He's rolling a cigarette. 'No need to make it complex if you've got good visibility like we have today. Just follow the coast.'

I do. Like a car, steering a plane is pretty easy. Well, at least in this fine weather. Taking off and landing, along with navigation, would be a lot harder. I'd love to learn some day.

He takes over when it's time to land.

We pile out and the pilot loads in the box of food he couldn't fit on the way over and I shove in Carl's carton of beer while he's not looking. Thankfully, he seems to have temporarily forgotten about it. We wait for him to return with Stephen. It's been a good trip, but I know I won't get back again. It was a one-off thing.

*

Five months later, having come off night shift, I'm dozing in the seat of my Pajero. Parked at the George Town aerodrome, I can hear the sound of a plane. I sit up straighter. Years of living on Clarke Island and I've come to realise that no two planes sound alike. I know the sound of this one. It's the black and white 172 Cessna that came and got Dad and Maree to take them to Flinders Island all those years ago.

Since Mum had flown off earlier, leaving Dad to finish out his contract, when the plane lands only Dad gets off clutching Jack. He's just got his bag of clothes; whatever food he's got left he's left behind, along with his bread maker. It's not just lack of room in the plane and weight limits. It's difficult to get things over there and so it's best to leave behind what you really don't need to take off.

'How was it?' I ask.

He shakes his head and launches into a tirade about the lack of a television and how Trudi wouldn't help him do things. I nod. I understand. Dad loves television and he'd always had us at his beck and call in our day. Having to do things on his own was a completely different experience.

'I've been offered a caretaking job on a private farm on Cape Barren Island.'

'You going to take it?'

'Not on your nelly. I'm done with islands.'

I understand, but I'm disappointed. I so wanted to go there but now he's turned the job down I probably never will. This time, we're truly done with islands. Well, at least for the time being.

About the Author

Dion Perry is an Australian who was born in Townsville, Queensland. He spent the first eight years of his life living in a caravan travelling around the eastern side of Australia, before moving to Tasmania when he was eight. He attended university in Hobart, where he did a BA with majors in sociology and Aboriginal studies. He writes mainly speculative fiction in the genres of science fiction and fantasy, but also dabbles in non-fiction. He has previously published three books: *Target 2013*, *Alien Love* and *Satellite Attack*. His day job is as a public servant in Canberra. He lives with his wife, two dogs and a cat on their ten-acre hobby farm on the beautiful Southern Tablelands of New South Wales.

https://dionperry.wordpress.com/

www.ingramcontent.com/pod-product-compliance
Lightning Source LLC
Chambersburg PA
CBHW030903080526
44589CB00010B/122